Joan Fisher's Guide to Crochet

Triune Books

Guide to Crochet

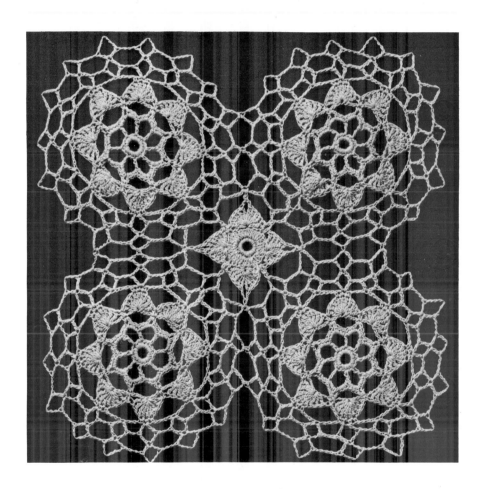

by Joan Fisher

Acknowledgements

The author acknowledges with thanks the help given with the preparation of this book by the following:

J. & P. Coats Ltd., 155 St. Vincent St., Glasgow C.2.
Emu Wools Ltd., Low Street Mills, Keighley, Yorkshire.
John C. Horsfall and Sons Ltd. (Hayfield Wools), Hayfield Mills, Glusburn, Nr. Keighley, Yorkshire.
Lister and Co. Ltd., Providence Mills, Wakefield, Yorkshire.
Patons and Baldwins, PO Box 22, Darlington, Co. Durham.

Robin Wools Ltd., Bradford, Yorkshire.
H. G. Twilley Ltd., Roman Mills, Stamford, Lincs.
Wendy and Peter Pan Knitting Wools, Carter and Parker Ltd., Gordon Mills, Guiseley, Yorkshire.
Abel Morrall Ltd. (Aero crochet hooks and other products).

The photographs on pages 55, 67, 72, 73, 85 and 128 were taken at the Westerham Riding Stables, Westerham, Kent.
The photographs on page 65, 89, 116, 117 and 121 were taken outside The Merry Harriers coaching inn, Cowbeech, East Sussex.

Photography by Rex Bamber

ISBN-0 85674 015 2
Published by
Triune Books, London, England
© Trewin Copplestone Publishing Ltd 1973
Printed in Spain
by Printer Industria Gráfica, S.A.   Tuset, 19   Barcelona
San Vicente dels Horts
Depósito legal B. 10317-1973
Mohn Gordon Ltd. London

Contents

Introduction

Crochet is easy to learn, quick to do and instantly effective for all manner of exciting designs – not only in its traditional form for fine lace edgings and insertions, but for top-fashion outfits and accessories, clothes for babies and children, and for elegant household furnishings too.

The technique which is based on a single stitch is extremely simple, although sometimes learning to hold and control the crochet hook is not so easy for a beginner. Once this has been mastered however, you can go on to work the limitless fascinating pattern variations of the single basic stitch.

In this book I show you with clear instructions, and easy-to-follow diagrams, exactly how to begin crochet, how to work the traditional stitch variations, and how to cope with the technical problems of the craft. The principles of Tunisian and hairpin crochet are also explained, and the dictionary of stitch patterns demonstrates the wonderful effects which are possible in crochet – these patterns should inspire you to go on to create your own designs.

Following the stitch dictionary are the pattern chapters, packed with exclusive new designs for you to make up for yourself, your family and your home. All the patterns are based on the stitches and techniques explained in the first chapter.

Take time not only to learn the basic principles of the age-old craft of crochet, but to experiment with both stitches and yarn types . . . discover how a single pattern motif can totally change its character by being worked in a variety of different yarns. Just one motif, for instance, worked in fine cotton could give you a beautiful cobwebby lace tablecloth, or, worked in multicoloured knitting yarns, the same motif could be used to produce a gay sweater or a waistcoat for a teenager. Worked again in a glitter or jewelled yarn, the same motif could give a glamorous, eyecatching long evening skirt. The possibilities are endless!

Why not try for yourself and see? All you need are a crochet hook and a ball of yarn . . .

JOAN FISHER

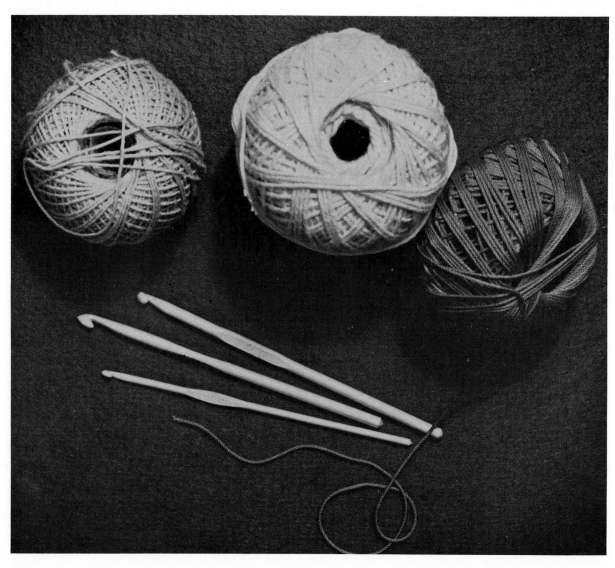

Chapter one
THE FACTS ABOUT CROCHET

BASIC EQUIPMENT

A crochet hook and a ball of yarn are all you need to begin to crochet, but you will find it useful also to have a tape measure for measuring your work as you go along (ideally, one marked with inches and centimetres), good-quality, rustless pins for pinning the finished work out to the correct size, plus an iron, ironing board and cloth for pressing the completed item, and a sewing needle for making it up.

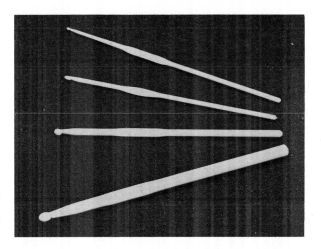

Crochet hooks

Hooks are available in many sizes from very thin to quite thick. The thin ones are used with fine cotton yarn, the thick with heavy wools or synthetics. In the system of sizing called International Standard Sizing the higher the size number the thicker the hook (see chart below). Hooks are available in steel, aluminium, bone or plastic; steel hooks are generally used for work with fine cotton yarns, and aluminium, plastic or bone for work with other yarns.

Although a pattern normally recommends a particular size of hook, it is important not necessarily to use this hook size, but to use the one with which you can achieve the correct tension as quoted in the pattern (see page 13).

Throughout the patterns in this book, the International Standard Sizing of hooks has been used; if it is wished to convert these sizes into other size ranges, please refer to the chart below.

International Standard Size	Old UK Sizes Wool	Old UK Sizes Cotton	American Sizes Wool	American Sizes Cotton
7.00	2	–	K	–
–	3	–	–	–
6.00	4	–	–	–
5.50	5	–	–	–
5.00	6	–	J	–
4.50	7	–	I	–
4.00	8	–	H	–
3.50	9	–	G	–
3.00	10	3/0	F	2/0
–	11	2/0	E	0
2.50	12	0	D	1
–	13	1	C	2
–	–	–	–	3
2.00	14	1½	B	4
–	–	2	A	5
1.75	15	2½	–	6
–	–	3	–	6
1.50	16	3½	–	7
–	–	4	–	8
1.25	–	4½	–	9
–	–	5	–	10
1.00	–	5½	–	11
–	–	6	–	12
0.75	–	6½	–	13
0.60	–	7	–	14
–	–	7½	–	–

Yarns

Traditionally very fine thread – usually cotton – is used for crochet trimmings and laces, but now that so many other items can be successfully crocheted, wool and synthetic yarns and mixtures can all be used as well. In fact the extensive range of yarn types, thicknesses and colours available for knitting can be used with equal success for crochet work. The choice of yarn is, of course, dependent on the article being made, and the amount of wear it will have to withstand. The following gives a guide to the principal yarn types available.

Acrylic yarns. These are man-made fibres, marketed under trade names such as Acrilan, Orlon, Courtelle and so on. Because of the way in which these yarns are manufactured there is usually more yardage in a ball of acrylic fibre than there is in a ball of natural yarn in the same weight. Acrylic yarns produce lightweight garments which are soft to the touch and are quick and easy to launder.

Angora. A fluffy yarn available in its pure natural form and also as a synthetic mixture in which the natural yarn is mixed with nylon. Although either version of the yarn is attractive for pretty, delicate garments, it is not an ideal yarn to use for crochet work – the fluffy characteristics of the yarn make it difficult to see and control stitches easily.

Bouclé. A textured yarn in which a normal smoothly-spun yarn is interspersed with tight clusters. Again, although the effect produced when a garment is crocheted in this type of yarn is attractive, because of the erratic thickness of a bouclé, it is not an easy yarn to crochet with.

Cotton. A natural yarn available in many weights which is ideally suited for crochet work. Cotton is a 'harder' yarn than wool, therefore stitches are easier to see and to work with and the finished result is a crisper look, with stitch detail clear and uniform. Cotton yarns are usually hardwearing and easy to launder.

Crêpe. This is another textured type of yarn, but because the texture (produced by tightly twisting a multi-ply yarn in natural or synthetic fibres) is uniform it is suitable for crochet work. A smooth fabric with a slightly crinkled surface is produced.

A selection of yarns suitable for crochet.

Double knitting yarns. These are ideal, everyday yarns suitable for most purposes. They may be produced from natural or synthetic fibres, or a mixture of both. The yarns are quick to work with but the finished fabric is not too bulky.

Linen. A natural fibre which is frequently spun into yarns suitable for crochet work. Sometimes the yarns are given a textured or novelty finish.

Marls. Marl yarns combine several strands of different colours twisted together after the spinning.

Mohair. A soft yarn spun from the hair of the Angora goat. Like Angora yarn, although the fabric produced is attractive, the yarn is not easy to crochet with unless a very openwork pattern is used (see, for example, design illustrated on page 83).

Novelty yarns. These yarns are intended to give special effects – sparkling, glitter and 'jewelled' yarns can all be termed novelty. So can most of the textured yarns. Often natural and man-made fibres are combined to give the particular effect required, or different colours are mixed. Glitter yarns are usually a combination of a natural yarn with a metal thread. Some novelty yarns can be successfully washed, others have to be dry-cleaned – be guided by the instructions on the label of each yarn type.

Nylon. A very strong and hardwearing fibre made from chemicals found in coal, air and water. It is resistant to bacteria and mildew, and is mothproof, also as it is a very white fibre it can be dyed successfully to brilliant white and vivid fluorescent shades. It can be used on its own, or combined with wool to give the advantages of both fibres. In either form, nylon is an excellent yarn to use for crochet work.

Tricel. This is another man-made fibre which is good for crochet work. It is hardwearing and very easy to launder.

Wool. A natural yarn available in many different weights and thicknesses, from the finest and softest baby yarns, usually of botany wool, to the sturdiest triple knitting weights which are good for chunky heavy sports sweaters.

HOLDING YOUR HOOK AND YARN

There is no hard and fast rule about the correct way to hold your crochet hook, and manipulate the yarn – really the ideal position is the one in which you feel comfortable, and you can produce even, regular work smoothly and quickly. The following method however is the one generally recommended: pass the yarn round the little finger of the left hand, under the middle two fingers then over the first finger. The hook is held in the right hand; it rests between thumb and first finger rather like holding a pencil, with the second finger on the tip of the hook. Initially the loose end of the yarn is held tight between thumb and first finger of the left hand. When work begins, the work is held by the left hand between thumb and first finger. The left hand also controls the yarn from the main ball while the right hand moves the hook.

Left-handed workers will work in reverse, holding the hook in the left hand and controlling yarn with the right hand. The easiest way for left-handed workers to follow diagrams intended for right-handed workers is to place a pocket mirror at right angles to the diagrams, and to follow the mirror-reflected diagrams. There is available a simple but clever gadget called a crochet tension

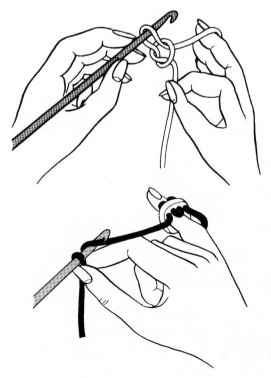

ring which is intended to help not only left-handed workers, but also arthritic and disabled people who are anxious to crochet but find difficulty in controlling the yarn. The tension ring is slipped over the little finger, and then the yarn is fed through the ring, so an even and regular tension is automatically maintained.

STITCHES

Chain

This is the foundation of all crochet work, and for this reason it is often called 'foundation chain', though this stitch is also used at other times in the course of a pattern.

When making foundation chain you must start with a slip loop. To make a slip loop, undo a short length of yarn from the ball. Hold yarn between thumb and first finger of left hand and take yarn from ball in the right hand; cross main yarn from ball over short length to make a loop then hold this loop firmly in the left hand. Take crochet hook in right hand and insert it into loop and with it pull through the main yarn so a loop forms on the hook. Pull short length of yarn to tighten loop on hook.

You are now ready to work your commencing chain – chain used as part of a pattern are worked in a similar way. Holding the short end of the yarn and the bottom of the slip loop between your left thumb and first finger, and yarn and hook in correct positions, take the hook under the yarn on the left hand first finger and pull the yarn and the hook through the loop on the hook. You have now worked one chain.

The action of taking the hook under the yarn is called 'yarn over hook'. Continue making chain in this way until you have the number you want. Move your first finger and thumb of left hand up the chain as you work so you are always holding the chain just made.

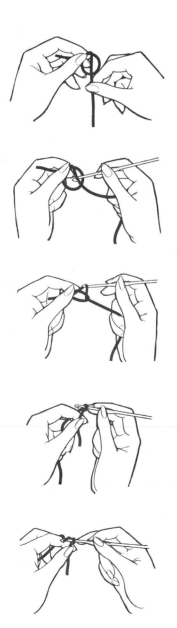

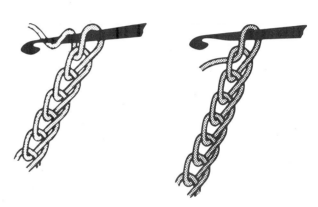

Slip stitch or single crochet

This stitch adds no height to the work, so can be used to take yarn across the work to another point, for joining or for making an edge firm. Work from right to left across foundation chain. Insert hook under top two loops of next chain (or stitch when working into a row of stitches instead of the foundation chain), yarn over hook and pull yarn through the chain stitch and through the loop on the hook. Insert hook into next stitch and repeat; continue in this way along row.

9

Double crochet

Insert hook into chain or stitch through top two loops, yarn over hook and draw through the stitch. This makes two loops on the hook. Take yarn over the hook again and draw through the two loops on the hook. Continue in this way along row.

Double crochet worked to give a dense, interlocked fabric.

Half treble

Take yarn over hook then insert hook into next stitch. Yarn over hook again and pull a loop through the stitch – three loops on the hook. Pass yarn over hook again and draw yarn through all three loops. Work along row in this way.

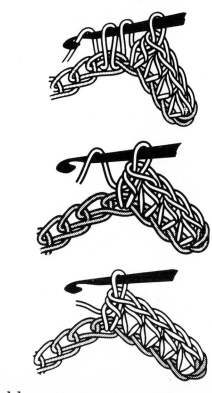

Treble

Pass yarn over hook then insert hook into next stitch. Yarn over hook and draw through stitch – three loops on hook. Yarn over hook again and draw through the first two loops on the hook. Yarn over hook once more and draw through remaining two loops on hook. Continue in this way along row.

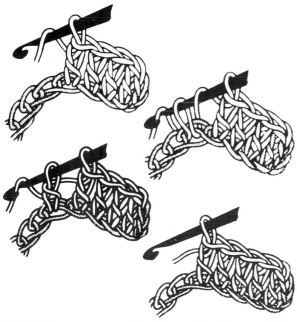

work another cluster, and continue along row in this way. On the next row work the clusters into the chain spaces of previous row.

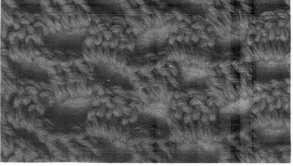

Example of a treble cluster pattern.

Treble between treble. Normally when working in a treble pattern, each consecutive row of stitches is worked into the top of the stitches of the previous row. To produce a denser fabric, the pattern can be varied by working each row of trebles into the spaces between the trebles worked in the previous row.

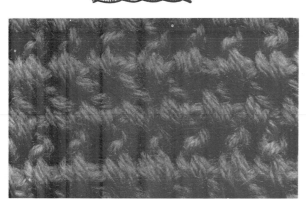

Example of treble between treble pattern.

Clusters or groups. This stitch variation is usually worked in trebles. If you are working into foundation chain, leaving last loop of each on hook, work three trebles into one chain (four loops on hook), yarn over hook and draw through all loops on hook, one chain, miss one chain,

Shell patterns. This is another traditional stitch pattern which is a combination of double crochets and trebles. Working into foundation chain, miss two chain, work one double crochet into the next chain, miss two chain, work five trebles into the next chain, and continue in this way to end of row. On next row, work the double crochet stitches into the centre trebles of the shells, and work the shells into the double crochet stitches.

Above: two shell pattern variations.

Double treble
(also sometimes called a long treble)

Take yarn over hook twice, then insert hook into next stitch. Yarn over hook and draw a loop through the stitch – four loops on hook. Yarn over hook and draw through two loops, yarn over hook again and draw through a further two loops, yarn over hook once more and draw through last two loops. Continue in this way all along row.

Triple treble

Yarn over hook three times, insert hook into next stitch, yarn over hook and draw through a loop – five loops on the hook. Yarn over hook and draw through two loops on the hook, yarn over hook and draw through two more loops on hook, yarn over hook and draw through two more loops, yarn over hook and draw through last two loops. Continue in this way along row.

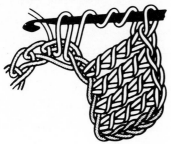

Quadruple treble

Yarn over hook four times, and complete as for triple treble until only one loop remains.

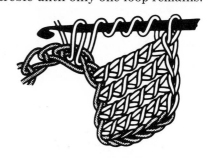

TURNING CHAIN

As crochet stitches are worked from the top down, when crocheting in rows a new row cannot start until the yarn has been taken up to the correct height to begin the new row. To do this, a number of chain stitches are worked and these chain count as the first stitch in the row. At the end of the following row, the last stitch is worked into the top of these 'turning chain' as they are called. The number of turning chain worked will depend on the depth of the stitch being used in the pattern. Most patterns will tell you how many chain to work, but as a general guide work two chain for a double crochet stitch or a half treble, three chain for a treble stitch, four chain for a double treble, and five chain for a triple treble.

INCREASING

The most usual method of increasing is to work two stitches into the same stitch of the previous row – or more if this is required. If extra stitches are required at the edge of the work, a length of chain can be made at the end of a row and these chain stitches worked into on the following row.

DECREASING

If several stitches are to be decreased at the edge of the work, this can be done in the following way: at the beginning of a row work slip stitches over the number of stitches you want decreased; at the end of a row stop working the required number of stitches before the end, turn and work next row. In some patterns, decreases can be made merely by missing a stitch, but a more successful method is to work two stitches together.

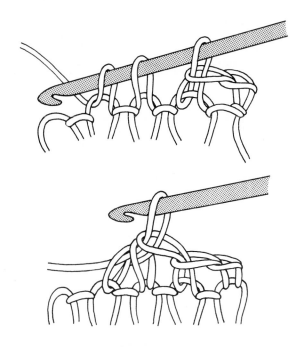

JOINING YARN

When your ball of yarn is running out, take the new ball and lay the end of it on top of your work. Crochet over this with the last of the old ball for a few stitches, then lay the end of the old ball over the top of the work and crochet over it with the new ball.

EDGINGS

A crochet edging worked round neck, sleeve and hem edges of a completed garment will give a decorative and neat finish not only to a crocheted garment but a knitted one as well. Simply work round the edge picking up stitches evenly through the loops of the last row of knitting or crochet worked on the garment (usually double crochet is used for this foundation row), then work in any crochet pattern as wished. Two or three rows of double crochet give a neat, plain border. For a more decorative border try a picot edging, as follows:

Work a foundation row of double crochet all round edge.

Next row or round: slip stitch to the required position for picot, then make four chain, and work a slip stitch into the fourth chain from the hook: a picot made. Slip stitch across stitches of previous row to required position for next picot, then repeat the picot.

Work the first stitch in the usual way but leave the last loop of it on the hook (so there are two loops on hook); move on to next stitch and work this but leave the last loop on the hook. Take yarn over hook and draw through the last three loops on the hook.

FASTENING OFF

When your piece of work is complete – or if you are changing the colour of your yarn, or for some other reason want to fasten off – cut the yarn a few inches from the work. Pull this end through the last loop on the hook and draw tightly. Darn this loose end in later.

TENSION

The tension is the number of stitches and rows which measure one square inch for a particular pattern. In order to make an item of the correct finished size, you must work to the tension measurement given – e.g. if a pattern gives a tension of 6 rows and 8 stitches to the square inch, then you must make sure that your work achieves exactly this measurement, being neither slacker nor tighter. Before starting work on any pattern, check your tension by working a 3 or 4-in. square in the stitch pattern, yarn and hook size given in the pattern. Press the square then mark off on it with pins a 2-in. square. Count the number of stitches and rows contained in this square and compare them with the tension measurement given in the pattern. If they are more than those given, work another square with a hook a size larger; if they are fewer try again with a hook a size smaller. Continue to make tension checks until you achieve exactly the right measurement. Do not ever start work on a pattern until you have found the right hook to give you the correct tension measurement.

A scalloped edging can be produced by working shell pattern round the edge. Work a foundation row of double crochet, as for picot edging. On the next row, work one slip stitch, then miss two stitches and work five treble all into the next stitch, miss two stitches, work a slip stitch into the next stitch. Continue in this way all round edge.

Crab stitch

This is double crochet worked from left to right. It makes a good edging, particularly for a jacket or similar item.

BUTTONHOLES

It is usual for buttonholes to be worked in a double crochet edging. Sometimes however a buttonhole will occur in the main body of a design, and in this case instructions are usually given in full within the pattern.

The principle of working buttonholes in crochet is fairly simple: work in pattern to the point where the buttonhole is required, then work a number of chain, and do not work into this same number of stitches on the previous row – i.e. if you work five chain, then miss five stitches, and resume pattern in the sixth stitch. Continue working into stitches of previous row in pattern until the next buttonhole position is reached; work the same number of chain as before, and miss the equivalent number of stitches. Continue in this way. On the subsequent row work in pattern across all stitches, including the chain stitches worked for the buttonholes. A short opening is thus formed in the work. The number of chain stitches worked will depend on the size of buttons being used.

WORKING WITH MORE THAN ONE COLOUR

Colour work in crochet is considerably easier than it is in knitting chiefly because the nature of crochet, where you work with only one stitch on the hook at a time, allows new colours to be easily joined in at the beginning of rows or rounds. If you are working in a simple regular stripe pattern (equal number of rows of each colour) then just carry the two colours of yarn up the sides of the work without breaking off the yarn. Loosely wind the two colours round each other when changing colours.

However if you are working in an irregular colour pattern where only occasional rows of a contrast colour are used then it is probably easier just to join in the contrast colour where required and break it off again at the end of the row. The loose ends can be darned into the seams afterwards when the garment is made up.

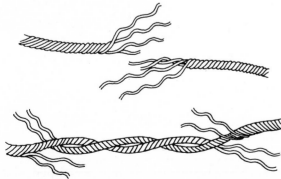

The same principle can be used when working in rounds. To work a multi-coloured square motif for instance, a different coloured yarn can be used for each round. If you wish to change colours in mid-round then splicing is the best joining method to use: to do this, untwist a few inches of yarn from

the two ends, cut away half the strands from each and overlaying the remaining strands in opposite directions, twist them together until they hold – the twisted yarn should thus be equivalent to the original thickness. Any loose ends can be trimmed away on the wrong side of work afterwards.

MOTIF CROCHET

The nature of the crochet technique in which it is easy to begin at a centre point and work round and round this central point, increasing stitches with each successive round, makes it particularly suitable for motif work. All sorts of motifs in plain or multiple colours can be quickly and easily worked, including not only plain squares but circles, stars and flower shapes as well. Also as only oddments of yarn are needed for each motif this is a good way to use up left-over yarns, and as motifs are easily portable this is an ideal form of crochet to take with you to do on a train or car journey. Save the assembling of multiple motifs into garments, blankets, pram covers, handbags, shawls, cushions covers or whatever you wish until later when you are home by your own fireside.

If you find a motif pattern which you particularly like, then it can be varied by working it in entirely different yarns and hook sizes – worked in fine cotton on a fine hook, for instance, will produce a small delicate lacy motif, suitable for a table runner, or edging for a party dress. The same motif worked in a chunky wool with a thick hook, will be totally different in size, texture and character – use it for a winter scarf or pullover, a cot blanket, or a handbag.

A simple round motif forms the basis for this elegant cheval set (see page 30).

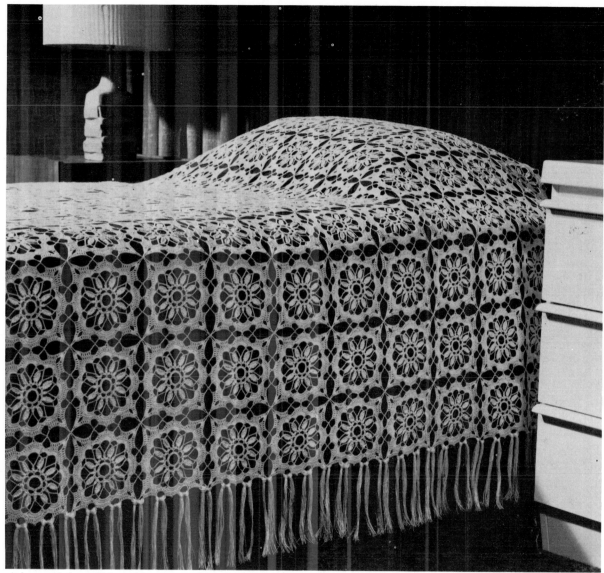

A beautiful traditional bedspread made from square motifs worked in fine crochet cotton (see page 33).

Several motif patterns are given in the stitch pattern dictionary, starting on page 20 – experiment with one or two of these, trying out different yarns and hook sizes to see the variety of effects which can be produced.

Joining motifs

Motifs may be either sewn together or crocheted together to form the finished design required.

To sew them together, place motifs together right sides facing, and using a large blunt-ended darning needle and thread to match the yarn used for the crochet (ideally use the same yarn, or a strand of it – if it is too thick to thread on to the darning needle, use a sewing thread in a colour as close as possible to the yarn colour), work overcasting stitches fairly loosely along the two edges.

To crochet motifs together, place motifs together right sides facing, and then insert hook into the loop at the edge of one motif and then into the corresponding loop on the other motif. Make a slip stitch with both stitches at once. Continue in this way along the edge.

FILET CROCHET

This is a traditional form of lace-work crochet in which designs are formed from a series of solid squares, produced by working blocks of trebles, and open areas, made by working individual trebles and chains. The resulting fabric is similar to net, and is suitable for all sorts of household furnishings, including tablecloths and curtains. Patterns are often given in the form of charts, one square on the chart representing one stitch in your work – the open or blank squares usually represent the spaces, the solid or black squares are the blocks.

To work the spaces in filet crochet

Work two chain, miss two stitches, one treble into next stitch.

Blocks and spaces

Work one treble into each of next four stitches, two chain, miss two stitches, one treble into next stitch, one treble into each of next three stitches.

Bars and lacet

A bar consists of five chain, miss five stitches or a lacet, one treble into next stitch. A lacet consists of three chain, miss two stitches, one double crochet into next stitch, three chain, miss two stitches, one treble into next stitch.

MAKING UP YOUR GARMENTS

When you have finished crocheting the individual parts of a garment or household design, they then have to be sewn together to make the complete item. First the individual pieces should be pressed: if specific instructions are given in the pattern, follow these as different yarns require different treatments. Wool is usually pressed with a warm iron over a damp cloth; synthetics with a cool iron over a dry cloth. Before pressing, pin out each piece of work to its correct measurements, with the wrong side up, then press in the appropriate way. Sew in any loose ends of yarn, and join seams using a large-eyed needle threaded with the same yarn as used for the crochet (or a strand of it). Use a backstitch seam to join side, sleeve and shoulder seams, an overcasting stitch to join edgings or trimmings to the main work.

AFTER-CARE

Never allow a crocheted garment to get too dirty. Careful washing does not damage any fabric but when a garment is very soiled, normal use of washing agents will not remove all the dirt without rubbing and it is this rubbing which causes damage to the fibres.

Make sure the washing agent, whether it is soap, soap flakes, soap powder or a detergent, is thoroughly dissolved in hot water, and then add cold water to reduce the temperature before placing the garment in the solution. Always make sure that enough washing water is prepared to cover the garment completely. Never boil a crocheted garment. The water temperature should be about 40 deg. C (104 deg. F.), just hot enough for your hand. Do not use any form of bleach.

Allow the washing agent to remove the dirt. Do not rub the fabric. Gently ease the fabric in the washing water, but do not lift the garment in and out of the water as this causes stretching. All fabrics are more easily harmed or distorted when wet than in a dry state.

Take the garment from the washing water and gently squeeze to remove as much of the water as possible. Rinse the garment in at least three changes of warm water. The third rinsing water should be quite clear after rinsing the garment in it. If it is not, it means that there is still some soap or detergent in the garment and another rinse is needed until the water is absolutely clear. Gently squeeze the garment on removing it from the final rinse and roll it in a clean dry white towel without twisting. This will absorb most of the excess moisture. Spread the garment out flat on a clean towel and ease it into the correct shape and size. Allow it to dry slowly in the shade or in an airing cupboard.

Items worked in fine crochet cotton should be carefully pinned out to shape when half-dry – place a piece of paper, either plain white or squared, on top of a clean, flat board. Following the correct measurements as given in the pattern, draw the shape of the finished article on to the paper. Using rustless pins, pin the crochet out to the pencilled shape, taking care not to strain the crochet. Pin out the general shape first, then finish by pinning each picot, loop or space into position.

If a slight stiffening is required, use a solution of starch (one dessertspoon to one pint of hot water), and dab lightly over the article. Raise the crochet up off the paper to prevent it sticking as it dries. When completely dry, remove the pins and press the article lightly with a hot iron.

Two-colour dress (see page 45) and yellow and white dress (see page 48).

TUNISIAN CROCHET

This technique – also known as tricot crochet, and sometimes as crochet-knitting – is in a way a combination of knitting and crochet. It is worked on a special Tunisian crochet hook which looks like a knitting needle with a knob at one end, but the other end instead of being pointed like a normal knitting needle is hooked like a crochet hook.

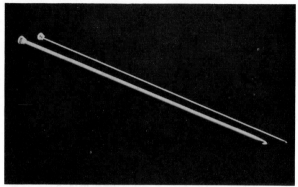

The principle of the technique is simple: all patterns including the basic plain Tunisian stitch are worked in two-row sequences – in the first row all the stitches across work are picked up and kept on the hook; in the second row the stitches are worked off one by one until you have at the end of the row only one stitch on the hook.

The fabric thus produced is firm and strong: it is in fact sometimes difficult to tell whether a fabric has been made by Tunisian crochet or by knitting, especially as many of the Tunisian stitch variations are worked to resemble knitting patterns – there is a stocking stitch variation, for example, which looks almost identical to knitting stocking stitch.

To work plain Tunisian stitch, work a chain to length required. Insert the hook into the second chain from the hook, and draw yarn through to form a loop on the hook; leave this loop on the hook and repeat the process into the next chain. Continue in this way all along the chain, so at the end of it you have a row of loops on the hook. Do not turn the work as you would normally do for conventional crochet.

Next row: take the yarn round hook and draw through the first stitch, take the yarn round the hook and draw it through the next two stitches, continue taking yarn round hook and drawing it through two stitches to the end of the row.

In the following row loops are taken back on to the hook by inserting the hook into each vertical stitch in turn and drawing through a loop. In the next row the stitches are worked off one by one as before. Continue in this way.

HAIRPIN CROCHET

This is a form of crochet worked with a normal crochet hook but the stitches are 'mounted' on a large steel hairpin or two-pronged fork. The hairpin acts as a frame for the work. Usually hairpin crochet is worked in fine cotton yarns, and it is possible to make pretty lace edgings and fringings. Strips can be joined together to give broader bands of lace fabric.

Begin as usual with a very loose chain stitch, then withdraw the crochet hook from the loop and insert the left prong of the fork upwards from below and take hold of it with the thumb and middle finger of the left hand. Now take the yarn in front of and round the right prong of the fork. Place the hook into the loop, lift up the yarn, take it through the stitch and fix it in place with a double crochet. Then take the yarn behind and over the left prong of the fork. Turn the fork, place the hook into the loop on the left prong and work another double crochet. Continue in this way. As the prong becomes covered with loops slip off the lower ones, to leave room for new loops as work progresses.

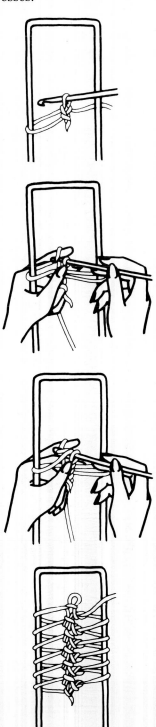

To join strips together, lay them side by side then, using a crochet hook, take two loops along the edge of the first strip and work a chain; take up two loops along the edge of the second strip and work a chain. Continue in this way.

ABBREVIATIONS

The following are the abbreviations normally used in crochet patterns.

alt.	alternate
beg.	beginning
blk(s).	block(s)
ch.	chain
cl.	cluster
cont.	continue
d.c.	double crochet
dec.	decrease(d)(ing)
d.tr.	double treble
foll.	following
gr(s).	group(s)
h.tr.	half treble
in.	inch(es)
inc.	increase(d)(ing)
p.	picot
patt.	pattern
qd.tr.	quadruple treble
rep.	repeat
sh.	shell
sp(s).	space(s)
sl.st.	slip stitch
st(s).	stitch(es)
tog.	together
tr.	treble
tr.tr.	triple treble
y.o.h.	yarn over hook

Pattern sizes. If a pattern gives a range of different sizes then normally instructions are given in size order, with the different instructions relating to larger sizes in brackets. Where only one set of figures occurs this refers to all sizes.

IMPORTANT NOTE

Stitch terminology in crochet varies not only from country to country, but also from region to region. For instance, a double crochet in some areas is called a single crochet in others. In all the patterns and instructions in this book, stitch terms used refer to the specific directions given within this chapter – e.g. wherever the instruction 'double crochet' occurs in a pattern, then work double crochet as described on page 10.

Opposite: *a selection of motifs. From top to bottom, left to right: flower-centre square (see page 26), Afghan square (see page 22), flower medallion (see page 26), flower motif (see page 26), wheel centre motif (see page 35), and six-point star (see page 33).*

Right: *matinee coat and bonnet (see page 39).*

Below: *orange and gold pram cover (see page 38).*

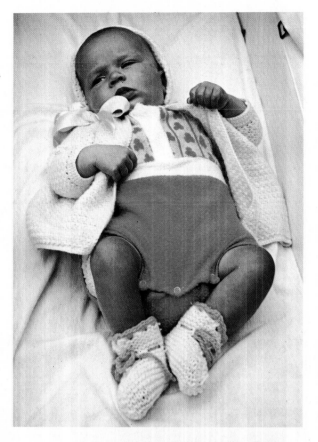

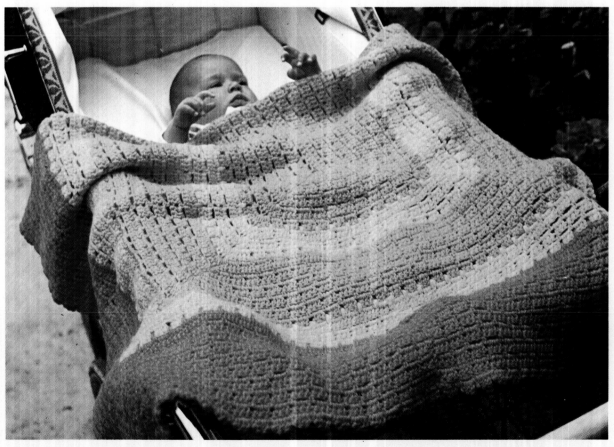

Chapter two
DICTIONARY OF STITCH PATTERNS

Note. For abbreviations used in stitch patterns throughout this chapter, see page 19.

Afghan square
illustrated in colour on page 20

This is the traditional multicoloured square which can be used to make all manner of household furnishings, including bedspreads, as well as fashion garments. Squares may all be made in single colours, or in two colours only, alternating the colours on rounds, or in multiple colours, having a different colour for every round. If multiple colours are used it is a good idea to finish each square with the same colour, and then to use this colour as the joining yarn – this creates the effect of a basic background colour, on which are superimposed all the other contrasting colours.
Our sample is worked in three colours: white, pink and blue.

With white, make 6 ch. Join into a ring with sl. st.
1st round: 2 ch., 2 tr., 3 ch., * 3 tr., 3 ch. into ring; rep. from * twice, sl.st. to first 2 ch. Join in pink.
2nd round: sl.st. to first sp., (2 ch., 3 tr., 3 ch., 3 tr.) into first 3 ch.sp., * (1 ch., 3 tr., 3 ch., 3 tr.) into next 3 ch.sp.; rep. from * twice, join with sl.st.
Join in blue.
3rd round: sl.st. to first sp., (2 ch., 2 tr., 3 ch., 3 tr.) into first 3 ch.sp., * 1 ch., 3 tr. into 1 ch.sp., (1 ch., 3 tr., 3 ch., 3 tr.) into each corner; rep. from * ending 1 ch., sl.st. to join. Join in white.
4th round: sl.st. to first sp., (2 ch., 2 tr., 3 ch., 3 tr.) into first 3 ch.sp., * 1 ch., 3 tr. into each 1 ch.sp., (1 ch., 3 tr., 3 ch., 3 tr.) into each corner; rep. from * ending 1 ch., sl.st. to join. Fasten off.

Arches

A regular openwork pattern in a firm, close fabric with a scalloped edge.

Work a ch. in a multiple of 6, plus 1 (e.g. 37).
1st row: 1 d.c. into 2nd ch. from hook, 1 d.c. into next st., * 3 ch., miss 3 sts., d.c. into each of the next 3 sts.; rep. from * ending 3 ch., miss 3 sts., 2 d.c. into each of next 2 sts., 1 ch., turn.
2nd row: 1 d.c. into first st., * 5 tr. into 3 ch.sp., miss 1 d.c., 1 d.c. into next st.; rep. from * ending 1 d.c. into centre of 3 d.c., 1 ch., turn.
3rd row: * 3 ch., 1 d.c. into each of 3 centre tr. of group; rep. from * ending 2 ch., 1 d.c. into last st., 3 ch., turn.
4th row: 2 tr. into 2 ch.sp., * 1 d.c. into centre of 3 d.c. of previous row, 5 tr., into 3 ch.sp.; rep. from * ending 1 d.c. into centre of 3 d.c., 3 tr. in last sp., 1 ch., turn.
5th row: as first row, beginning with 2 d.c.
Rep. 2nd-5th rows until work is length required.

Balancing trebles

Alternating sets of treble groups give a firm yet lacy fabric.

Work a ch. in a multiple of 4, plus 3 (e.g. 27).
1st row: (2 tr., 1 ch., 1 tr.) into 4th ch. from hook, * miss 3 ch., (3 tr., 1 ch., 1 tr.) into next st.; rep. from * ending miss 2 sts., 1 tr. in last st., 3 ch., turn.
2nd row: (2 tr., 1 ch., 1 tr.) into 1 ch.sp., * (3 tr., 1 ch., 1 tr.) into next 1 ch.sp.; rep. from * ending 1 tr. into turning ch., 3 ch., turn.
Rep. 2nd row until work is length required.

Clusters

Groups of stitches set above each other in even rows.

Work a ch. of an even number.

1st row: miss 3 ch., y.o.h., insert hook into next ch., * (y.o.h., draw through a loop, y.o.h., draw through 2 loops) 3 times into the same st., y.o.h., draw through 4 loops: 1 cluster made; 1 ch., miss 1 ch.; rep. from * ending with 1 tr., 1 ch., turn.

2nd row: work 1 d.c. on each cluster and 1 d.c. on each single ch. to end, 3 ch., turn.

3rd row: * miss 1 ch., work cluster into next st., 1 ch.; rep. from * ending 1 tr., 1 ch., turn.

Rep. 2nd and 3rd rows until work is length required.

Clusters and spaces

This stitch pattern combines clusters and open-work. The fabric produced is firm enough for a sports sweater, yet open and light enough for an evening dress.

Work a ch. in a multiple of 6, plus 1 (e.g. 37).

1st row: work 1 d.c. in 2nd ch. from hook and then 1 d.c. in each ch. to end, 6 ch., turn.

2nd row: miss first 2 d.c., 1 d.c. in next d.c., * 3 ch., miss 2 d.c., (y.o.h., draw up loop, y.o.h. and draw through 2 loops) twice in next st., y.o.h. and draw through 3 loops: 1 cluster made; 3 ch., miss 2 d.c., 1 d.c. in next d.c.; rep. from * to last 3 sts., 3 ch., 1 tr. in last d.c., 1 ch., turn.

3rd row: 1 d.c. in first tr., * 3 ch., make cluster in next d.c., 3 ch., 1 d.c. in top of next cluster; rep. from * ending 1 d.c. in 3rd ch. of turning 6 ch., 6 ch., turn.

4th row: 1 d.c. in top of first cluster, * 3 ch., make cluster in next d.c., 3 ch., 1 d.c. in top of next cluster; rep. from * ending 3 ch., 1 tr. in next d.c., 1 ch., turn.

Rep. 3rd and 4th rows until work is length required.

Double shell

An interesting use of shells to give an alternating, balanced effect.

Work a ch. in a multiple of 7, plus 5 (e.g. 26).

1st row: 1 d.c. into 2nd st., miss 2 sts., 3 tr. into next st., * 3 ch., miss 3 sts., 1 d.c. into next st., miss 2 sts., 3 tr. into next st.; rep. from * to end, 1 ch., turn.

2nd row: 1 d.c. into first tr., 3 tr. into next d.c., * 3 ch., 1 d.c. into 3 ch.sp., 3 tr. into next d.c.; rep. from * to end, 1 ch., turn.

Rep. 2nd row until work is length required.

Fancy squares

A spectacular stitch pattern which is nevertheless simple to work, giving open squares in a regular sequence.

Work a ch. in a multiple of 9, plus 2 (e.g. 38).

1st row: work 1 tr. in 3rd ch. from hook and 1 tr. in each ch. to end, 4 ch., turn.

2nd row: miss first tr., 1 d.tr. in next tr., * 4 ch., miss 1 tr., 1 tr. in each of next 3 tr., 4 ch., miss 1 tr., 1 d.tr. in each of next 4 tr.; rep. from * ending 4 ch., miss next tr., 1 d.tr. in next tr., 1 d.tr. in top of turning ch., 1 ch., turn.

3rd row: 1 d.c. in each of first 2 d.tr., * 4 ch., 1 tr. in each of next 3 tr., 4 ch., 1 d.c. in each of next 4 d.tr.; rep. from * ending 4 ch., 1 d.c. in last d.tr., 1 d.c. in top of turning ch., 1 ch., turn.

4th row: 1 d.c. in each of first 2 d.c., * 4 ch., 1 tr. in each of next 3 tr., 4 ch., 1 d.c. in each of next 4 d.c.; rep. from * ending 4 ch., 1 d.c. in each of last 2 d.c., 1 ch., turn.

5th row: rep. 4th row, 4 ch., turn.

6th row: 1 d.tr. in 2nd d.c., * 1 d.c., 1 tr. in each of next 3 tr., (1 ch., 1 d.tr.) in next d.c. 4 times; rep. from * ending (1 ch., 1 d.tr. in next d.c.) twice, 3 ch., turn.

7th row: 1 tr. in next d.tr., * 1 tr. in next 1 ch.sp., 1 tr. in each of next 3 tr., (1 tr. in next 1 ch.sp., 1 tr. in next d.tr.) 4 times; rep. from * ending 1 tr. in each of next 3 tr., 1 tr. in next 1 ch.sp., 1 tr. in next d.tr., 1 tr. in top of turning ch., 4 ch., turn.

8th row: 1 d.tr. in 2nd tr., * 4 ch., miss next tr., 1 tr. in each of next 3 tr., 4 ch., (miss next tr., 1 d.tr. in next tr.) 4 times; rep. from * ending 4 ch., 1 d.tr. in last tr., 1 d.tr. in top of turning ch., 1 ch., turn.

Rep. 3rd-8th rows until work is length required.

Above and right: *pink bolero and hat (see page 54).*

Opposite: *pink and white dress and hat (see page 51).*

Flower-centre square
illustrated in colour on page 20

A multicoloured square with a central, raised flower. Particularly attractive for cushion covers, bedspreads and so forth. Our square is worked in four colours: yellow, dark green, white and purple.

With yellow, make 5 ch., and sl.st. to form a ring.
1st round: (1 d.c., 1 tr., 1 d.c.) in each of 4 ch.
2nd round: * 2 ch., from wrong side sl.st. to base of 2nd d.c. of next st.; rep. from * 3 times.
3rd round: * 4 tr. and 1 sl.st. under next 2 ch.; rep. from * 3 times, draw dark green yarn through loop on hook, and fasten off yellow.
4th round: * 3 ch., sl.st. in base of next sl.st. of previous round; rep. from * 3 times.
5th round: * 8 tr. and 1 sl.st. under next ch.; rep. from * 3 times.
6th round: as 4th round.
7th round: * 10 tr. and 1 sl.st. under next ch.; rep. from * 3 times, draw white yarn through loop on hook, and fasten off dark green.
8th round: 3 tr. in sl.st. just made, * 2 ch., 3 tr. in 5th tr. of next petal, 1 ch., 3 tr. in same tr., 2 ch., 3 tr. in sp. before next petal; rep. from * ending 2 ch., sl.st. in top of first tr. Fasten off white yarn.
9th round: attach purple yarn in any corner ch. (between two 3 tr. groups). Work 3 ch. and in same sp. work (2 tr., 1 ch., 3 tr.), 2 ch., * (3 tr. in next sp., 2 ch.) twice, in next sp. work (3 tr., 1 ch., 3 tr.), 2 ch.; rep. from * all round, join with sl.st. to top of first tr. and fasten off.

Flower medallion

A light and lacy motif with eight petal points.

Work 6 ch., and join into a ring with sl.st.
1st round: 7 ch., (1 d.tr. into ring, 3 ch.) 7 times, sl.st. into 4th of 7 ch.
2nd round: 3 ch., * miss 3 ch., (1 tr., 6 ch., 1 tr.) into top of d.tr.; rep. from * ending last rep. miss 3 ch., 1 tr. into first d.tr., 6 ch., sl.st. into top of 3 ch.
3rd round: * (3 tr., 5 ch., 3 tr.) into next ch.sp., 1 sl.st. into 2nd tr.; rep. from * to end. Fasten off.

Flower motif
illustrated in colour on page 20

A regular, eight-petalled flowerhead shape which can be used as a trimming or, joined together, to form an attractive fabric.

Work 6 ch. and join into ring with sl.st.
1st round: 2 ch., work 23 tr. into ring, join into ring with sl.st. to 2 ch. at beg. of round.
2nd round: 4 ch., 1 tr. into same st. as sl.st., 1 ch., * miss 2 sts., (1 tr., 2 ch., 1 tr.) into next st., 1 ch.; rep. from * 6 times, sl.st. to 2 ch. at beg. of round.
3rd round: 2 ch., (1 tr., 2 ch., 2 tr.) into first 2 ch.sp., 1 d.c. into 1 ch.sp., (2 tr., 2 ch., 2 tr.) into next 2 ch.sp.; rep. from * 6 times, 1 d.c. into last 1 ch.sp., sl.st. to 2nd ch. of first 2 ch.
4th round: * (3 tr., 1 ch., 3 tr.) into 2 ch.sp., 1 d.c. on d.c. of previous round; rep. from * 7 times, sl.st. to join. Fasten off.

Lace and bars

A combination of close work and lacy sections alternating in vertical panels.

Work a ch. in a multiple of 13, plus 1 (e.g. 27).
1st row: 1 tr. into 3rd ch. from hook, 1 tr. into each st., 3 ch., turn.
2nd row: 1 tr. into first 3 sts., * 3 ch., miss 3 tr., 1 d.c. into next st., 3 ch., miss 3 tr., 6 tr. on 6 tr.; rep. from * ending with 3 ch., 1 d.c., 3 ch., 3 tr., 1 tr. into turning ch., 3 ch., turn.
3rd row: 1 tr. into each of next 3 sts., * 1 ch., 1 d.c. into 3 ch.sp., 3 ch., 1 d.c. into next 3 ch.sp., 1 ch., 6 tr. on 6 tr.; rep. from * ending with 4 tr. as 2nd row, 3 ch., turn.
4th row: 3 tr. on 3 tr., * 7 tr. into 3 ch.sp., 6 tr. on 6 tr.; rep. from * ending with 4 tr., 3 ch., turn.
Rep. 2nd-4th rows until work is length required.

Lace and picot

An ideal stitch pattern for babywear and delicate evening tops.

Work a ch. in a multiple of 7, plus 2 (e.g. 23).
1st row: 2 ch., * 1 h.tr. into each of next 2 sts., 3 ch., miss 2 sts., 1 d.c. into next st., 3 ch., miss 2 sts.; rep. from * ending with 1 h.tr. into each of last 2 sts., 2 ch., turn.
2nd row: 1 h.tr. on 2nd h.tr., * 3 ch., (1 d.c., 3 ch., 1 d.c.) on d.c., 3 ch., 2 h.tr. on 2 h.tr.; rep. from * to end, 1 ch., turn.
3rd row: 1 d.c. on 2nd h.tr., * 1 d.c. into 3 ch.sp., 5 ch., 1 d.c. into next 3 ch.sp., 1 d.c. into each of next 2 h.tr.; rep. from * to end, 1 ch., turn.
4th row: 1 d.c. on 2nd d.c., * 7 d.c. into ch. arch, 2 d.c. on 2 d.c.; rep. from * to end, 2 ch., turn.
5th row: 1 h.tr. on 2nd d.c., * 3 ch., miss 3 d.c., 1 d.c. into centre d.c. of arch, 3 ch., miss 2 d.c., 2 h.tr. on 2 d.c.; rep. from * to end, 2 ch., turn. **6th row:** as 2nd row.
Rep. 2nd-6th rows until work is length required.

Lattice and loops

Vertical bars of clusters set in lattice panels.

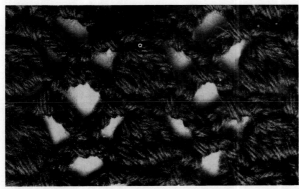

Work a ch. in a multiple of 8.
1st row: 1 d.c. in 8th ch. from hook, * 4 ch., miss 3 ch., 1 d.c. in next ch.; rep. from * to end, 4 ch., turn.
2nd row: (y.o.h., draw loop under first 4 ch. loop, y.o.h. and draw through 2 loops) 4 times, y.o.h. and draw through 4 loops, y.o.h. and draw through 2 loops: a cluster made; * 4 ch., 1 d.c. under next loop, 4 ch., work cluster under next loop; rep. from * ending with a cluster under turning ch., d.tr. in 5th ch. of turning ch., 4 ch., turn.
3rd row: * 1 d.c. under next 4 ch. loop, 4 ch.; rep. from * ending 4 ch., 1 d.c. under turning ch., 4 ch., turn.
4th row: * work cluster under next loop, 4 ch., 1 d.c. under next loop, 4 ch.; rep. from * ending with a cluster under turning ch., 1 d.tr. in top of d.tr. of last cluster row, 4 ch., turn.
Rep. 3rd and 4th rows until work is length required.

Lattice squares

A firm, openwork stitch pattern which is ideal for tailored garments.

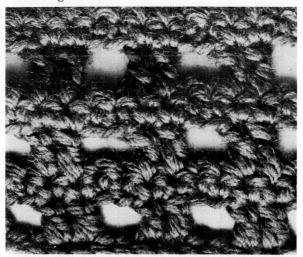

Work a ch. in a multiple of 4.
1st row: 1 tr. in 4th ch. from hook, * 2 ch., miss 2 ch., 1 tr. in each of next 2 ch.; rep. from * to end, 1 ch., turn.
2nd row: 1 d.c. in each of first 2 tr., * 1 d.c. in each ch. of 2 ch., 1 d.c. in each of next 2 tr.; rep. from * ending 1 d.c. in last tr., 1 d.c. in top of turning ch., 2 ch., turn.
3rd row: miss first ch., 1 tr. in next d.c., * 2 ch., miss 2 d.c., 1 tr. in each of next 2 d.c.; rep. from * to end, 1 ch., turn.
Rep. 2nd and 3rd rows until work is length required.

Open shells

Groups of shells spaced to give an open, lacy texture.

Work a ch. in a multiple of 5, plus 4 (e.g. 34).
1st row: 1 d.c. in 2nd ch. from hook and in each ch. to end, 3 ch., turn.
2nd row: miss first d.c., 1 tr. in next d.c., * 5 ch., miss 4 d.c., (2 tr., 1 ch., 2 tr.) in next d.c. (shell): a shell made; rep. from * ending 5 ch., 1 tr. in last 2 d.c., 3 ch., turn.
3rd row: miss first tr., 1 tr. in next tr., * 5 ch., make shell under 1 ch.sp. of next shell; rep. from * ending 5 ch., 1 tr. in last tr., 1 tr. in top of turning ch., 3 ch., turn.
4th row: miss first tr., 1 tr. in next tr., * 2 ch., 1 d.c. in centre ch. of 5 ch. of 2nd row, working over the 5 ch. of 3rd row, 2 ch., make a shell in centre of next shell; rep. from * ending 1 tr. in last tr., 1 tr. in top of turning ch., 3 ch., turn.
5th row: miss first tr., 1 tr. in next tr., * 5 ch., make shell in next shell; rep. from * ending 1 tr. in last tr., 1 tr. in top of turning ch., 3 ch., turn.
Rep. 3rd-5th rows until work is length required.

Three-colour play suit (see page 43).

Smockeasy dress (see page 46).

Pique stitch

This pattern is excellent for skirts, jackets, coats or any garment which needs a firm, stable texture.

Work a ch. to any length.
1st row: work 1 d.c. into each ch., beg. with 2nd ch. from hook.
2nd row: 2 ch., * draw loop through each of next 2 ch., y.o.h. draw through 2 loops, y.o.h. and draw through last 2 loops, 1 ch.; rep. from * to end, 1 ch., turn.
3rd row: work 1 d.c. on each group and 1 d.c. on each ch. between groups all along, 1 ch., turn.
4th row: as first row, working first 2 loops on 2nd and 3rd d.c. of previous row, 1 ch., turn.
Rep. 3rd and 4th rows until work is length required.

Popcorn stitch

In this pattern raised bobbles stand out from a flat fabric thus giving a three-dimensional effect.

Work a ch. in a multiple of 4.
1st row: beg. with 2nd ch. from hook, 1 d.c. in each ch. to end, 1 ch., turn.
2nd row: * 1 d.c. in each of first 3 d.c., 3 tr. in next d.c., take hook out of st. and insert it in first of the 3 tr., pick up loop and pull through tr.: a popcorn st. made; 1 ch. to tighten st.; rep. from * to last 3 d.c., 1 d.c. in each of last 3 d.c., 1 ch., turn.
3rd row: * 1 d.c. in each of first 3 d.c., 1 d.c. in popcorn st.; rep. from * to last 3 d.c., 1 d.c. in each of last 3 d.c., 1 ch., turn.

4th row: 1 d.c. in first d.c., * popcorn st. in next d.c., 1 d.c. in each of next 3 d.c.; rep. from * to end, ending with 1 d.c. instead of 3 d.c., 1 ch., turn.
5th row: 1 d.c. in first d.c., * 1 d.c. in popcorn st., 1 d.c. in each of next 3 d.c.; rep. from * to last 2 sts., 1 d.c. in popcorn st., 1 d.c. in last d.c., 1 ch., turn.
Rep. last 4 rows until work is length required.

Round motif in fine crochet cotton
illustrated opposite and also on page 14

Our sample is worked in No. 20 mercer-crochet cotton, with a steel crochet hook International Standard Size 1.25, and shows four round motifs joined together with a central diamond filling motif. The motifs are joined as work progresses and the filling worked between the joined motifs.

Make 7 ch., and join with sl.st. to form a ring.
1st round: 16 d.c. into ring, 1 sl.st. into first d.c.
2nd round: 8 ch., * miss 1 d.c., 1 tr. into next d.c., 5 ch.; rep. from * ending with 1 sl.st. into 3rd of 8 ch.
3rd round: * into next loop work 3 d.c., 3 ch. and 3 d.c.; rep. from * ending with 1 sl.st. into first d.c.
4th round: 1 sl.st. into each of next 2 d.c., 1 sl.st. into next loop, 1 d.c. into same loop, * 7 ch., 1 d.c. into next loop; rep. from * ending with 7 ch., 1 sl.st. into first d.c.
5th round: 1 d.c. into same place as sl.st., * 9 d.tr. into centre ch. of next loop, 1 d.c. into next d.c.; rep. from * omitting 1 d.c. at end of last rep., 1 sl.st. into first d.c.
6th round: 1 sl.st. into each of next 3 d.tr., * 1 d.c. into each of next 3 d.tr., 7 ch., miss 7 sts.; rep. from * ending with 1 sl.st. into first d.c.
7th round: 1 sl.st. into next d.c., 8 ch., 1 tr. into same place as last sl.st., * 2 ch., into centre ch. of next loop work 1 tr., 5 ch. and 1 tr., 2 ch., miss next d.c., into next d.c. work 1 tr., 5 ch. and 1 tr.; rep. from * omitting 1 tr., 5 ch. and 1 tr. at end of last rep., 1 sl.st. into 3rd of 8 ch.
8th round: 1 sl.st. into each of next 3 ch., 8 ch., 1 tr. into same place as last sl.st., * 3 ch., miss next 2 ch.sp., into centre ch. of next loop work 1 tr., 7 ch. and 1 tr., 3 ch., miss next 2 ch.sp., into centre ch. of next loop work 1 tr., 5 ch. and 1 tr.; rep. from * omitting 1 tr., 5 ch. and 1 tr. at end of last rep., 1 sl.st. into 3rd of 8 ch. Fasten off.
This completes the basic circular motif.
To make second motif and join it on to the first as you work, complete as for first motif to the end of the 7th round.
8th round: 1 sl.st. into each of next 3 ch., 8 ch., 1 tr. into same place as last sl.st., * 3 ch., miss next 2 ch.sp., 1 tr. into centre ch. of next loop, 3 ch., 1 d.c. into corresponding loop on first motif, 3 ch., 1 tr. into same place as last tr. on second motif, * 3 ch., miss next 2 ch.sp., 1 tr. into centre ch. of next loop, 2 ch., 1 d.c. into corresponding loop on first motif, 2 ch., 1 tr. into same place as last tr. on second motif; rep. from * to * once more, complete as first motif.
Make a second row of two motifs below the first, joining motifs as second motif was joined to the first and leaving one 5 ch. loop free on each motif between joinings.

To work filling motif
Work as for first motif for one round.
2nd round: 3 ch., 1 tr. into same place as sl.st., 2 tr. into each d.c., 1 sl.st. into 3rd of 3 ch.
3rd round: 1 d.c. into same place as sl.st., 1 ch., 1 d.c. into any free 5 ch. loop between joinings, * 1 ch., 1 d.c. into same place as last d.c. on filling, miss 3 tr., 5 d.tr. into next tr., 2 ch., 1 d.c. into next joining between motifs, 2 ch., 5 d.tr. into same place as last d.tr. on filling, miss 3 tr., 1 d.c. into next tr., 1 ch., 1 d.c. into next free 5 ch. loop on next motif; rep. from * omitting 1 d.c., 1 ch. and 1 d.c. at end of last rep., 1 sl.st. into first d.c. Fasten off.

Scalloped edging

An attractive finish for the edge of a sweater, dress, blouse or even a tablecloth.

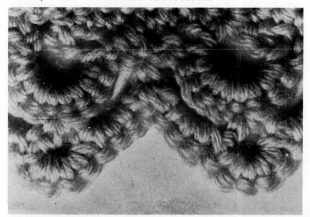

Work a ch. in a multiple of 8, plus 2 (e.g. 26).

1st row: 1 d.c. in 2nd ch., from hook and work 1 d.c. into each ch. to end, 1 ch., turn.

2nd row: working through front loops of sts., 1 d.c. in each of first 4 d.c., * (1 d.c., 7 ch., 1 d.c.) in next d.c., 1 d.c. in each of next 7 d.c.; rep. from * to last 5 d.c., (1 d.c., 8 ch., 1 d.c.) into next d.c., 1 d.c. in each of last 4 d.c., 3 ch., turn.

3rd row: working through back loops of sts., miss first d.c., 1 d.c. in next d.c., * miss 3 d.c., 9 d.c. under 7 ch.sp., miss next 3 d.c., 1 d.c. in next d.c., 1 tr. in next d.c., 1 d.c. in next d.c.; rep. from * ending miss next 3 d.c., 9 d.c. under 7 ch.sp., miss next 3 d.c., 1 d.c. in next d.c., 1 tr. in last d.c., 1 ch., turn.

4th row: 1 d.c. in first d.c., * 4 ch., (1 d.c., 5 ch., 1 d.c.) in centre d.c. of next 9 d.c., 1 d.c. in next d.c.; rep. from * working last d.c. in top of turning ch. instead of a tr., 1 ch., turn.

5th row: 1 d.c. in first d.c., * 3 d.c. under next 4 ch.sp., 5 d.c. under next 5 ch.sp., 3 d.c. under next 4 ch.sp., 1 d.c. in next d.c.; rep. from * to end. Fasten off.

Four round motifs joined together with a diamond filling in the centre.

Top: *the same square motif worked in (from left to right) No. 40,*
No. 20 and No. 10 cotton (see instructions opposite).
Bottom: *green square with diagonals and pale blue square with trebles (see page 34).*

Single shell

A delicate and pretty stitch pattern, but firm enough for most purposes.

Work a ch. in a multiple of 6, plus 3 (e.g. 27).
1st row: work 2 tr. in 3rd ch. from hook, * miss 2 ch., 1 d.c. in next ch., miss 2 ch., 5 tr. in next ch.: a shell made; rep. from * ending miss 2 ch., 3 tr. in last ch., 1 ch., turn.
2nd row: 1 d.c. in first tr., * 5 tr. in next d.c., 1 d.c. in centre tr. of shell; rep. from * ending 1 d.c. in top of turning ch., 2 ch., turn.
3rd row: 2 tr. in first d.c., * 1 d.c. in centre tr. of shell, shell in next d.c.; rep. from * ending 3 tr. in top of turning ch., 1 ch., turn.
Rep. 2nd and 3rd rows until work is length required.

Six-point star
illustrated in colour on page 20

An attractive motif which is easy to make and which can be used as a trimming.

Centre piece
Make 25 ch.
1st row: 1 d.c. in 2nd ch. from hook, 1 d.c. in each ch. to end: 24 sts.
** **2nd row**: 1 ch., 1 d.c. in first st., miss next st., 1 d.c. in each st. to last 2 sts., miss next st., 1 d.c. in last st.
3rd row: 1 ch., 1 d.c. in each st. to end. **
Rep. last 2 rows until 4 sts. remain ending with a 3rd row.
*** **Next row**: 1 ch., 1 d.c. in first st., 1 d.c. in last st.
Next row: 1 ch., draw loop through first st., draw loop through last st., yarn round hook and draw loop through 3 loops on hook. Fasten off.

First side piece
Rejoin yarn in 9th st. of first ch. and work 1 d.c. in this st., 1 d.c. in each of next 7 sts., turn: 8 sts.
Work as Centre Piece from ** to **.
Rep. last 2 rows once: 4 sts. Complete as for Centre Piece from *** to end.

Second and third side pieces (make both alike)
Rejoin yarn to 8th row of one side of Centre Piece and work 1 d.c. into this row, 1 d.c. in each of next 7 rows, turn: 8 sts.
Work as for Centre Piece from ** to **. Rep. last 2 rows once: 4 sts. Complete as Centre Piece from *** to end.

Square motif in fine crochet cotton

This delicate lacy motif is ideal for making up into a bedspread (see page 15). Our sample is in No. 10 mercer-crochet cotton, with a steel crochet hook International Standard Size 1.50. This produces a motif of about $4\frac{1}{2}$ in. square. If the motif is worked in No. 20 cotton (same hook size) you will get a $3\frac{3}{4}$ in. square; and in No. 40 cotton, a 3-in. square. See illustrations on page opposite.

Make 20 ch. and join with a sl.st. to form a ring.
1st round: work 32 d.c. into ring, 1 sl.st. into first d.c.
2nd round: 1 d.c. into same place as sl.st., * 5 ch., miss 3 d.c., 1 d.c. into next d.c.; rep. from * ending with 5 ch., 1 sl.st. into first d.c.
3rd round: 1 sl.st. into first loop, into same loop work 3 d.c., 3 ch. and 3 d.c., * 1 ch., into next loop work 3 d.c., 3 ch. and 3 d.c.; rep. from * ending with 1 ch., 1 sl.st. into first d.c.
4th row: 1 sl.st. into each of next 2 d.c., 1 sl.st. into next loop, 6 ch., leaving the last loop of each on hook, work 4 quadruple tr. into same loop, yarn over and draw through all loops on hook: a 4 quad. tr. cluster made; * 9 ch., a 3 tr. cluster into next 1 ch.sp., 9 ch., a 5 quad. tr. cluster into next loop; rep. from * omitting 9 ch. and a 5 quad. tr. cluster at end of last repeat, 6 ch., 1 tr. into first cluster.
5th row: 1 d.c. into last tr. made, * 7 ch., 1 d.c. into 3rd ch. of next loop, 7 ch., 1 d.c. into 7th ch. of next loop; rep. from * omitting 1 d.c. at end of last repeat, 1 sl.st. into first d.c.
6th row: 1 sl.st. into each of next 2 ch., 5 d.c. into same loop, * 13 tr. into next loop, 5 d.c. into next loop; rep. from * omitting 5 d.c. at end of last rep., 1 sl.st. into first d.c.
7th row: 1 sl.st. into next d.c., * 1 d.c. into next d.c., 1 tr. into each of next 6 tr., into next tr. work 1 tr., 7 ch. and 1 tr., 1 tr. into each of next 6 tr., miss 2 d.c., 1 d.c. into next d.c., 1 tr. into each of next 13 tr., miss 2 d.c.; rep. from * ending with 1 sl.st. into first d.c.
8th round: 1 sl.st. into each of next 3 tr., 3 ch., * 1 tr. into each of next 4 tr., into next loop work 4 tr., 7 ch. and 4 tr., 1 tr. into each of next 5 tr., 7 ch., miss 5 sts., 1 d.c. into each of next 4 tr., into next tr. work 1 d.c., 3 ch. and 1 d.c., 1 d.c. into each of next 4 tr., 7 ch., miss 5 sts., 1 tr. into next tr.; rep. from * omitting 1 tr. at end of last rep., 1 sl.st. into 3rd of 3 ch.
Fasten off.

Square with diagonals

illustrated in colour on page 32

The central flower of this square motif has 'arms' that radiate out towards the corners.

Make 8 ch., and join into a ring with sl.st.

1st round: 3 ch., * (y.o.h. and insert hook into ring, y.o.h. and draw through a loop, y.o.h. and draw through 1 loop, y.o.h. and draw through 2 loops) * twice, y.o.h. and draw through 3 loops, ** 5 ch., work from * to * 3 times, y.o.h. and draw through 4 loops, 2 ch., work from * to * 3 times, y.o.h. and draw through 4 loops; ** rep. from ** to ** twice, 5 ch., work from * to * 3 times, y.o.h. and draw through 4 loops, 2 ch., sl.st. to 3rd ch. of first 3 ch.

2nd round: 2 sl.st. over 2 tr., 3 ch., work from * to * of first round twice into 5 ch.sp., y.o.h., and draw through 3 loops, 2 ch., work from * to * 3 times into same ch.sp., y.o.h. and draw through 4 loops, 2 ch., 3 tr. into 2 ch.sp., 2 ch.

Continue in this way working (1 cluster, 2 ch., 1 cluster) into 5 ch.sp. and (2 ch., 3 tr., 2 ch.) into 2 ch.sp. to end of round, join with sl.st. into 3rd of 3 ch.

3rd round: 1 sl.st., 3 ch., * work (1 cluster, 2 ch., 1 cluster) into corner ch., 2 ch., 2 tr. into 2 ch.sp., 3 tr. on 3 tr. of previous round, 2 tr. into 2 ch.sp., 2 ch.; rep. from * to end, join with sl.st.

4th round: work as previous round, working tr. in tr. of previous round with 2 tr. on either side in 2 ch.sp., join with sl.st.

5th round: as 4th round.

Subsequent rounds are worked in a similar way to enlarge the square to size required.

Square with trebles

illustrated in colour on page 32

This is a close-textured square motif which can be made into any size required.

Make 10 ch. and join into a ring with sl.st.

1st round: 10 ch., (4 d.tr., 7 ch.) 3 times into ring, 3 d.tr., sl.st. to 3rd st. of first 10 ch., sl.st. over 3 sts. and turn work.

2nd round: 10 d.c. along each side, join with sl.st.

3rd round: 10 ch., (2 d.tr. into first d.c., 1 d.tr. in each of next 8 d.c., 2 d.tr. into next d.c., 7 ch.) 3 times, 2 d.tr. into first d.c. of next 10 d.c., 1 d.tr. into each of next 9 d.c., sl.st. to 3rd ch. of first 10 ch., turn work.

4th round: as 2nd round, with 18 d.c. worked on each side instead of 10.

5th round: 3 ch., 1 d.tr. into each st. and 6 into each corner. Fasten off.

Trebles and arches

An open, delicate stitch pattern.

Work a ch. in a multiple of 10, plus 7 (e.g. 37).

1st row: 1 tr. in 4th ch. from hook, 1 tr. in each of next 3 ch., * 3 ch., miss 2 ch., 1 d.c. in next ch., 3 ch., miss 2 ch., 1 tr. in each of next 5 ch.; rep. from * to end, 2 ch., turn.

2nd row: miss first tr., 1 tr. in each of next 4 tr., * 4 ch., 1 tr. in each of next 5 tr.; rep. from * ending 1 tr. in each of last 4 tr., 1 tr. in top of turning ch., 6 ch., turn.

3rd row: 1 d.c. in centre tr. of 5-tr. group, * 3 ch., 5 tr. under 4 ch.sp., 3 ch., 1 d.c. in centre tr. of next 5 tr. group; rep. from * ending 3 ch., 1 tr. in top of turning ch., 6 ch., turn.

4th row: miss 1 d.c., * 1 tr. in each of next 5 tr., 5 ch.; rep. from * ending 4 tr., 1 tr. in 3rd ch. of turning ch., 3 ch., turn.

5th row: 4 tr. in first ch.sp., * 3 ch., 1 d.c. in centre tr. of 5 tr. group, 3 ch., 5 tr. under next 5 ch.sp.; rep. from * ending 4 tr. under turning ch., 1 tr. in 3rd ch. of turning ch., 3 ch., turn.

Rep. 2nd–5th rows until work is length required.

Trebles and spaces

A pleasing, tailored stitch pattern which is excellent for men's wear and also fashion jackets and coats.

Make a ch. of an even number.

1st row: 1 tr. in 6th ch. from hook, * 1 ch., miss 1 ch., 1 tr. in next ch.; rep. from * to end, 3 ch., turn.

2nd row: miss first tr., * 2 tr. in next tr.; rep. from * ending 2 tr. in last tr., miss next ch. of turning ch., 1 tr. in next ch., 3 ch., turn.

3rd row: miss first 2 tr., 1 tr. in next tr., * 1 ch., miss 1 tr., 1 tr. in next tr.; rep. from * ending 1 tr. in last tr., 1 ch., 1 tr. in 2nd ch. of turning ch., 3 ch., turn.

Rep. 2nd and 3rd rows until work is length required.

Triangle stitch

A classic stitch pattern which is regular and firm but has a look of lightness.

Work a ch. in a multiple of 3, plus 2 (e.g. 23).
1st row: 1 tr. in 5th ch. from hook, * miss 2 ch., (1 tr., 1 ch., 1 tr.) in next ch.; rep. from * to end, turn with 5 ch.
2nd row: 1 tr. in first ch.sp., * (1 tr., 1 ch., 1 tr.) in next ch.sp.; rep. from * ending (1 tr., 2 ch., 1 tr.) into loop of 5 ch., turn with 5 ch.
Repeat 2nd row until work is length required.

Two-colour drop stitch

Stripes in two colours – use more if you wish – with an interesting stepped effect.

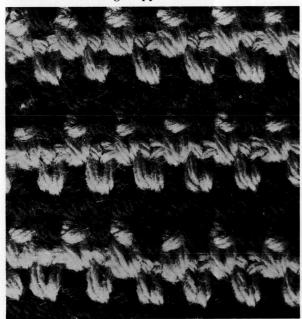

With first colour, work a ch. in a multiple of 8, plus 4 (e.g. 36).
1st row: 1 d.c. in 4th ch. from hook, * 1 ch., miss next ch., 1 d.c. in next ch.; rep. from * to end, 2 ch., turn.
2nd row: * 1 d.c. in next 1 ch.sp., 1 ch.; rep. from * ending 1 d.c. under turning ch., draw second colour through loop, and drop first colour, 2 ch., turn.
Repeat 2nd row until work is length required, alternating colours after every two rows.

Two-colour octagon

An attractive eight-sided motif which could be used as a trimming.

With first colour, work 6 ch., and join into a ring with sl.st.
1st round: 2 ch., work 15 tr. into ring, join with sl.st., joining in second colour.
2nd round: (2 ch., 1 tr., 1 ch., 2 tr.) into first st., miss 1 st., * (2 tr., 1 ch., 2 tr.) into next st., miss 1 st.; rep. from * 6 times, sl.st. to join, joining in first colour.
3rd round: (2 ch., 1 tr., 1 ch., 2 tr.) into first ch.sp., * 1 tr. between 4 tr. groups, (2 tr., 1 ch., 2 tr.) into next ch.sp.; rep. from * 7 times, 1 tr. between last 4 tr. group, sl.st. to join, joining in second colour.
4th round: work 1 d.c. into each tr. and ch.
Fasten off.

Wheel centre motif
illustrated in colour on page 20

Another version of the Afghan square, using three colours.

With first colour, make 8 ch., and join into a ring with sl.st.
1st round: 6 ch., * (1 tr., 3 ch.) 7 times into ring, sl.st. to join, joining in second colour.
2nd round: 2 ch., 3 tr., 2 ch. into first sp., * 4 tr., 2 ch. into next sp.; rep. from *, sl.st. to join, joining in third colour.
3rd round: 2 ch., 5 tr., 1 ch. into first sp., * 6 tr., 3 ch. into next sp., 6 tr., 1 ch. into next sp.; rep. from * 3 times, 6 tr., 3 ch. into next sp., sl.st. to join, joining in first colour.
4th round: 2 ch., 1 tr., 3 ch., 2 tr. into 3 ch.sp. at corner, * 3 ch., 1 d.c. between 3rd and 4th tr. of next group, 3 ch., 1 d.c. into 1 ch.sp., 3 ch., 1 d.c. between 3rd and 4th tr. of next group, 3 ch., (2 tr., 3 ch., 2 tr.) into 3 ch.sp. at corner; rep. from * 3 times, sl.st. to join. Fasten off.

Chapter three
FIRST THINGS FIRST
pretty and practical baby clothes

Cotton cot blanket

MATERIALS
15 oz. Twilleys Lyscordet fine knitting cotton. One crochet hook International Standard Size 2.50.

MEASUREMENTS
Finished shawl is approx. 41 in. square.

TENSION
1 patt. measures $1\frac{1}{4}$ in.

ABBREVIATIONS
See page 19.

TO MAKE
Centre
Begin with 230 ch. (to measure 41 in.).
Foundation row: 1 d.c. into 7th ch. from hook, * 1 d.c. into each of next 4 ch., 5 ch., miss 2 ch., 1 d.c. into next ch.; rep. from * to within last 6 ch., 1 d.c. into each of next 4 ch., 2 ch., 1 tr. into last ch., turn: 32 groups.
1st row: 1 d.c. into first tr., 3 ch., * miss next d.c., 1 d.c. into each of next 3 d.c., 3 ch., 1 d.c. into next 5 ch. loop, 3 ch.; rep. from * ending with miss next d.c., 1 d.c. into each of next 3 d.c., 3 ch., 1 d.c. into 3rd of 5 ch., turn.
2nd row: 1 d.c. into first d.c., * 1 d.c. into next 3 ch. loop, 3 ch., miss next d.c., 1 d.c. into next d.c., 3 ch., 1 d.c. into next 3 ch.sp., 1 d.c. into next d.c.; rep. from * to end, turn.
3rd row: 1 d.c. into first d.c., 1 d.c. into next 3 ch.sp., 5 ch., 1 d.c. into next 3 ch.sp., 1 d.c. into each of next 3 d.c.; rep. from * omitting last d.c. of last rep., turn.
4th row: 1 d.c. into first d.c., * 1 d.c. into next d.c., 3 ch., 1 d.c. into next 5 ch. loop, 3 ch., miss next d.c., 1 d.c. into next 2 d.c.; rep. from * to end, turn.

5th row: 1 d.c. into first d.c., * 3 ch., 1 d.c. into next 3 ch.sp., 1 d.c. into next d.c., 1 d.c. into next 3 ch.sp., 3 ch., miss next d.c., 1 d.c. into next d.c.; rep. from * to end, turn.
6th row: 5 ch., * 1 d.c. into next 3 ch.sp., 1 d.c. into each of next 3 d.c., 1 d.c. into next 3 ch.sp., 5 ch.; rep. from * ending with 1 d.c. into next 3 ch.sp., 1 d.c. into each of next 3 d.c., 1 d.c. into next 3 ch.sp., 2 ch., 1 tr. into last d.c., turn.
Repeat 1st–6th patt. rows 31 times more, then work first patt. row once.
Fasten off.

EDGING
1st round: with right side facing attach yarn to one corner, 3 d.c. into same place, * work 223 d.c. evenly along until next corner is reached, 3 d.c. into corner; rep. from * omitting 3 d.c. at end of last rep., 1 d.c. into first d.c.
2nd and 3rd rounds: working in continuous rounds, make 1 d.c. into each d.c., sl.st. into first d.c.
Fasten off.

Fringed shawl

MATERIALS
5 oz. Wendy Double Knit Nylonised in first shade, 7 oz. in second shade and 5 oz. in third shade. One crochet hook International Standard Size 4.00.

MEASUREMENTS
32 in. wide; 36 in. long.

TENSION
16 sts. to 3 in. when stretched and pressed.

ABBREVIATIONS
See page 19; A., first shade; B., second shade; C., third shade.

TO MAKE
Commence with 176 ch.
1st row: 1 d.c. into 2nd ch. from hook, 1 d.c. into each ch. to end, 1 ch.; turn.

2nd row: working into back loops only of all sts., insert hook into each of next 2 d.c. but do not put yarn over hook (3 loops on hook), y.o.h. and draw through all loops on hook (1 st. dec.), 1 d.c. into each of next 5 sts., * 3 d.c. into next st., 1 d.c. into each of next 6 sts., insert hook into each of next 3 d.c. but do not put yarn over hook (4 loops on hook), y.o.h. and draw through all loops on hook (2 sts. dec.), 1 d.c. into each of next 6 d.c.; rep. from * 9 times, 3 d.c. into next st., 1 d.c. into each of next 5 d.c., insert hook into each of next 2 d.c. but do not put yarn over hook (3 loops on hook), y.o.h. and draw through all loops on hook (1 st. dec.).

The 2nd row forms the patt. Rep. 2nd row throughout. Work 10 rows in A., 10 rows in B., 10 rows in C. Cont. in this colour patt. until Cover measures 36 in., ending with 10 rows in A. Fasten off.

FRINGE

Cut B. into 8-in. strands. Taking 6 strands at a time, knot at ¾-in. intervals along side of Cover: fold strands in half, insert hook into edge and pull through folded end of strands then pull ends through loop.

TO COMPLETE

Stretch Cover out to correct measurements, pin sides and press with a steam iron held ½ in. above work or with a warm iron over a damp cloth.

Angel top

also illustrated on previous page

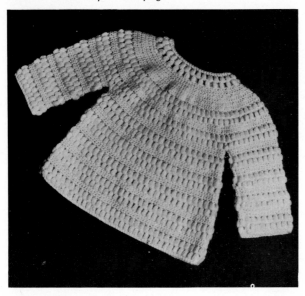

MATERIALS

7 (8) balls (25 gr.) Twilleys Cortina Super Crochet Wool. Crochet hooks International Standard Sizes 3.50 and 3.00. Four small buttons.

MEASUREMENTS

To fit birth to 9 months (9 to 18 months); length 11 (12½) in.; sleeve seam 6 (7½) in.

TENSION

5 sts. to 1 in.; 6 rows (1 patt.) to 1½ in.

ABBREVIATIONS

See page 19.

BACK AND FRONT (make 2 pieces alike)

With No. 3.00 hook make 72 (78) ch.
1st row: 1 d.c. in 2nd ch. from hook, 1 d.c. in each d.c. to end.
2nd row: 1 ch., 1 d.c. in each d.c. to end.
Cont. in patt. as follows:
1st patt. row: 2 ch., * (y.o.h., insert hook into next d.c. and draw through long loop) 4 times, y.o.h., draw through 8 loops, y.o.h., draw through 2 loops, 1 ch., miss 1 d.c.; rep. from * to last st., 1 tr. in last st.
2nd patt. row: 2 ch., * (y.o.h., insert hook into next ch.sp. and draw through long loop) 4 times, y.o.h., draw through 8 loops, y.o.h., draw through 2 loops, 1 ch.; rep. from * to last st., 1 tr. in last st. Change to No. 3.50 hook.
3rd patt. row: 1 ch., 1 d.c. in each st. to end.
Repeat 3rd row 3 times more. **
These 6 rows form pattern.
Change to No. 3.00 hook.
Work 5 (11) rows more in patt.
Next row: 1 ch., 1 d.c. in each of first 1 (7) d.c., (miss 1 d.c., 1 d.c. in each of next 6 d.c.) to end: 61 (67) sts. Work 11 rows straight in patt., beg. with a first patt. row.
Next row: 1 ch., 1 d.c. in each of first 1 (7) d.c., (miss 1 d.c., 1 d.c. in each of next 5 d.c.) to end: 51 (57) sts. Work 5 rows more in patt., beg. with a first patt. row.
Fasten off.

SLEEVES (make 2 alike)

With No. 3.00 hook make 42 (48) ch.
Work as for Back and Front to **.
Work 17 (23) rows more in patt.: 3 (4) patts. and 5 rows in all.
Fasten off.

YOKE

Tie a length of coloured thread to centre st. of Back as a marker. With No. 3.50 hook, work d.c. across 25 (28) sts. at left-hand side of marker then work in d.c. across one sleeve, front, then second sleeve, then work across 25 (28) sts. at right-hand side of back to marker: 183 (207) sts. Work 5 rows in patt., beg. with a first patt. row.
Next row: 1 ch., 1 d.c. in each of first 3 d.c., (miss 1 d.c., 1 d.c. in each of next 5 d.c.) to end: 153 (173) sts.
Work 5 rows in patt., beg. with a first patt. row.
Next row: 1 ch., 1 d.c. in each of first 3 d.c., (miss 1 d.c., 1 d.c. in each of next 4 d.c.) to end: 123 (139) sts.
Now continue in d.c. for every row on No. 3.50 hook.
Work 3 (5) rows d.c.
Next row: 1 ch., work 1 d.c. in each of first 3 d.c., (miss 1 d.c., 1 d.c. in each of next 3 d.c.) to end: 93 (105) sts.
Work 3 (5) rows d.c.
Next row: 1 ch., 1 d.c. in each of first 3 d.c., (miss 1 d.c., 1 d.c. in each of next 2 d.c.) to end: 63 (71) sts.
Change to No. 3.00 hook and work first and 2nd patt. rows.
Change to No. 3.50 hook and work 1 row d.c.
Fasten off.

TO COMPLETE

Press very lightly.
Join side and sleeve seams.
With No. 3.00 hook work 2 rows d.c. round back opening, making 4 evenly-spaced buttonholes on right side of opening on 2nd row (make buttonholes to fit buttons – see page 14).
Fasten off.
Press border and seams. Sew on buttons.

Gold pram cover

illustrated in colour on page 21

MATERIALS

19 oz. Emu Scotch double knitting in main shade, 11 oz. in first contrast shade and 8 oz. in second contrast shade. One crochet hook International Standard Size 5.50.

MEASUREMENTS

Length 64 in. approx.; width 43 in. approx.

TENSION

Three 3-tr. gr. measure 2 in.; 1 tr. is 1 in. deep.

ABBREVIATIONS

See page 19; M., main shade; A., first contrast shade; B., second contrast shade.

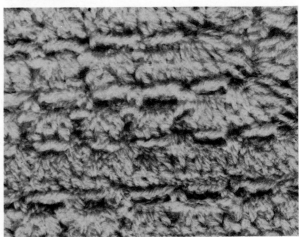

TO MAKE

With A., commence with 60 ch.

1st round: working through upper loops of ch., 1 d.c. into 2nd ch. from hook, 1 d.c. into each ch. to end, working along other side of ch. through upper loops, 1 d.c. into each ch. to end, sl.st. to first d.c.

2nd round: * 3 ch., miss 1 d.c., 1 d.c. into next d.c.; rep. from * 29 times, 3 ch., 1 d.c. across end of work, 3 ch., 1 d.c. into first d.c. on other side, ** miss 1 d.c., 3 ch., 1 d.c. into next d.c.; rep. from ** to end, 1 d.c. across end of work, 3 ch., sl.st. into ch.sp.

3rd round: 6 tr. into first 3-ch.sp., 3 tr. into each 3-ch.sp. to last sp. of first side, 6 tr. into next sp., 3 tr. into next sp., 6 tr. into next sp., 3 tr. into each ch.sp. to last sp. of 2nd side, 6 tr. into next sp., 3 tr. into next 3 ch. sp., sl.st. to first tr.

4th round: 3 ch., 1 d.c. into centre sp. of corner 6 tr., * 3 ch., 1 d.c. into sp. between next 3 tr.; rep. from * to corner 6 tr., 3 ch., 1 d.c. into centre sp. of corner 6 tr., 3 ch., 1 d.c. into sp. between next 3 tr., 3 ch., 1 d.c. into centre sp. of corner 6 tr., ** 3 ch., 1 d.c. into sp. between next 3 tr.; rep. from ** to corner, 3 ch., 1 d.c. into centre sp. of corner tr., 3 ch., 1 d.c. into sp. between next 3 tr., sl.st. to first ch.

5th round: work 6 tr. into each d.c. at centre of previous corner 6 tr. and 3 tr. into each 3-ch.sp. all round, sl.st. to first tr.

The 4th and 5th rounds form the patt.

Work 8 more rounds.

Change to B.

Note. When changing colour, on the 2nd round of the new colour (tr. round), work 1 tr. into sp. between each 3 tr. of previous tr. round (making a long st.) and between each of the 3 tr. of round being worked.

Work 6 rounds with B.

Change to A. and work 12 rounds.

Change to B. and work 6 rounds.

Change to M. and work 18 rounds, then 1 more 4th patt. round.

EDGING

With M. work 1 d.c., 3 tr. and 1 d.c. into each 3-ch.sp. and 6 tr. into each corner d.c., sl.st. to first d.c.

Fasten off.

TO COMPLETE

Press lightly.

Matinee coat and bonnet
illustrated in colour on page 21

MATERIALS

5 oz. Emu Baby Nylon 3 ply. One crochet hook International Standard Size 3.00. ¾ yd. narrow ribbon for jacket. 1½ yd. ribbon, 1 in. wide, for bonnet.

MEASUREMENTS

To fit chest size 16–18 in. **Bonnet:** face edge measures 11 in.

TENSION

7 cl. to 2 in.

ABBREVIATIONS

See page 19.

COAT BACK

Make 98 ch., turn, * miss 1 st., 1 d.c. and 1 tr. into next st.; rep. from * ending 1 d.c. into last st., 1 ch.: 97 sts. and 48 cls. This row forms the patt. Cont. in patt. until 40 rows of patt. have been completed, always remembering to turn with 1 ch.

Shape Waist

Next row: 1 d.c. into first st., (miss 1 st., 1 d.c. on each of next 2 sts., miss 1 st., 1 d.c. on each of next 2 sts., miss 1 st., 1 d.c. on next st.) to end: 61 d.c.

Work 5 more rows in d.c. still turning each row with 1 ch. Change back to main patt. and work 4 rows.

Shape Armholes

Next row: patt. to within 3 sts. of end of previous row, 1 d.c. into next st., turn leaving 2 sts. unworked.

Rep. this row 5 times more: 49 sts.

Cut yarn and leave for yoke.

COAT RIGHT FRONT

Make 50 ch. and work exactly as for Back until the 40th row has been worked, then dec. for waist as for Back: 31 d.c.

Work 5 rows of d.c. on d.c., then change back to patt. for 4 rows.

Shape Armhole

Next row: as first row of Back armhole shaping.

Next row: in patt.

Rep. the last 2 rows twice more, thus leaving 2 sts. unworked at armhole edge 3 times: 25 sts. and 12 cls.

Cut yarn and leave for yoke.

COAT LEFT FRONT

Work exactly as for Right Front (as work is reversible).

COAT SLEEVES (make 2 alike)

Make 38 ch. and work in patt. as for Back until 30 rows are completed, shaping sides by inc. on 5th row thus: 1 d.c. and 1 tr. into each of the first 3 sts., patt. to last 3 sts., 1 d.c. and 1 tr. into each of the next 2 sts., 1 d.c. in last st.: 41 sts.

Work 5 rows straight. Rep. last 6 rows twice more, then 5th row again. There are now 53 sts. and 26 cls.

Work 1 more row. (Cont. for more rows for longer sleeve.)

Shape Top

Work as for Back armhole shaping until 41 sts. and 20 cls. rem.

Cut yarn and leave for yoke.

COAT YOKE

Arrange all pieces in order, 25 sts. of Right Front, 41 sts. of one Sleeve, 49 sts. of Back, 41 sts. of other Sleeve, and 25 sts. of Left Front. Across these, joining yarn work thus: 1 ch., 12 cls., hook through last st. of Front and first st. of Sleeve, yarn over hook and pull through 2 loops, yarn over hook and pull through last 2 loops (as for d.c.), 1 tr. into same st., miss 1 thus completing a cl., 1 cl. 19 times, hook through last d.c. of sleeve and first d.c. of back, yarn over hook and pull through, yarn over

hook and pull through 2 loops as for d.c., 1 tr. into same st. (another cl. completed), 23 cls., hook through last of back and first of second sleeve, complete cl. as before then work other side to match: 177 sts. and 88 cls. Work 1 row in patt. Now dec. thus on every alt. row and always working 1 row in patt. between each dec. row always turning with 1 ch.

Next row (3rd yoke row): 4 cl., (miss 3 sts., 7 cl.) 10 times, miss 3 sts., patt. 3 cl., 1 d.c.: 155 sts.

5th yoke row: 3 cl., (miss 3 sts., 6 cl.) 10 times, miss 3 sts., patt. to end, ending 1 d.c. in last st.: 133 sts.

7th yoke row: 2 cl., (miss 3 sts., 5 cl.) 10 times, patt. to end working 1 d.c. in last st.: 111 sts.

9th yoke row: 1 cl., (miss 3 sts., 4 cl.) 10 times, patt. to end working 1 d.c. in last st.: 89 sts.

11th yoke row: (miss 3 sts., 3 cl.) 10 times, patt. to end working 1 d.c. in last st.: 67 sts.

13th yoke row: (miss 3 sts., 2 cl.) 11 times, 1 d.c. in last st.

15th yoke row: 2 ch. instead of 1 turning ch., * 1 tr., 1 ch., miss 1 st.; rep. from * ending 1 tr. in last st.

This completes yoke, but do not cut yarn. Beg. with last loop on hook, work 3 rows d.c. along centre front edge, lower edge and along other front edge, working 3 d.c. into each of the 2 lower corners on both rows and turning with 1 ch. Fasten off.

Work 6 rows of d.c. along wrist edge of each sleeve, always turning with 1 ch. Fasten off.

BONNET

Make 76 ch. and work in patt. as for Back: 75 sts. and 37 cl.

Work 22 rows straight, then always turning with 1 ch. shape top on every alt. row thus:

23rd row: 3 cl., (miss 3 sts., 7 cl.) 4 times, miss 3 sts., 1 cl. on next st., 1 d.c. on last st.: 65 sts.

25th row: 2 cl., (miss 3 sts., 6 cl.) 4 times, miss 3 sts., 1 cl. on next st., 1 d.c. on last st.: 55 sts.

27th row: 1 ch., (miss 3 sts., 5 cl.) 4 times, miss 3 sts., 1 cl., 1 d.c. in last st.: 45 sts.

29th row: (miss 3 sts., 4 cl.) 4 times, miss 3 sts., 1 cl., 1 d.c. in last st.: 35 sts.

31st row: (miss 3 sts., 3 cl.) 4 times, miss 2 sts., 1 d.c. in last st.: 25 sts. **33rd row:** (miss 3 sts., 1 cl.) to last st., 1 d.c. in st. Fasten off.

TO COMPLETE

Press work lightly with dry cloth and cool iron.

Coat. Join side and sleeve seams, then neatly join the 4 tiny armhole seams. Thread narrow ribbon through neck edge.

Bonnet. Sew back seam for about 2 in. from tip. Work 2 rows of d.c. along lower edge. Fold back brim for about 1½ in. and catch neatly in place. Work 1 row of d.c. round back neck edge. Sew on ribbon at each side.

Lacy dress

MATERIALS

4 (5, 6) balls Emu Machine Washable Baby Quickerknit. One crochet hook International Standard Size 3.50. Six buttons.

MEASUREMENTS

To fit chest size 20 (22, 24) in.; sleeve seam 1½ in.; length from shoulder 12 (15, 18) in.

TENSION

2 patt. to 1 in.

ABBREVIATIONS

See page 19.

BACK

Commence with 92 (98, 104) ch. to measure 16 (17, 18) in.

Foundation row: 1 d.c. into 2nd ch. from hook, * 5 ch., miss 2 ch., 1 d.c. into next ch.; rep. from * to within last 3 ch., miss 2 ch., 1 d.tr. into last ch., turn: 30 (32, 34) 5 ch. loops.

1st patt. row: 5 ch., 1 sl. st. into 2nd ch. from hook, 1 tr. into first d.tr., (1 tr., 2 ch., 1 sl.st. into last tr. made, 1 tr.) into centre ch. of each loop to end, turn.

2nd patt. row: 1 d.c. into first tr., 5 ch., miss next tr., * 1 d.c. into next sp., 5 ch., miss 2 tr.; rep. from * ending with 1 d.c. into next sp., 2 ch., 1 d.tr. into 3rd of 3 ch., turn.

Sizes 22 and 24 only. Rep. last 2 rows once more.

All sizes. ** Dec. row: 5 ch., 1 sl.st. into 2nd ch. from hook, 1 tr. into first d.tr., (1 tr., 2 ch., 1 sl.st. into last tr. made, 1 tr.) into centre ch. of each of next 5 loops, 1 tr. into centre sp. of next loop, 2 ch., 1 sl.st. into last tr. made, 1 tr. into centre ch. of next loop, (1 tr., 2 ch., 1 sl.st. into last tr. made, 1 tr.) into centre ch. of each loop to within last 8 loops, end with 1 tr. into centre ch. of next loop, 2 ch., 1 sl.st. into last tr. made, 1 tr. into centre ch. of next loop, (1 tr., 2 ch., 1 sl.st. into last tr. made, 1 tr.) into centre ch. of each loop to end, turn: 2 loops dec. Rep. 2nd patt. row once.

Rep. first and 2nd patt. rows 1 (1, 2) times. **

Rep. from ** to ** 3 times more.

Rep. dec. row once then cont. in patt. until work measures 8½ (11, 13½) in. from beg. ending with first patt. row. Fasten off.

Shape Armholes and Back Opening

Mark sp. at centre of row.

1st row: miss first 4 tr. and attach yarn to next sp., * 5 ch., miss 2 tr., 1 d.c. into next sp.; rep. from * ending with 2 ch., miss 2 tr., 1 d.tr. into marked sp., turn.

Rep. first patt. row once.

3rd row: sl.st. across first 2 tr., 1 sl.st. into next sp., * 5 ch., miss 2 tr., 1 d.c. into next sp.; rep. from * to end, turn.

For size 24 only. Rep. last 2 rows once more.

For all sizes. Cont. in patt. until armhole measures 3½ (4, 4½) in. from beg., ending with 2nd patt. row. Fasten off.

Second Side of Opening

1st row: attach yarn to marked sp., then patt. to within last 2 patt., turn.

Repeat first patt. row once.

3rd row: patt. to within last patt., turn.

For size 24 only. Rep. last 2 rows once more.

For all sizes. Complete as for first side. Fasten off.

FRONT

Work as for Back to armhole shaping. Fasten off.

Shape Armholes

1st row: miss first 4 tr. and attach yarn to next sp., * 5 ch., miss 2 tr., 1 d.c. into next sp.; rep. from * to within last 3 patt., end with 2 ch., miss 2 tr., 1 tr. into next sp., turn.

Rep. first patt. row once.

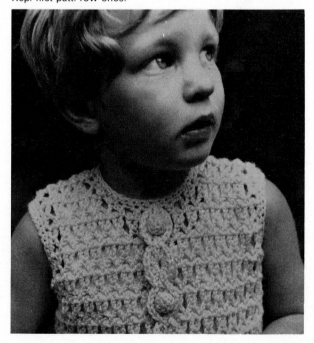

3rd row: sl.st. across first 2 tr., 1 sl.st. into next sp., * 5 ch., miss 2 tr., 1 d.c. into next sp.; rep. from * to within last 2 sp., end with 2 ch., miss 2 tr., 1 d.tr. into next sp., turn.
For size 24 only. Rep. last 2 rows once more.
For all sizes. Cont. in patt. until 2 rows less than back.

Shape Neck
1st row: work as for first patt. row until 5 (6, 6) patts. are completed, turn.
Rep. 3rd row of first side of back armhole shaping once.
Rep. first patt. row once. Fasten off.
Second Side of Neck
1st row: attach yarn to centre ch. of 5 (6, 6) loop working from other edge then patt. to end, turn.
Rep. 3rd row of 2nd side of back armhole shaping once then rep. first patt. row once. Fasten off.
BIB
Commence with 32 ch. to measure 5½ in.
1st row: 1 d.c. into 2nd ch. from hook, * miss 2 ch., 6 tr. into next ch., miss 2 ch., 1 d.c. into next ch.; rep. from * to end, then working along other side of commencing ch., ** miss 2 ch., 6 tr. into next ch., miss 2 ch., 1 d.c. into next ch.; rep. from ** to end. Fasten off.

TO COMPLETE
Join side and shoulder seams. Sew bib down centre front of dress from neck edge. Sew 3 buttons down bib for decoration.
Lower Edging
1st round: with right side facing attach yarn to edge then work d.c. evenly round having a multiple of 6, 1 d.c. into first d.c.
2nd round: * miss 2 d.c., 6 tr. into next d.c., miss 2 d.c., 1 d.c. into next d.c.; rep. from * all round omitting 1 d.c. at end of last rep., sl.st. into first d.c.
Fasten off.
Armhole Edgings (make both alike)
1st round: with right side facing attach yarn to edge then work d.c. evenly round, 1 d.c. into first d.c.
2nd round: make 1 d.c. into each d.c., sl.st. into first d.c.
Fasten off.
Neck Edging
1st row: with right side facing attach yarn to base of back opening then work d.c. up back, round neck and down 2nd side, turn.
2nd row: make 1 d.c. into each d.c. all round working 3 d.c. into centre d.c. at both corners. Fasten off. Sew 3 buttons evenly down back opening and use sps. in patt. as buttonholes.

Chapter four
PICKED FOR PLAYTIME
attractive designs to make for younger children

Flower motif dress

MATERIALS
6 (7, 8, 9, 10) balls (25 gr.) Twilleys Cortina Super Crochet Wool. Crochet hooks International Standard Sizes 3.00, 3.50 and 4.00.

MEASUREMENTS
To fit chest size 18 (21, 24, 27, 30) in.; length 15 (18½, 22, 25½, 29) in.

TENSION
1 patt. (9 sts.) to 1½ in.; 13 sts. and 6½ rows to 2 in. over treble.

ABBREVIATIONS
See page 19.

YOKE
With No. 3.00 hook make 60 (69, 78, 87, 96) ch. loosely for front.
1st row: 2 ch. for first st., 1 tr. in 3rd ch., (1 tr. in next ch.) to end.
2nd row: 2 ch. (for first tr.), 1 tr. in 2nd tr., (1 tr. in next tr.) to end. This row forms tr. patt.
Work 2 rows more in tr.

Front Armhole Shaping
Next row: sl.st. across first 8 (9, 10, 11, 12) tr., 2 ch., 1 tr. in 2nd tr., (1 tr. in next tr.) to last 8 (9, 10, 11, 12) sts., turn: 44 (51, 58, 65, 72) sts.
Work on these sts. only for 1½ (2, 2, 2½, 3) in.
Neck dividing row: 2 ch., 1 tr. in 2nd tr., (1 tr. in next tr.) 6 (7, 8, 9, 10) times, turn. Work on these sts. only.
Work 1 row.
Next row: work to last tr., turn.
Rep. last 2 rows once more: 6 (7, 8, 9, 10) sts.
Work 1 (2, 2, 2, 2) in. straight in tr., ending at armhole edge.
Next row: work to last tr., 2 tr. in last tr. Work 1 row straight.
Rep. last 2 rows once more. **
Fasten off.
Return to neck dividing row, leave centre 28 (33, 38, 43, 48) sts., rejoin yarn and work across remaining 8 (9, 10, 11, 12) sts. Work other side of neck to match first side to **, ending at armhole edge.
Next row: work to end, make 28 (33, 38, 43, 48) ch., work across 8 (9, 10, 11, 12) sts. of other side.
Work 1½ (2, 2, 2½, 3) in. straight.

Back Armhole Shaping
Next row: break yarn, make 8 (9, 10, 11, 12) ch., work across row, make 8 (9, 10, 11, 12) ch.: 60 (69, 78, 87, 96) sts. Work 4 rows in tr. across all sts.

BACK SKIRT
*** **Next row:** work in d.c. across row, inc. 5 (3, 1) sts. for first, 2nd and 3rd sizes respectively and dec. 1 (3) sts. for 4th and 5th sizes respectively across row: 65 (72, 79, 86, 93) sts.
Patt. foundation row (wrong side): 2 ch., 1 h.tr. in each of first 2 d.c., (3 ch., miss 2 d.c., 1 d.c. in next d.c., 3 ch., miss 2 d.c., 1 h.tr. in each of next 2 d.c.) to end.
Now patt. as follows:
1st row: 2 ch., 1 h.tr. in 2nd h.tr., (3 ch., work 1 d.c., 3 ch., 1 d.c. all in next d.c., 3 ch., 1 h.tr. in each of next 2 h.tr.) to end.
2nd row: 1 ch., 1 d.c. in 2nd h.tr., (1 d.c. in 3-ch.sp., 5 ch., miss centre d.c. group, 1 d.c. in 3 ch.sp., 1 d.c. in each of next 2 h.tr.) to end.
3rd row: 1 ch., 1 d.c. in 2nd d.c., (miss 1 d.c., 7 d.c. in 5 ch.sp., miss 1 d.c., 1 d.c. in each of next 2 d.c.) to end.
4th row: 2 ch., 1 h.tr. in 2nd d.c., (3 ch., miss 3 d.c., 1 d.c. in next d.c., 3 ch., miss 3 d.c., 1 h.tr. in each of next 2 d.c.) to end.
These 4 rows form the patt.
Continue in patt. until work measures 3 (4, 5, 6, 7) in. from start of patt.
Change to No. 3.50 hook and work 4 (5, 6, 7, 8) in. more in patt. Change to No. 4.00 hook and continue in patt. until work measures 15 (18½, 22, 25½, 29) in. from shoulder, ending with a first patt. row. Adjust length here if required. (To measure, fold yoke in half and measure shoulder at centre of neck shaping.)
Fasten off.

FRONT SKIRT
Rejoin yarn to front yoke ch. edge and work as Back from ***.

TO COMPLETE
Borders
With No. 3.00 hook work d.c. all around neck edge.
Next row: (1 d.c. in next d.c., 5 ch., miss 1 d.c.) all round, sl.st. to first d.c., fasten off.
Join side seams and work 2 rows d.c. around armholes.

Flower Motif
With No. 3.00 hook make 6 ch. and sl.st. into a ring.
1st round: (4 ch., 1 d.c. into ring) 5 times, sl.st. to first ch.
2nd round: work (1 d.c., 5 ch., 1 d.c.) in each sp., sl.st. to first d.c.
3rd round: (5 ch., 1 d.c. into foundation ring between d.c.) 5 times, sl.st. to first ch.
4th round: work (2 d.c., 7 ch., 2 d.c.) into each sp., sl.st. to first d.c.
5th round: (6 ch., 1 d.c. into foundation ring between d.c.) 5 times, sl.st. to first ch.
6th round: work (2 d.c., 9 ch., 2 d.c.) into each sp., sl.st. to first d.c. Fasten off.

To Make Up
Press lightly. Sew flower motif to side of front yoke, as shown in illustration, left. Press seams.

Three-colour play suit
illustrated in colour on page 28

MATERIALS
4 (4, 5) 50-gr. balls Patons Promise in main shade, and 1 ball in each of two contrasting shades. Crochet hooks International Standard Sizes 3.00 and 4.00. A 6-in. (7-in., 8-in.) zip fastener. A 2-in. buckle.

MEASUREMENTS
To fit chest size 23 (26, 29) in.; length from top of shoulders 18 (20, 22) in.

TENSION
8½ sts. and 12 rows to 2 in. over d.c. on No. 4.00 hook.

ABBREVIATIONS

See page 19; M., main shade; C., contrast shade; dec. 1 on d.c. rows, decrease 1 stitch on double crochet rows as follows: (draw loop through next st.) twice, y.o.h., and draw through all 3 loops on hook; dec. 1 on h.tr. rows, decrease 1 stitch on half treble rows as follows: y.o.h., draw loop through next st., y.o.h., draw loop through 2 loops, y.o.h., draw loop through next st., y.o.h., draw through all 4 loops on hook.
Note. The turning ch. counts as 1 st., the first st. being missed on every row unless otherwise stated.

STRIPE PATTERN

1st row: join 1st C. in first st., and work 2 ch., 1 h.tr. in each rem. st. to end. Break 1st C.
2nd row: join 2nd C. in first st., and work 1 ch., 1 d.c. in each rem. st. to end, turn with 2 ch.
3rd row: 1 h.tr. in each st. to end, turn with 1 ch.
4th row: 1 d.c. in each st. to end.
Break 2nd C.
5th row: join 1st C. in first st. and work 2 ch., 1 h.tr. in each remaining st. to end.
Break 1st C.
These 5 rows form stripe patt.

LEFT LEG

With No. 4.00 hook and M., make 75 (77, 79) ch.
Foundation row (right side): 1 d.c. in 2nd ch. from hook, 1 d.c. in each remaining ch., turn with 1 ch.: 74 (76, 78) sts.
1st row: 1 d.c. in each st. to end, turn with 1 ch.
2nd row: 2 d.c. in next st., 1 d.c. in each st. to last 2 sts., 2 d.c. in next st., 1 d.c. in last st., turn with 1 ch.
Rep. first and 2nd rows once more, then first row again, omitting turning ch. on last row: 78 (80, 82) sts.
Fasten off.

RIGHT LEG

Work as for Left Leg.

MAIN PART

With right side facing, leaving first 7 sts. of Right Leg free, join 1st C. to next st. and work 2 ch., dec. 1, 1 h.tr. in each st. to last 3 sts., leave these 3 sts. unworked and continue across Left Leg as follows: leaving first 3 sts. free, work 1 h.tr. in each st. to last 10 sts., dec. 1, 1 h.tr. in next st., turn: 134 (138, 142) sts.
Break 1st C.
Next row: as 2nd row of stripe patt.
Next row: dec. 1, 1 h.tr. in each st. to last 3 sts., dec. 1, 1 h.tr., turn with 1 ch.
Next row: as 4th row of stripe patt.
Next row: join 1st C. in first st. and work 2 ch., dec. 1, 1 h.tr. in each st. to last 3 sts., dec. 1, 1 h.tr. in next st.: 130 (134, 138) sts.
Break 1st C.
Next row: join M. in first st. and work 1 ch., 1 d.c. in each st. to end, turn with 1 ch.
Next row: 14 (14, 15) d.c., (dec. 1, 31 (32, 33) d.c.) 3 times, dec. 1, d.c. to end, turn with 1 ch.
Work 2 (3, 4) rows straight in d.c.
Next row: 13 (14, 14) d.c., (dec. 1, 30 (31, 32) d.c.) 3 times, dec. 1, d.c. to end, turn with 1 ch.
Work 2 (3, 4) rows straight in d.c.
Next row: 13 (13, 14) d.c., (dec. 1, 29 (30, 31) d.c.) 3 times, dec. 1, d.c. to end, turn with 1 ch.: 118 (122, 126) sts.
Next row: 1 d.c. in each st. to end, turn.
Break M.

Shape Front Opening

Next row: leaving first 3 sts. free, join 1st C. to next st. and work 2 ch., 1 h.tr. in each st. to last 3 sts., turn: 112 (116, 120) sts.
Break 1st C.
Work 4 rows stripe patt., starting with a 2nd row.
Next row: join M. in first st. and work 1 ch., 1 d.c. in each st. to end, turn with 1 ch.
Next row: 10 d.c., (dec. 1, 28 (29, 30) d.c.) 3 times, dec. 1, d.c. to end, turn with 1 ch.: 108 (112, 116) sts.
Work 2 (3, 4) rows straight in d.c.
Next row: 9 d.c., (dec. 1, 27 (28, 29) d.c.) 3 times, dec. 1, d.c. to end, turn with 1 ch.
Work 2 (3, 4) rows straight in d.c.
Next row: 9 d.c., (dec. 1, 26 (27, 28) d.c.) 3 times, dec. 1, d.c. to end, turn with 1 ch.: 100 (104, 108) sts.
Work 3 rows straight in d.c., omitting turning ch. at end of last row.
Break M. (2 extra rows in M. have been worked here for position of Belt).
Work 5 rows stripe patt.
1st size only. Join in M. and work 9 rows d.c., omitting turning ch. on last row.
Work 5 rows stripe patt.
Join in M. and work 5 rows d.c.
2nd and 3rd sizes only. Join in M. and work (5, 6) rows straight in d.c.
Next row: (12, 13) d.c., (2 d.c. in next st., (25, 26) d.c.) 3 times, 2 d.c. in next st., d.c. to end, turn with 1 ch.: (108, 112) sts.

Work (3, 4) rows straight in d.c.
Next row: (12, 13) d.c., (2 d.c. in next st., (26, 27) d.c.) 3 times, 2 d.c. in next st., d.c. to end, turn with 1 ch.: (112, 116) sts.
Next row: 1 d.c. in each st. to end, turn.
Break M.
Work 5 rows stripe patt.
Join in M. and work 1 row in d.c.
2nd size only. Work 6 rows more in d.c.
3rd size only. Next row: 14 d.c., (2 d.c. in next st., 28 d.c.) 3 times, 2 d.c. in next st., d.c. to end, turn with 1 ch.
Work 3 rows straight in d.c.
Next row: 14 d.c., (2 d.c. in next st., 29 d.c.) 3 times, d.c. to end, turn with 1 ch.: 124 sts.
Work 3 rows straight in d.c.
All sizes. Divide for right front and shape as follows:
Next row: dec. 1, 18 (21, 24) d.c., dec. 1, 1 d.c., turn with 1 ch.: 22 (25, 28) sts.
Next row: 1 d.c. in each st. to end, turn with 1 ch.
Next row: dec. 1, 16 (19, 22) d.c., dec. 1, 1 d.c., turn with 1 ch.
Next row: 1 d.c. in each st. to end, turn.
Break M. Work 5 rows stripe patt. Join in M. and work 1 row in d.c.
Dec. 1 st. at each end as before on next and every following 3rd (4th, 5th) row until 14 (17, 20) sts. remain.
Next row: 1 d.c. in each st. to end, turn.
Break M. Work 5 rows stripe patt.
Join in M. and work 1 row in d.c.
Next row: dec. 1, 8 (11, 14) d.c., dec. 1, 1 d.c., turn with 1 ch.: 12 (15, 18) sts.
Work 4 (6, 8) rows straight in d.c., omitting turning ch. at end of last row.

Shape Shoulder
Next row: sl.st. over 4 (5, 6) sts., d.c. to end, turn with 1 ch.
Next row: 3 (4, 5) d.c., 4 (5, 6) sl.st.
Fasten off.

Left Front
With right side facing, join M. to 24th (27th, 30th) st. from end and work 1 ch., dec. 1, 18 (21, 24) d.c., dec. 1, 1 d.c.: 22 (25, 28) sts.
Complete to match Right Front reversing shapings.

Back
With right side facing, leaving 2 sts. free at underarm, join M. to next st. and work 1 ch., dec. 1, 42 (48, 54) d.c., dec. 1, 1 d.c., turn with 1 ch.: 46 (52, 58) sts.
Next row: in d.c. to end, turn with 1 ch.
Next row: dec. 1, 1 d.c. in each st. to last 3 sts., dec. 1, 1 d.c., turn with 1 ch.
Next row: in d.c. to end, turn with 1 ch.
Break M. Work 5 rows stripe patt. Join in M. and work 1 row d.c.
Dec. 1 st. at each end as before on next and every following 3rd (4th, 5th) row until 38 (44, 50) sts. remain.
Next row: in d.c. to end, turn. Break M.
Next row: join 1st C. in first st. and work 2 ch., 13 (16, 19) h.tr., turn.
Break 1st C. Work 4 rows stripe patt., starting with a 2nd row. Join in M. and work 1 row d.c.
Next row: dec. 1, 1 d.c. in each st. to last 3 sts., dec. 1, 1 d.c., turn with 1 ch.
Work 4 (6, 8) rows straight in d.c.

Shape Shoulder
Next row: d.c. to last 4 (5, 6) sts., turn.
Next row: sl.st. over 4 (5, 6) sts., 1 d.c. in each st. to end.
Fasten off.
With right side facing, leaving 10 sts. free, join in 1st C. to next st. and work 2 ch., 1 h.tr. in each st. to end.
Complete to match first side reversing shapings.

TO COMPLETE
Block each piece by pinning out round edges and press lightly using a warm iron and slightly damp cloth.
Join shoulder, leg and crutch seams, join front seam to opening.
Using 1st C. work a running stitch through each 3rd row of stripe patt.

Armhole Borders
With right side facing, No. 3.00 hook and M., start at underarm and work 1 row d.c. all round armhole, turn with 1 ch.
Work 4 rows more in d.c., omitting ch. at end of last row.
Fasten off.

Front Border
With right side facing, No. 3.00 hook and M., start at base of opening on Right Front and work in d.c. up Right Front, round neck and down Left Front, turn with 1 ch.
Work 4 rows more in d.c. omitting ch. at end of last row.
Fasten off.

Leg Borders
With right side facing, No. 3.00 hook and M., work 1 round d.c. all round leg working into remaining loop of starting ch.
Fasten off. Neatly join armhole borders. Stitch front borders to base of opening. Press seams. Sew zip in position.

BELT
With No. 4.00 hook and M., make 8 ch.
1st row: 1 d.c. in 2nd ch. from hook, 1 d.c. in each st. to end, turn with 1 ch.: 7 sts.
2nd row: 1 d.c. in each st. to end, turn with 1 ch.
Rep. last row until Belt measures 29 (32, 35) in. or required length, when slightly stretched.
Dec. 1 st. at each end of next 3 rows.
Fasten off.
With No. 3.00 hook and M., work 1 round d.c. all round Belt, working 1 d.c., 1 ch., 1 d.c. at corners.
Fasten off. Attach buckle.

Belt Tabs (make 4 alike)
With No. 3.00 hook and M., make 13 ch.
1st row: 1 d.c. in 2nd ch. from hook, 1 d.c. in each remaining ch., 1 d.c., 1 ch., 1 d.c. into row end, work 1 d.c. in each remaining ch. loop of starting ch., 1 d.c., 1 ch., 1 d.c. into row end, join with a sl.st. Fasten off. Attach 2 tabs to wide strip of M. approximately 3 in. from opening. Sew remaining tabs at back to correspond.

Two-colour dress
illustrated in colour on page 17

MATERIALS
9 (10, 10) 25-gr. balls Wendy Invitation Cotton in main colour, and 1 ball in a contrasting colour. One crochet hook International Standard Size 3.00. Six buttons.

MEASUREMENTS
To fit chest size 20 (22, 24) in.; length 14 (16, 18) in.

TENSION
9 tr. measure 1 in.

ABBREVIATIONS
See page 19; cr.tr., crossed trebles (1 tr. in 2nd st., 1 tr. in first st.); p., picot (3 ch., 1 d.c. in first ch.); cl., cluster (make 1 d.tr. leaving last loop on hook, then make one more d.tr. pulling all loops through); M., main colour; C., contrast colour.

BACK BODICE

With M., make 56 (60, 64) ch.

1st row: 1 tr. in 3rd ch., 1 tr. in each ch. to end.

2nd row: 3 ch., miss 2 tr., 1 tr. in next tr., 1 tr. in last of 2 missed tr., * miss 1 tr., 1 tr. in next tr., 1 tr. in missed tr.; rep. from * to end, finishing with 1 tr. in top of 3 ch.

3rd row: 3 ch., then work 1 tr. in each tr. to end.

Rep. 2nd and 3rd rows once.

Shape Armholes

1st row: sl.st. to 5th tr., 3 ch., work in cr.tr. to the last 5 sts., 1 tr. in first of 5 sts., turn. **

Rep. 3rd and 2nd rows 3 times.

Rep. 3rd row then work 3 ch., 8 patts., 1 tr.

Fasten off.

To Make Other Shoulder

Miss 14 tr., attach yarn to 15th tr., 3 ch., work 8 patts.

Fasten off.

FRONT BODICE

Work as for Back Bodice to **.

Rep. 3rd and 2nd rows twice.

Rep. 3rd row then work 3 ch., 8 patts., 1 tr., turn.

Work 3rd and 2nd rows on these 8 patts. Fasten off.

Work other side to match, missing 14 tr.

Fasten off. Sew sides of bodice.

SKIRT

Begin at right under-arm seam of bodice.

1st row: 3 ch., * 2 tr. in next tr., 1 tr. in next tr.; rep. from * all over bodice, turn.

2nd row: 4 ch., miss 2 tr., * into next st. work 1 cl. (see Abbreviations), work 1 p., then work 1 cl., 1 ch., 1 d.tr. (all in same tr.), miss 3 sts.; rep. from * to end, finishing with 1 d.tr. in top of 3 ch., turn.

3rd row: 4 ch., * 1 cl., 1 p., 1 cl., 1 ch., 1 d.tr. in 1 ch. loop; rep. from * to end, finishing with 1 d.tr. in top of 4 ch.

Rep. 3rd row 12 times (adjust length here, if required).

Fasten off.

TO COMPLETE

Sew seam of skirt.

Edgings

With C., make edgings round neckline and armholes as follows:

1st row: work all round evenly in d.c., commencing on seam of bodice.

2nd row: commencing at left under-arm work 3rd row of patt. making 1 patt. in every other d.c. up to shoulder, work 3 buttonholes in shoulder by working 1 d.c., 2 ch., miss 1 d.c., work 6 d.c., 2 ch., miss 1 d.c., work 6 d.c., 2 ch., miss 1 d.c., work in d.c. to next shoulder, 3 d.c., 2 ch., miss 1 d.c., work 6 d.c., 2 ch., miss 1 d.c., work 6 d.c., 2 ch., miss 1 d.c., 1 d.c. in next d.c., 1 d.tr., work in patt. over armhole as on other armhole to top of shoulder, work in d.c. over shoulder without buttonholes to other end on second shoulder, work other half of armhole as on first half. Join to start of work and fasten off.

Sew on buttons to correspond with buttonholes.

Smockeasy dress

also illustrated in colour on page 29

MATERIALS

5 (6, 7) balls Emu Tricel with Nylon in main shade, 1 ball in a contrast shade. Crochet hooks International Standard Sizes 4.00, 3.50, 3.00 and 2.50.

MEASUREMENTS

To fit chest size 24 (25, 26) in.

TENSION

7 sts. to 1 in. on No. 2.50 hook.

ABBREVIATIONS

See page 19; M., main; C., contrast.

BACK AND FRONT (make 2 pieces alike)
Bodice

With M. and No. 2.50 hook, make 90 (94, 98) ch.

Next row: 1 tr. in 6th ch. from hook, (1 ch., miss 1 ch., 1 tr. in next st.) to end.

Next row: 4 ch., 1 tr. in first tr., (1 ch., 1 tr. in next tr.) to end.

Cont. to rep. last row until work is 2 (2½, 3) in.

Break yarn and rejoin at 5th (6th, 7th) tr. along, work to corresponding point at end of row, turn.

Cont. on these sts. till work is 2½ in. from beg. of armhole shaping.

Next row: work 4 ch., 1 tr. in first tr., (1 ch., 1 tr. in next tr.) 7 (8, 9) times, turn.

Work on this 'shoulder' until it is 2½ (2¾, 3) in.

Fasten off. Work second 'shoulder' to correspond.

Skirt

With M. and No. 3.00 hook, work along base of bodice making 44 (48, 52) d.c.

1st row: 5 ch., * miss 1 d.c., (2 tr., 2 ch., 2 tr.) into next d.c., 2 ch., miss 1 d.c., 1 tr. into next d.c., 2 ch.; rep. from * to last 4 sts., miss 1 d.c., (2 tr., 2 ch., 2 tr.) into next d.c., 2 ch., miss 1 d.c., 1 tr. into last d.c.

2nd row: 5 ch., * (2 tr., 2 ch., 2 tr.) into centre of first group, 2 ch., 1 tr. into single tr., 2 ch.; rep. from * to last 4 sts., (2 tr., 2 ch., 2 tr.) into centre of group, 2 ch., 1 tr. into single tr.

Now rep. last row until skirt is 2 in., change to No. 3.50 hook for next 2 in., and then to No. 4.00 hook and cont. until skirt is 9½ (10¾, 12) in. Fasten off.

TO COMPLETE
Join shoulder seams and side seams of dress.

Bodice Trim
With C. and No. 2.50 hook, work round neck and armhole edges as follows:

1st round: work all round evenly in d.c. making a multiple of 4 sts.

Next round: 1 ch., * 1 d.c. into next 4 d.c., 3 ch., sl.st. into 3rd ch. from hook· rep. from * all round.

Hem Edging
With C. and No. 2.50 hook work a picot edge as follows: * 2 d.c. into 2 ch., 1 d.c. into each of 2 tr., then in 2 ch.sp. work (1 d.c., 3 ch., sl.st. into 3rd ch. from hook, 1 d.c.), 1 d.c. into each of 2 tr., 2 d.c. into 2 ch., 1 d.c. into single tr.; rep. from * to end, finishing 1 d.c. into top of ch. Fasten off.

Smocking
With No. 2.50 hook and C., work smocking over dress front bodice, following chart and instructions on page 48, and working in the following sequence:

1st row: chain stitch.

2nd-6th rows: zig-zag stitch.

7th-8th rows: feather stitch.

9th-13th rows: zig-zag stitch.

14th row: chain stitch.

If required, further rows of chain stitch or another row of feather stitch can be worked above and below this block for the two larger sizes.

Rows

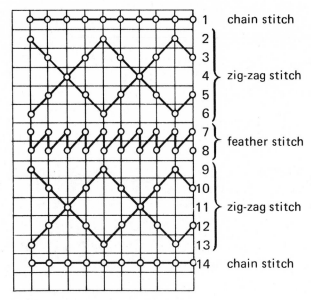

1 — chain stitch

2 ⎫
3 ⎬ zig-zag stitch
4
5
6 ⎭

7 ⎫
8 ⎬ feather stitch

9 ⎫
10
11 ⎬ zig-zag stitch
12
13 ⎭

14 — chain stitch

Smocking chart

1 square = 1 hole in the crochet

TO WORK SMOCKEASY CROCHET
Smockeasy is worked over the treble section of the garment. When following the chart always work from right to left keeping yarn to right side of work. All stitches are worked over the surface by putting the crochet hook under a complete treble and pulling yarn through, following the lines on the chart and working in the correct colour. Each square on the chart represents one hole in the crochet.

The Stitches
Chain stitch: 1 d.c., 1 ch. over each tr.
Zig-zag stitch: 1 d.c., 2 ch., moving from right to left.
Feather stitch: this is worked over 2 rows in the following way: 1 d.c. (from right to left) over first tr. in first row, 1 ch., 1 d.c. (from left to right) over first tr., in row above, * 1 ch., 1 d.c. (from right to left) over 2nd tr. in first row, 1 ch., 1 d.c. (from left to right) over 2nd tr. in row above; rep. from * to end, working over each tr. in the correct sequence.

Yellow and white dress
also illustrated on page 17

MATERIALS
7 (9) 25-gr. balls Twilleys Cortina in white, 1 ball in yellow. One crochet hook International Standard Size 3.00 (3.50). Two buttons.

MEASUREMENTS
To fit chest size 22 (24) in.; length 16½ in.; width right round underarms 24 in.

TENSION
4 d.c. and 6 rows to 1 in. on No. 3.00 hook; 4 patt. to 1 in. on No. 3.50 hook.

ABBREVIATIONS
See page 19; W., white; Y., yellow.

FRONT
With No. 3.00 (3.50) hook and W. make 90 ch. loosely.

1st row: 1 d.c. into 3rd ch. from hook, * 1 ch., miss 1 ch., 1 d.c. into next ch.; rep. from * to end: 44 sps.
2nd row: 1 ch., * 1 d.c. into next sp., 1 ch.; rep. from * to end, 1 d.c. into end.
Rep. 2nd row twice more.

Shape Armholes
1st row: sl.st. into 1 sp., 1 d.c., 1 sp. and 1 d.c., patt. until 4 sts. remain, turn.
2nd row: sl.st. into sp., patt. until 1 sp remains, turn.
Rep. 2nd row twice more: 34 sps.
Continue without shaping until 28 rows have been worked from beginning edge.

Shape Neck (left side)
Work in patt. over 12 sps., turn.
Next row: 1 d.c. into sp., patt. to end.
Next row: patt. to last sp., 1 d.c. into sp.
Rep. the last 2 rows until 8 sps. remain.
Continue without dec. until 36 rows have been worked.
Fasten off.

Shape Neck (right side)
Join yarn into 12th sp. from end.
Next row: patt. to the last sp., 1 d.c. into sp.
Complete as for left side.

BACK
Work as for Front until 14 rows have been worked.
Patt. over 17 sps., turn.
Cont. in patt. on these 17 sps. until 34 rows have been worked from beginning edge. Patt. until 10 sps. have been worked, turn, 1 d.c. into sp., patt. to end. Fasten off.
Join yarn into next sp. for opening, patt. to end, cont. until 34 rows have been worked.
Sl.st. until 10 sps. remain.
Continue to end as for first side; join side seams together.

SKIRT

Using lengths of coloured cotton, mark each row at side edges as work progresses.
Do not join rounds with sl.st.
Join yarn to one side seam.
1st round: * 1 ch., 1 d.c. into next sp.; rep. from * to end.
2nd round: 1 ch., 1 d.c., 1 ch., 1 d.c. into next sp., cont. in patt. to next marker, 1 ch., 1 d.c., 1 ch., 1 d.c. into next sp., cont. in patt. to next marker.
3rd round: as first round.
4th round: 1 ch., 1 d.c., 1 ch., 1 d.c. into next sp., place marker, 1 ch., 1 d.c., 1 ch., 1 d.c. into next sp., patt. until 1 sp. remains from next marker, 1 ch., 1 d.c., 1 ch., 1 d.c. into next sp., place marker, 1 ch., 1 d.c., 1 ch., 1 d.c. into next sp., patt. to end.
5th round: rep. first round.
6th round: inc. each side of markers, work as 4th round.
****Work 10 rounds without inc.
Next round: as 4th round. **
Rep. from ** to ** until work measures 16½ in. from shoulder.

Edging

1st round: * 1 d.c. into sp., 1 d.c. into d.c.; rep. from * to end.
2nd round: 1 d.c. into each d.c. to end, sl.st. into next d.c.
Fasten off.

SLEEVES (make 2 alike)

With No. 3.00 (3.50) hook and W., make 58 ch.
1st row: 1 d.c. into 3 ch. from hook, * 1 ch., miss 1 ch., 1 d.c. into next ch.; rep. from * to end.
2nd and 3rd rows: join in Y. work in patt.
4th and 5th rows: join in W., work in patt.
6th and 7th rows: as 2nd and 3rd rows.
Join W., sl.st. into 1 sp., 1 d.c., 1 sp., 1 d.c., patt. until 4 sts. remain, turn.
Next row: sl.st. into sp., patt. to last sp., turn.
Cont. dec. as last row working 2 rows Y. and 2 rows W., until there are 8 patts. Y. and 8 patts. W., without the first row.
Fasten off.

POCKETS (make 2 alike)

With W., make 12 ch.
1st row: 1 d.c. into 3rd ch. from hook, * 1 ch., 1 d.c. into next ch.; rep. from * to end.
2nd row: join Y. Inc. into first d.c., patt. to last d.c., inc. into d.c.
3rd row: as 2nd row.
4th and 5th rows: join W., and rep. 2nd and 3rd rows.
Cont. without inc. using alt. colours until 5 patts. of Y. have been worked. Work 1 row in W.
Work 2 rows of Edging as for lower edge of Skirt.
Fasten off.

TO COMPLETE

Press with a warm iron over a damp cloth.
Join shoulders, sleeve seams and sew sleeves into armholes.

Neck Edging

1st round: with W., work in patt. round neck edge, 1 d.c. into each row on each side of back opening.
2nd round: 1 d.c. into corner, * 1 d.c. into sp., 1 d.c. into d.c.; rep. from * to top of opening, 1 d.c. into corner, 2 ch., miss 2 d.c., 1 d.c. into each of next 7 d.c., 2 ch., miss 2 d.c., 1 d.c. into each d.c. to end of first side, 1 d.c. into each d.c. to end of second side. Join with sl.st.

To Make Up

Turn edges of pockets in about ¼ in., and sew on to skirt front positioning each 3 in. down from waist and 1½ in. from side marker. Sew on buttons to back opening to correspond with buttonholes worked in edging. Press seams.

Loopy-fringed midi coat

illustrated in full length overleaf

MATERIALS

15 (16, 17) balls (50 gr. each) Robin Aran Pure New Wool. One crochet hook International Standard Size 5.00.

MEASUREMENTS

To fit chest size 26 (28, 30) in.; length 29 (31, 33) in.; length of sleeve seam 12½ (13½, 14½) in.

TENSION

8 sts. and 9 rows to 2 in. over d.c.

ABBREVIATIONS

See page 19; m. loop, make loop st.: insert hook into next st., draw up a 1-in. loop on first finger of left hand, draw yarn through st. as in making d.c., y.o.h., draw through 2 loops on hook and drop 1-in. loop from finger (loop patt. is formed at back of work).

BACK

Commence with 69 (73, 77) ch. made fairly loosely.
Foundation row: 1 d.c. into 2nd ch. from hook, 1 d.c. into each ch. to end; turn: 68 (72, 76) d.c.
1st row: 2 ch. (to stand as first d.c.), 1 d.c. into each d.c. to end; turn.
2nd row: 2 ch., m. loop into each d.c. to last d.c., 1 d.c. into last d.c.; turn.
Rep. the last 2 rows twice.
Cont. in d.c., dec. 1 st. (by working 2 sts. leaving last loop of each on hook, y.o.h. and draw through all loops on hook) at each end of 10th and then every foll. 12th row until 64 sts. remain, then every foll. 10th row until 52 (56, 60) sts. remain (work should measure 20 (21, 22) in.).
Cont. straight until work measures 23½ (25, 27½) in., ending with a right-side row.

Shape Armholes
Next row: sl.st. over 3 (4, 4) sts., d.c. to last 3 (4, 4) sts.; turn: 46 (48, 52) d.c.
Work 1 row straight.
Dec. 1 st. at each end of the next 4 rows: 38 (40, 44) sts.
Work straight until armholes measure 5½ (6, 6½) in.

Shape Shoulders
Next row: sl.st. over 5 (5, 6) d.c., 1 d.c. into each of next 28 (30, 32) d.c.; turn.
Next row: sl.st. over 5 (6, 6) d.c., 1 d.c. into each of next 18 (18, 20) d.c.; break yarn and fasten off.

LEFT FRONT
Commence with 37 (39, 41) ch. and work the first 7 rows as given for Back: 36 (38, 40) sts.
Work 1 row in d.c.
** **Next row:** 2 ch., m. loop into each of next 4 sts., 1 d.c. into each d.c. to end; turn.
Cont. working in d.c. keeping the front border of 4 loops and *at the same time* dec. 1 st. at end of the 10th and every foll. 12th row until 34 sts. remain, then every foll. 10th row until 28 (30, 32) sts. remain.
Now work straight until Front measures same as Back to armhole, ending at side edge.

Shape Armhole and Neck

Next row: sl.st. over 3 (4, 4) sts., d.c. to within 2 sts. of loop border, dec. 1, work to end; turn.

Work 1 row straight.

*** Dec. 1 st. at armhole edge on the next 4 rows and *at the same time* dec. 1 st. at neck edge inside border on every foll. 5th row until 16 (17, 18) sts. remain.

Cont. straight until armhole measures same as Back armhole to shoulder, ending at armhole edge ***

Shape Shoulder

Next row: sl.st. over 5 (5, 6) sts., work to end; break yarn and fasten off.

Rejoin yarn to 6th st. from front edge and cont in patt. (4 loops) on the last 6 sts. Work until band when slightly stretched fits to centre back neck. Break yarn and fasten off.

RIGHT FRONT

Work as Left Front to **.

Next row: 2 ch., 1 d.c. into each d.c. to last 5 d.c., m. loop into each of next 4 d.c., 1 d.c. into last d.c.; turn.

Now work as Left Front, but dec. at beg. of rows until 28 (30, 32) sts. remain. Work straight until Right Front measures same as Left Front to armhole, ending at front edge.

Shape Neck and Armhole

Next row: dec. 1 inside loop border, work to last 3 (4, 4) d.c.; turn.

Work 1 row straight.

Now work as Left Front from *** to ***, but end at front edge.

Shape Shoulder

Next row: work to last 5 (5, 6) sts.; break yarn and fasten off.

Cont. with loops on last 6 sts. as for Left Front.

SLEEVES (make 2 alike)

Commence with 27 (29, 31) ch. and work the first 7 rows as for Back: 26 (28, 30) sts.

Now work in d.c., inc. 1 st. at each end of the 5th and every foll. 7th row until there are 36 (40, 44) sts. Work straight until Sleeve measures 12½ (13½, 14½) in., ending with a wrong-side row.

Shape Top

Next row: sl.st. over 3 (4, 4) d.c., d.c. to last 3 (4, 4) d.c.; turn.

Work 1 row straight.

Now dec. 1 st. at beg. of next 12 rows: 18 (20, 24) sts., then dec. 1 st. at each end of every row until 8 (8, 10) sts. remain. Break yarn and fasten off.

TO COMPLETE

Press d.c. parts only on wrong side using a warm iron over a damp cloth.

Join shoulder, side and sleeve seams. Set in Sleeves. Join ends of band and st. band to back of neck. Press seams.

Pink and white dress and hat
illustrated in colour on page 24

MATERIALS

For dress: 6 (7, 8) 1-oz. balls Patons Fiona in pink, and 3 balls in white. Three small buttons. **For hat:** 1 ball of same yarn in pink, and 1 ball in white. **For both:** crochet hooks International Standard Sizes 4.00 and 3.50.

MEASUREMENTS

Dress: to fit chest size 22 (24, 26) in.; length from top of shoulders 16½ (18½, 20½) in.; sleeve seam 1½ in.

Hat: to fit an average size child's head.

TENSION

8 sts. and 4 rows to 2 in. measured over tr. on No. 4.00 hook.

ABBREVIATIONS

See page 19; P., pink; W., white.

Note. Turning ch. of previous row counts as 1 stitch, and the first stitch is missed on every row.

DRESS BACK YOKE

With No. 4.00 hook and P., make 49 (53, 57) ch., marking the 23rd (25th, 27th) ch., turn.

** **1st row (right side):** 1 tr. in 5th ch. from hook, 1 tr. in each ch. to end, turn with 3 ch.: 46 (50, 54) sts.

2nd row: miss first st., * 1 tr. in next st.; rep. from * ending 1 tr. in top of 3 ch., turn with 3 ch.

Rep. last row once more, omitting turning ch.

Shape Armholes

Next row: sl.st. over 4 sts., 3 ch., patt. to last 4 sts., turn.

Next row: sl.st. over 1 st., 3 ch., patt. to last st., turn.

Rep. last row until 32 (36, 40) sts. remain, turn with 3 ch. ** Work straight until Yoke measures 5½ (6, 6½) in., omitting turning ch. on last row, and ending with wrong side facing.

Shape Shoulders

Next row: sl.st. over 4 (4, 5) sts., 3 ch., patt. to last 4 (4, 5) sts., turn.

Next row: sl.st. over 4 (5, 5) sts., 3 ch., patt. to last 4 (5, 5) sts.

Fasten off.

FRONT YOKE

With No. 4.00 hook and P., make 49 (53, 57) ch., turn.

Work as for Back Yoke from ** to **.

Work a few rows straight until Yoke measures 4 (4½, 5) in., ending with right side facing.

Divide for Neck

Next row: patt. 10 (11, 12), turn.

Next row: sl.st. over 2 sts., 3 ch., patt. to end, turn with 3 ch.

Next row: in patt.

Shape Shoulder

Next row: patt. 4 (5, 5).

Fasten off.

Leaving centre 12 (14, 16) sts. unworked, rejoin yarn in next st. and finish to correspond with first side, reversing shapings.

Join side seams.

SKIRT (worked in one piece)

With right side of Yoke facing, No. 4.00 hook and P., rejoin yarn in marked st. on Back Yoke.

1st round: 3 ch., 2 tr. in st. just worked into, * miss 1 st., 3 tr. in next st.; rep. from * all round yoke edge, ending sl.st. in top of 3 ch.: 46 (50, 54) groups of 3 tr.

Join in W.

2nd round: in W., 4 ch., 1 tr. in sp. between first and last groups of 3 tr. of previous round, * (1 tr., 1 ch., 1 tr.) in sp. between next 2 groups of 3 tr. of previous round; rep. from * ending sl.st. in 3rd of 4 ch.

3rd round: in P., 3 ch., 2 tr. in sp. between first and last groups of previous round, * 3 tr. in sp. between next 2 groups of 1 tr., 1 ch., 1 tr. of previous round; rep. from * ending sl.st. in top of 3 ch.

4th round: in W., work sl.st. into ch.sp. of last group of 1 tr., 1 ch., 1 tr. of 1 round below, 4 ch., 1 tr. in same ch.sp., * (1 tr., 1 ch., 1 tr.) in ch.sp. of next group of 1 round below; rep. from * ending sl.st. in 3rd of 4 ch.

The last 2 rows form patt.

Work straight in patt. until Dress measures 10½ (12, 13½) in. from yoke line, ending with a 4th round.

** Change to No. 3.50 hook.

Next round: in P., 1 ch., 1 d.c. in st. just worked into, * 1 d.c. in next ch.sp., 1 d.c. in each of next 2 tr.; rep. from * ending 1 d.c. in last tr., join with sl.st. in first ch.

Next round: in P., 1 ch., 1 d.c. in each d.c., ending sl.st. in first ch.

Rep. last round twice more.

Fasten off. **

SLEEVES (make 2 alike)

With No. 3.50 hook and P., make 31 (33, 35) ch., turn.

1st row (right side): 1 d.c. in 2nd ch. from hook, 1 d.c. in each ch. to end, turn with 1 ch.: 30 (32, 34) sts.

2nd row: 1 d.c. in each d.c., turn with 1 ch.

Rep. last row twice more, turning with 3 ch. on last row.

Change to No. 4.00 hook.

5th row: 1 tr. in first d.c., * 1 tr. in next d.c.; rep. from * to last d.c., 2 tr. in last d.c., turn with 3 ch.: 32 (34, 36) sts.

6th row: miss first st., * 1 tr. in next tr.; rep. from *, ending 1 tr. in top of 3 ch., turn.

Shape Top

7th row: sl.st. over 4 sts., 3 ch., patt. to last 4 sts., turn.

8th row: sl.st. over 1 st., 3 ch., patt. to last st., turn.

Rep. last row until 20 sts. remain.

Next row: sl.st. over 2 sts., 3 ch., patt. to last 2 sts., turn.

Rep. last row once more: 12 sts. Fasten off.

TO COMPLETE

With wrong side of work facing, block each piece by pinning out round edges, and press each piece lightly using a warm iron and slightly damp cloth.

Join right shoulder seam, then join left shoulder seam for ½ in. from side edge.

With right side facing for next row, No. 3.50 hook and P., work 4 rows d.c. all round neck.

Back Shoulder Border

With right side facing for first row, No. 3.50 hook and P., work 2 rows d.c. along back shoulder.

Fasten off.

Front Shoulder Border

Work as for Back Shoulder Border with the addition of 3 buttonloops on last row.

First mark position of buttons on back shoulder with pins to ensure even spacing, then work buttonloops to correspond.

To make a buttonloop: 2 ch., miss 1 d.c.

Join sleeve seams.

Insert sleeves.

Press seams.

Sew on buttons to correspond with buttonloops.

Using 5 strands of yarn, make a chain and slot through row of trebles at underarm. Make and attach a pompon to each end of cord.

HAT

With No. 4.00 hook and P., make 4 ch., join in a ring with sl.st.

1st round: 3 ch., into ring work 15 tr., join with sl.st. in top of 3 ch.: 16 sts.

2nd round: 3 ch., * 2 tr. in next st., 1 tr. in next st.; rep. from * to last st., 2 tr. in last st., join with sl.st. in top of 3 ch.: 24 sts.

3rd round: as 2nd round: 36 sts.

4th round: as 2nd round: 54 sts.

5th round: 3 ch., 1 tr. in next st., 2 tr. in next st., * 1 tr. in each of next 2 sts., 2 tr. in next st.; rep. from * ending sl.st. in top of 3 ch.: 72 sts.

6th round: 3 ch., 2 tr. in st. just worked into, * miss 2 sts., 3 tr. in next st.; rep. from * ending miss 2 sts., sl.st. in top of 3 ch.: 24 groups of 3 tr.

Join in W.

Work straight in patt. as for Skirt, starting with 2nd round, until Hat measures 6½ in., ending with a 4th round.

Work as for Skirt from ** to **

Press as for Dress.

Miss Muffet hat and bag set

MATERIALS

6 balls (20 gr. each) Coats Chain Mercer-Crochet No. 20. One steel crochet hook International Standard Size 1.25. 1 yard lining material 36 in. wide. 1 yard interfacing 32 in. wide. 1 yard ribbon ½ in. wide.

MEASUREMENTS

Finished crochet 20 in. in diameter before making up.

TENSION

First 3 rows 2 in. in diameter.

ABBREVIATIONS

See page 19.

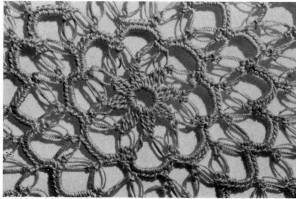

HAT

Commence with 10 ch., join with sl.st. to form a ring.

1st round: 3 ch., leaving the last loop of each on hook work 2 d.tr. into ring, y.o.h. and draw through all loops on hook (a 2-d.tr.cl. made), * 1 ch., draw loop up ¼ in., y.o.h. and draw through loop on hook, insert hook between loop and single thread of this ch. and complete as d.c. (knot st. made), work another knot in same manner (a solomon's knot made), a 3-d.tr.cl. into ring; rep. from * 6 times, 1 ch., a knot st., y.o.h., insert hook into first cl., y.o.h. and draw loop through cl. to measure ¼ in., y.o.h. and draw through all loops on hook (a long h.tr. made).

2nd round: 1 d.c. between loops of h.tr. just made, * 8 ch., 1 d.c. over double loop at right of centre of next knot, 1 d.c. over double loop at left of same knot (2 d.c. made over knot); rep. from * ending with 8 ch., 1 d.c. to right of last knot, sl.st. into first d.c.

3rd round: 1 d.c. into same place as last sl.st., * 11 d.c. into next loop, (insert hook into next d.c. and draw yarn through) twice, y.o.h. and draw through all loops on hook (a joint d.c. made); rep. from * ending with 11 d.c. into next loop, insert

hook into next d.c. and draw yarn through, insert hook into first d.c. and draw yarn through all loops on hook.

4th round: sl.st. into each of next 2 d.c., * 1 d.c. into next d.c., 1 solomon's knot, miss next 5 sts.; rep. from * all round omitting 1 solomon's knot at end of last rep., 1 knot st., a long h.tr. into first d.c. **5th and 6th rounds:** as 2nd and 3rd rounds.

7th round: sl.st. into each of next 2 d.c., * 1 d.c. into next d.c., 1 solomon's knot, miss next 5 d.c., 1 d.c. into next d.c., 1 solomon's knot, miss next 8 sts., 1 d.c. into next d.c., 1 solomon's knot, miss next 8 sts.; rep. from * all round omitting 1 solomon's knot at end of last rep., 1 knot st., a long h.tr. into first d.c.

8th and 9th rounds: as 2nd and 3rd rounds.

10th round: as 7th round.

11th and 12th rounds: as 2nd and 3rd rounds.

13th round: sl.st. into each of next 5 d.c., * 1 d.c. into next d.c., 1 solomon's knot, miss next 11 sts.; rep. from * all round omitting 1 solomon's knot at end of last rep., 1 knot st., a long h.tr. into first d.c.

Rep. 8th to 13th rounds twice, then rep. 11th to 13th rounds 5 times, and 2nd and 3rd rounds again.

43rd round: sl.st. into each of next 5 d.c., * 1 d.c. into next d.c., 8 ch., miss 11 sts.; rep. from * all round ending with sl.st. into first d.c.

44th round: 1 d.c. into same place as last sl.st., * 11 d.c. into next loop, 1 d.c. into next d.c.; rep. from * all round ending with 11 d.c. into next loop, sl.st. into first d.c.

45th round: as 13th round.

46th and 47th rounds: as 2nd and 3rd rounds. Fasten off.

TO COMPLETE

Damp and pin out to measurements (½ in. has been allowed for seams). Cut 2 circles of lining and 1 circle of interfacing each 17 in. in diameter. Place and baste interfacing to wrong side of 1 piece of lining. Place lining circles right sides tog. and st. round leaving an opening. Trim interfacing to seam line, turn to right side and st. opening. Place lining centrally on wrong side of crochet and st. to edge of 40th row. Thread ribbon through spaces between 42nd and 43rd rows of crochet, draw up to size of head and tie ribbon ends in a bow.

BAG

Work as Hat.

Make lining up as Hat. Make 2 twisted cords (see page 126) each approx. 32 in. long. Thread through spaces between 42nd and 43rd rows and draw up.

Pink bolero and hat

illustrated in colour on page 25

MATERIALS

For bolero: 7 (8, 8) oz. Robin Vogue Double Knitting or Robin Tricel-Nylon Perle Double Knitting. **For hat:** 3 oz. of the same yarn. **For both:** crochet hooks International Standard Sizes 4.00 and 3.00.

MEASUREMENTS

Bolero: to fit chest size 24 (26, 28) in.; length 11¼ (12¼, 13¼) in.

Hat: to fit an average size child's head.

TENSION

9 sts. and 10 rows to 2 in. with No. 4.00 hook.

ABBREVIATIONS

See page 19; m. loop, make loop by inserting hook into next st., draw up a 1-in. loop on first finger of left hand, draw yarn through st. as in working d.c., y.o.h. and draw through 2 loops on hook, drop loop from finger (loops are formed at back of work); dec. 1, decrease 1 stitch by inserting hook into next st., draw through loop (if working a loop st. row, then make a loop), insert hook into next st. and draw through a loop, y.o.h. and draw through 3 loops on hook.

BOLERO BACK

With No. 4.00 hook commence with 59 (63, 68) ch.

Foundation row: 1 d.c. into 2nd ch. from hook, 1 d.c. into each ch. to end: 58 (62, 67) d.c.

1st patt. row: 2 ch. (to stand as first d.c.), m. 1 loop into each st. to last st. (see Abbreviations), 1 d.c. into last st.; turn.

2nd patt. row: 2 ch., 1 d.c. into each st. to end; turn.

These 2 rows form patt. Rep. patt. rows throughout. Work straight until Back measures 7 (7½, 8) in. from beg., ending with a first patt. row.

Shape Armholes

Next row: sl.st. over first 4 sts., 2 ch., patt. to last 4 sts., turn. Dec. 1 st. at each end of the next 8 (7, 7) rows: 34 (40, 45) sts. Now work straight until armholes measure 4¼ (4¾, 5¼) in., ending with a first patt. row.

Shape Shoulders

Next row: sl.st. over first 6 (8, 9) sts., 2 ch., 1 d.c. into each of next 22 (24, 27) sts. Break yarn and fasten off.

BOLERO LEFT FRONT

With No. 4.00 hook commence with 13 (13, 15) ch.

Work foundation row as given for Back: 12 (12, 14) d.c.

Work the first row of patt.

Next row: 2 ch., 1 d.c. into each st. to last 3 sts., 2 d.c. into

each of last 3 sts., turn: 15 (15, 17) sts.

Work 1 row straight.

Rep. the last 2 rows 4 times more: 27 (27, 29) sts.

Next row: 2 ch., 1 d.c. into each st. to last st., 2 d.c. into last st.; turn.

Work 1 row straight.

Rep. the last 2 rows 1 (3, 3) times more: 29 (31, 33) sts.

Now work straight until Front measures same as Back to armhole, ending with a first patt. row.

Shape Neck and Armhole

Next row: sl.st. over next 4 sts., patt. to last 2 sts., dec. 1 (see Abbreviations).

** Dec. 1 st. at each end of every row until 8 (12, 14) sts. remain, then at neck edge only until 6 (8, 9) sts. remain.

Now work straight until armhole measures same as Back armhole ending with a first patt. row.

Break yarn and fasten off.

BOLERO RIGHT FRONT

With No. 4.00 hook commence with 13 (13, 15) ch.

Work foundation row as given for Back: 12 (12, 14) d.c.

Work the first row of patt.

Next row: 2 ch., 2 d.c. into each of next 3 sts., 1 d.c. into each st. to end, turn: 15 (15, 17) sts.

Work 1 row straight.

Rep. the last 2 rows 4 times more: 27 (27, 29) sts.

Next row: 2 ch., 2 d.c. into first st., 1 d.c. into each st. to end; turn.

Work 1 row straight.

Rep. the last 2 rows 1 (3, 3) times more: 29 (31, 33) sts.

Now work straight until Right Front measures same as Left Front to armhole, ending with a first patt. row.

Shape Armhole and Neck

Next row: 2 ch., dec. 1, patt. to last 4 sts., turn. Now work from ** to end.

TO COMPLETE

Press work lightly on wrong side using a warm iron over a damp cloth. Join shoulder and side seams. Press seams.

Edgings

With No. 3.00 hook and right side of work facing, beg. at right side seam at lower edge and work d.c. right round lower edge, front and neck edges, working 1 d.c. to each st. and 1 d.c. to each row.

Work d.c. round armholes.

HAT

With No. 4.00 hook make 65 ch.

Work the foundation row of patt. as given for Bolero: 64 d.c.

Work in patt. to 4½ in. from beg., ending on a first patt. row.

Shape Top

Next row: 2 ch., * work 4 d.c., dec. 1; rep. from * to last 4 sts., 1 d.c. into each of last 4 sts.: 52 d.c.; turn.

Next row: as first patt. row, turn.

Next row: 2 ch., * work 3 d.c., dec. 1; rep. from * to last 4 sts., 1 d.c. into each of last 4 sts.: 40 d.c.; turn.

Next row: as first patt. row, turn.

Next row: 2 ch., * work 2 d.c., dec. 1; rep. from * to last 4 sts., 1 d.c. into each of last 4 sts.: 28 d.c.; turn.

Next row: as first patt. row, turn.

Next row: 2 ch., * work 1 d.c., dec. 1; rep. from * to last 2 sts., 1 d.c. into each of last 2 sts.: 15 d.c.; turn.

Next row: as first patt. row, turn.

Next row: 2 ch., miss first st., dec. 1 to end.

Break yarn and fasten off.

Draw top together.

TO COMPLETE

Press as for Bolero. Join back seam.

Chapter five
FASHIONS FOR ALL SEASONS
a selection of flattering outfits to make and wear all the year round

Button-up jacket (instructions start overleaf).

Button-up jacket
illustrated on previous page

MATERIALS
12 (13, 14) 50-gr. balls Pingouin Jaspee or Multipingouin. One crochet hook International Standard Size 4.00. Five medium buttons.

MEASUREMENTS
To fit bust size 34 (36, 38) in.; length 25½ (26, 26½); sleeve seam 17 (17½, 17½) in.

TENSION
4 tr. to 1 in., 2 clusters to 1 in.

ABBREVIATIONS
See page 19; cl., cluster: work 3 tr. leaving the last loop of each tr. on hook, y.o.h. and draw through all 4 loops on hook; work 3 tog., work 3 together by working 1 tr. into each of next 3 tr., leaving the last loop of each tr. on hook, y.o.h. and draw through all 4 loops on hook.

POCKETS (make 2 alike)
Make 26 ch. Work in cl. patt. thus:
Foundation row: 1 cl. into 4th ch. from hook, * 1 ch., miss 1 ch., 1 cl. into next ch.; rep. from * to end: 12 cl.
Patt. row: 3 ch., 1 cl. into first sp., * 1 ch., 1 cl. into next sp.; rep. from * to end, working last cl. into turning ch. loop.
Rep. last row 8 times. Fasten off.

BACK
Make 93 (97, 101) ch.
Foundation row: 1 tr. into 4th ch. from hook, 1 tr. into each ch. to end: 91 (95, 99) tr.
Tr. row: 3 ch. for first tr., 1 tr. into each tr. to end.
Rep. last row twice more. Cont. in tr. and dec. thus:
Dec. row: sl.st. into next tr., 3 ch., 1 tr. into each tr. until 1 tr. remains (omitting to work into top of turning ch. at end): 1 st. dec. at both ends.
Cont. to dec. at both ends in a similar manner on every foll. alt. row 8 times more: 73 (77, 81) tr. Work 2 rows straight. Now work in cl. patt. thus:
Next row: 3 ch., 1 cl. into 2nd tr., * 1 ch., miss 1 tr., 1 cl. into next tr.; rep. from * to end: 36 (38, 40) cl.
Work another 4 rows in cl. patt. as for Pockets.
Cont. in tr. again thus:
Next row: 3 ch. for first tr., * 1 tr. into next sp., 1 tr. into next cl.; rep. from * to end, 1 tr. into turning ch.: 72 (76, 80) tr. Work another 3 rows in tr.

Shape Armholes
Next row: sl.st. along and into 5th tr., 3 ch. for first tr., 1 tr. into each tr. until 4 tr. remain, turn.
Next row: 3 ch., miss first tr., 1 tr. into each of next 2 tr., leaving the last loop of each tr. on hook, y.o.h. and draw through all 3 loops on hook, 1 tr. into each tr. until 3 tr. remain, work 3 tog. Rep. last row once more: 56 (60, 64) tr.
Work 10 (11, 12) rows in tr. Fasten off.

LEFT FRONT
Make 52 (54, 56) ch. Work foundation row as for Back: 50 (52, 54) tr.
Work 3 rows in tr. Now dec. 1 st. at beg. of next and then every foll. alt. row until the 9th dec. has been completed: 41 (43, 45) tr. Work 2 rows straight.
Next row: work in cl. patt. as for Back: 20 (21, 22) cl.
Work another 4 rows in cl. patt. as for Pockets.
Next row: work in tr. as for Back: 40 (42, 44) tr.
Work another row in tr.

Shape Neck
Dec. 1 st. (working dec. as for side shapings) at neck edge on next 2 rows. **

Shape Armholes and Continue to Shape Neck
1st row: sl.st. along and into 5th tr., 3 ch. for first tr., work to last tr., turn.
2nd row: sl.st. into next tr., 3 ch., work to last 3 tr., work 3 tog.
3rd row: 3 ch. and miss first tr., 1 tr. into each of next 2 tr. leaving the last loop of each tr. on hook, y.o.h. and draw through all 3 loops on hook, work to last tr., turn (8 tr. dec. at armhole edge). *** Keeping armhole edge straight, continue to dec. 1 st. at neck edge on every row until 18 (19, 20) tr. remain. Work 0 (1, 2) rows straight. Fasten off.
With pins mark the positions of 5 buttons along front edge, the top button ½ in. below first neck dec., the bottom button approx. 3 in. from lower edge and the others equally spaced between.

RIGHT FRONT
Work as for Left Front to **, but reversing side shapings by dec. at end of rows and making buttonholes to correspond with marked positions thus (ending at front edge): 3 ch. for first tr., 1 tr. into each of next 2 tr., * 2 ch. (loosely), miss 2 tr., 1 tr. into each tr. to next buttonhole position, and rep. from *. In following row work 1 tr. into each ch. over buttonhole. Where buttonhole is worked on cluster band, work thus: 3 ch., 1 cluster into first sp., 3 ch., miss 1 ch.sp. and work 1 cluster into following sp., patt. to end. In following row work 1 cluster, 1 ch., 1 cluster, 1 ch. into ch.sp. over buttonhole.

Shape Armhole and Continue to Shape Neck
Next row: sl.st. into next tr., 3 ch., work until 4 tr. remain, turn.
Next row: 3 ch., miss first tr., 1 tr. into each of next 2 tr. leaving the last loop of each tr. on hook, y.o.h. and draw through all 3 loops on hook, work until 1 tr. remains, turn.
Next row: sl.st. into next tr., 3 ch., patt. until 3 tr. remain, work 3 tog. (8 tr. dec. at armhole edge).
Now work as for Left Front from *** to end.

SLEEVES (make 2 alike)
Make 60 (62, 62) ch. Work foundation row as for Pocket: 29 (30, 30) clusters.
Work 1 row in cluster patt. as for Pockets, then dec. at both ends thus:
1st row: as patt. row, but work only 2 tr. for the first and last cluster.
2nd row: 3 ch., 1 tr. into first sp., * 1 ch., 1 cluster into next sp.; rep. from * until 1 cluster and turning ch. remain, 1 tr. into turning ch.
3rd row: 3 ch., miss first tr. and cluster, 1 cluster into next sp., patt. to end, working last cluster into last ch.sp., turn (1 patt. dec. at both ends).
Rep. last 3 rows 3 times more: 21 (22, 22) clusters. Continue straight until sleeve measures 17 (17½, 17½) in.

56

Shape Top

1st row: sl.st. into 2nd ch.sp., 3 ch., 1 cluster into next sp., patt. until 2 clusters remain, turn.

2nd row: sl.st. into first ch.sp., 3 ch., 1 cluster into next sp., patt. until 1 cluster and turning ch. remain, turn.

Rep. last row 5 times more. Fasten off.

COLLAR

Make 6 ch. Now shape work thus:

1st row: 1 cluster into 4th ch. from hook, 1 ch., 1 tr. into last ch.

2nd row: 1 cluster into first sp., 1 ch., 1 cluster into turning ch.

3rd row: 3 ch., 1 cluster into first sp., 1 ch., 1 cluster into turning ch., 1 ch., 1 tr. into same turning ch. (1 patt. increased at this side).

4th row: cluster patt. to end.

5th row: patt. to end, but work 1 cluster, 1 ch. and 1 tr. into turning ch.

Rep. last 2 rows until there are 9 clusters. Now continue straight, working in patt. as for Pockets, until shaped side of collar will be long enough to fit from first neck dec. of front to centre of back. Fasten off. Work second side of collar in exactly the same way. Join top edges of collar.

TO COMPLETE

Join shoulder, side and sleeve seams. Set in sleeves. Beginning at first neck dec., work a row of d.c. down left front edge, along lower edge of jacket and up right front edge, ending at 1st neck dec. Work a row of d.c. round pockets, along lower edge of sleeves and along straight edge of collar. Pin centre of collar to centre of back neck and points at first neck dec., now sew shaped edge of collar to neck edge. Sew pockets to fronts. Sew on buttons.

Batwing sweater

MATERIALS

12 oz. Hayfield Courtier Bri-Nova Double Knitting. One crochet hook International Standard Size 4.00.

MEASUREMENTS

To fit bust size 32–34 in.; length 18 in.; length of side seam (including sleeve) 20 in.

TENSION

2 patt. reps. measure 2 in. across, 1 in. deep.

ABBREVIATIONS

See page 19.

Note. Use yarn double throughout.

BACK

With 2 strands yarn commence with 57 ch.

1st row: miss 8 ch., work 1 d.c., 3 ch. and 1 d.c. into next ch. (1 p. made), * 5 ch., miss 3 foundation ch., work 1 d.c., 3 ch. and 1 d.c. into next ch.; rep. from * to last 4 ch., miss 3 ch., 1 d.c. into last ch.: 12 p.

2nd row: * 5 ch., work 1 d.c., 3 ch. and 1 d.c. into 3rd ch. of next 5-ch. loop; rep. from * to end, ending with 1 d.c. into last ch.

3rd row: * 5 ch., work 1 d.c., 3 ch. and 1 d.c. into 3rd ch. of next 5-ch. loop; rep. from * ending with 1 d.c., 3 ch. and 1 d.c. into 5th ch., 12 ch.; turn.

4th row: miss 8 ch., 1 d.c., 3 ch. and 1 d.c. into next ch., miss 3 ch., * 5 ch., work 1 d.c., 3 ch. and 1 d.c. into 3rd ch. of next 5-ch. loop; rep. from * to end, 12 ch.; turn. Rep. last row until there are 32 p. omitting ch. at end of last row. Work 8 rows straight **.

Shape Shoulders

Next row: patt. to last 4 p., 1 d.c.; turn.

Next row: sl.st. over first 4 p., 1 d.c., patt. to last 4 p., 1 d.c.; turn.

Rep. last row once.

Next row: patt. to last 4 p., 1 d.c.; turn.

Work 1 row across rem. 8 p. Fasten off.

FRONT

Work as Back to **.

Shape Neck

Next row: patt. across 12 p., 1 d.c.; turn.

Next row: patt. across 8 p., 5 ch., 1 d.c.; turn.

Next row: sl.st. across 4 p., patt. to end.

Fasten off.

Miss 8 centre p. and rejoin yarn to 2nd side of neck.

Next row: patt. to last 4 p., 1 d.c.; turn.

Next row: sl.st. across 4 p., patt. to end.

Fasten off.

TO COMPLETE

Press lightly with a warm iron and a damp cloth.

Join underarm and side seams.

Join shoulder seams: with 2 strands yarn work d.c. across one shoulder seam beg. at armhole edge as follows.

* 1 d.c. into next ch. of Front, 1 ch., 1 d.c. into next ch. of Back, 1 ch., 1 d.c. into first d.c., 5 ch.; rep. from * to neck edge. Fasten off.

Work other shoulder in the same way.

Lower Border

With 2 strands yarn work 1 round of d.c. round lower edge.

Next round: 1 tr. into each d.c., sl.st. to first tr.

Next round: * 1 tr. into each of next 3 tr., miss 1 tr.; rep. from * to end, sl.st. to first tr.

Work 3 rows straight in tr. Fasten off.

Sleeve Borders

With 2 strands yarn work 1 round d.c. round one sleeve edge, then work 3 rounds of tr. Work other sleeve in the same way.

Neck Border

With 2 strands yarn work round neck edge as follows: * 3 ch., work 1 d.c., 3 ch. and 1 d.c. into 3rd ch. of 5-ch. loop; rep. from * to end.

Mother and daughter jackets

MATERIALS

11 (12, 14, 15, 17, 19, 20, 21, 22) balls Robin Tricel-Nylon Perle 4-ply. Crochet hooks International Standard Sizes 4.00 and 3.00. $\frac{3}{4}$ ($\frac{3}{4}$, 1, 1, 1, 1, 1$\frac{1}{4}$, 1$\frac{1}{4}$) yd. facing ribbon, 1 in. wide.

MEASUREMENTS

To fit chest/bust size 24 (26, 28, 30, 32, 34, 36, 38, 40) in.; sleeve seam 10$\frac{1}{2}$ (12, 13, 14$\frac{1}{2}$, 16, 17, 17, 17$\frac{1}{2}$, 17$\frac{3}{4}$) in.; length from shoulder 13$\frac{1}{2}$ (15, 16$\frac{1}{2}$, 18, 19$\frac{3}{4}$, 20$\frac{1}{2}$, 21, 21$\frac{3}{4}$, 22) in.

TENSION

6 d.c. and 7 rows to 1 in. over patt. on No. 4.00 hook.

ABBREVIATIONS

See page 19.

BACK

With No. 4.00 hook make 80 (86, 92, 98, 104, 110, 116, 122, 128) ch.

Foundation row: work 1 d.c. into 2nd ch. from hook then 1 d.c. into every ch. to end: 79 (85, 91, 97, 103, 109, 115, 121, 127) d.c., 1 ch., turn.

1st row (wrong side): work 1 d.c. into first d.c., * 2 ch., miss 2 d.c., 1 d.c. into next d.c.; rep. from * to end, 1 ch., turn.

2nd row: work 1 d.c. into first d.c., * 2 d.c. into 2 ch.sp., 1 d.c. into next d.c.; rep. from * to end, 1 ch., turn.

Rep. these 2 rows 4 (4, 4, 5, 5, 5, 6, 6, 6) times more, then work 2 rows d.c. These 12 (12, 12, 14, 14, 14, 16, 16, 16) rows complete the patt. and are repeated throughout.

Work straight to 9 (10, 11, 12, 13, 13, 13, 13$\frac{1}{2}$, 13$\frac{1}{2}$) in. from beg., ending on a wrong-side row.

Shape Armholes

Sl.st. over 3 sts., work to last 3 sts., turn.

Dec. 1 d.c. at beg. of every row until 61 (67, 73, 79, 85, 85, 85, 91, 91) d.c. remain.

Work straight to 13 (14½, 16, 17½, 19, 20, 20½, 21, 21½) in. from beg.

Shape Shoulders

Sl.st. over 6 (7, 7, 8, 9, 9, 9, 9, 9) sts., work to last 6 (7, 7, 8, 9, 9, 9, 9, 9) sts., turn; rep. the last row twice more.

Fasten off.

LEFT FRONT

With No. 4.00 hook make 44 (47, 50, 53, 56, 59, 62, 65, 68) ch.

Work foundation row as Back: 43 (46, 49, 52, 55, 58, 61, 64, 67) d.c., 1 ch., turn.

Work in patt. to same length as back to underarm ending on same patt. row.

Shape Armhole

Sl.st. over 3 sts., work to end, then dec. 1 st. at armhole edge on every alternate row until 34 (37, 40, 43, 46, 46, 46, 49, 49) d.c. remain.

Work straight until armhole measures 2¾ (2¾, 3¼, 3½, 3¾, 4¼, 4½, 5, 5½) in. from beg. of shaping, ending at front edge.

Shape Neck

Next row: sl.st. over the first 6 (6, 6, 9, 9, 9, 9, 9) sts., patt. to end. Dec. 1 st. at neck edge on every row until 18 (21, 21, 24, 27, 27, 27, 27, 27) d.c. remain. Work straight to 13½ (15, 16½, 18, 19¾, 20½, 21, 21¾, 22) in. from beg. ending at side edge.

Shape Shoulder

Next row: sl.st. over 6 (7, 7, 8, 9, 9, 9, 9, 9) sts., work to end.

Next row: work to last 6 (7, 7, 8, 9, 9, 9, 9, 9) sts., turn, work to end. Fasten off.

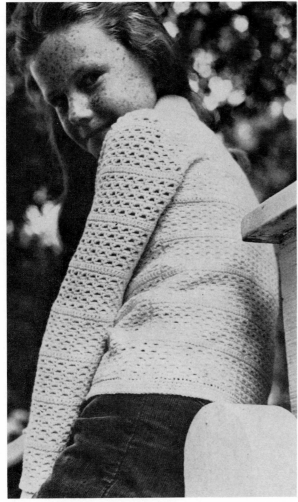

Edging
With No. 3.00 hook begin at right side seam and work 1 row d.c. on lower edge, up right front, round collar, down left front, and all round lower edge to right side seam, work 3 more rows working twice into the 2 corner sts. of fronts and collar and work last st. of front neck and first st. of collar tog. to keep edging correct. Fasten off.
Face fronts with ribbon. Cut and neaten buttonholes.

Crochet buttons
With No. 3.00 hook make 3 ch., sl.st. into a ring and work 6 d.c. into ring.
Next round: work 2 d.c. into every d.c.
Next 2 rounds: work 1 d.c. in every d.c.
Next row: work 1 d.c. into every alternate d.c. Cut yarn.
Stuff firmly with cotton wool or insert a small button; using a wool needle gather up last round, draw up tightly and fasten off.
Sew on buttons. Press seams and edges.

Fringed bolero

MATERIALS
11 (13) balls (20 gr. each) Wendy Tricel Nylon D.K. One crochet hook International Standard Size 3.50 (3.50, 4.00).

MEASUREMENTS
To fit bust size 34 (36, 38) in.

TENSION
$1\frac{1}{2}$ in. over patt. of 12 sts., 6 rows to 1 in.

ABBREVIATIONS
See page 19.

Note. Instructions are given for bust size 34 in., with bust size 36 in. in brackets. For bust size 38 in., follow directions given for bust size 36 but use a No. 4.00 hook.

BACK
Make 102 (108) ch. and work 2 rows in d.c.

The Pattern
1st row: 3 (6) d.c., * 9 ch., miss 6 d.c., 3 d.c.; rep. from * ending row 3 (6) d.c.
2nd–4th rows: rep. first row, making 3 d.c. into the 3 d.c. in row below.
5th row: 3 (6) d.c., * 5 ch., 1 d.c. placing yarn under the 4 preceding rows and completing st. by pulling 4 rows tog., 5 ch.; rep. from * ending 3 (6) d.c.
These 5 rows form the patt.
Cont. in patt. until Back measures approx. $11\frac{1}{2}$ in. ending after a complete patt. Fasten off.

RIGHT FRONT
Work to match Left Front reversing shapings and working buttonholes on the 5th (5th, 5th, 5th, 5th, 5th, 7th, 7th, 7th) row of each patt. repeat as follows: patt. to last 6 d.c., 4 ch., miss 4 d.c., 1 d.c. in each of next 2 d.c., 1 ch., turn.
Next row: 2 d.c., 4 d.c. into buttonhole space, patt. to end.

SLEEVES (make 2 alike)
With No. 4.00 hook make 32 (38, 44, 50, 50, 50, 50, 56, 56) ch. Work foundation row and 1 inch patt. as given for Back.
Inc. 1 d.c. at each end of the next and every following 5th (6th, 6th, 7th, 8th, 7th, 7th, 7th, 7th) row 12 (12, 12, 12, 12, 15, 15, 15, 15) times in all: 55 (61, 67, 73, 73, 79, 79, 85, 85) d.c.
Work straight to $10\frac{1}{2}$ (12, 13, $14\frac{1}{2}$, 16, 17, 17, $17\frac{1}{2}$, $17\frac{1}{2}$) in. from beg.

Shape Sleeve Top
Sl.st. over 3 sts., work to last 3 sts., turn.
Dec. 1 d.c. at each end of every row until 9 (9, 9, 9, 9, 11, 11, 13, 13) d.c. remain. Fasten off.

TO COMPLETE
Press work on wrong side using a warm iron over a damp cloth. Join shoulder seams.

Collar
With wrong side facing using No. 3.00 hook work 1 row fairly close d.c. all round neck edge beg. and end $\frac{3}{4}$ in. from front edge. Continue in d.c. for $1\frac{1}{2}$ (2, 2, 2, $2\frac{1}{2}$, $2\frac{1}{2}$, $2\frac{1}{2}$, 3, $3\frac{1}{2}$) in.
Fasten off.
Set in sleeves. Join sleeve and side seams.

Rejoin yarn at 13th (15th) st., leaving 2 (3) d.c. to commence patt., work in patt. to last 13 (15) sts. in row; turn.

Cont. working on these sts. until Back measures 7½ in. from start of armhole shaping, ending after a complete patt.

Next row: sl.st. over 1 (3) d.c., 6 ch., * sl.st. over 3 d.c., 6 ch.; rep. from * across row, ending with 6 ch., sl.st. over 1 (3) d.c. Now work 2 (5) rows of d.c. to form edging.

To Shape Shoulders

With right side facing, sl.st. over 7 (8) sts., work in d.c. to last 7 (8) sts., turn. Sl.st. over 7 (8) sts., work in d.c. to last 14 (16) sts., turn. Sl.st. over 7 (8) sts., work in d.c. to last 21 (24) sts. Fasten off.

LEFT FRONT

Make 39 (43) ch. and work as given for Back but when commencing patt. for size 36, commence with 4 d.c. and finish with 6 d.c. When Front measures 14 in. dec. 1 st. at beg. of every alt. row at centre front edge until 21 (24) sts. rem.

When front measures 19 in., finishing after a complete patt., work edging of 2 (5) rows of d.c. as for Back (sl.st. over d.c. of patt. and work ch. of 6 between, as given for Back, first of all to give a foundation in which to work the d.c. edging).

With right side of work facing, shape shoulder by sl.st. over 7 (8) sts. at armhole edge, work in d.c. over rest of sts.

In the foll. row, work d.c. only on 7 (8) sts. at centre front edge. Sl.st. over these sts. and fasten off.

RIGHT FRONT

Work as for Left Front, reversing shapings.

TO COMPLETE

Press lightly with a cool iron, and join side and shoulder seams. Work 2 rows of d.c. down each side of centre front neck shaped edge.

Fringe

Cut yarn into 8-in. lengths, and using 8 strands at a time, make fringe along lower edge of Bolero, inserting groups of strands into spaces in patt.

Lace-panelled blouse

MATERIALS
9 (10, 10) oz. Emu 4-ply crochet wool. One crochet hook International Standard Size 3.50.

MEASUREMENTS
To fit bust size 34 (36, 38) in.; length at side 24 (25, 26) in.

TENSION
5½ sts. and about 4½ rows to 1 in.

ABBREVIATIONS
See page 19.

BACK

Commence with 100 (106, 112) ch.

1st row: 1 h.tr. into 3rd ch. from hook, 1 h.tr. into each ch. to end: 98 (104, 110) h.tr.

Cont. in h.tr., turning with 2 ch.

Work straight until Back measures 16 (16½, 17) in.

Shape Armholes

Next row: 2 ch., patt. to last 4 (5, 6) sts.; turn.

Rep. last row once: 90 (94, 98) sts.

3rd row: miss first st., patt. to last st.; turn.

Rep. last row 4 times. Work 1 row straight. Rep. 3rd row again. Rep. last 2 rows 4 times: 70 (72, 74) sts.

Work straight until Back measures 23½ (24½, 25½) in.

Shape Neck and Shoulders

1st row: 2 ch., patt. 24 h.tr.; turn.

2nd row: 2 ch., miss 1 st., patt. 15 h.tr.; turn.

3rd row: 2 ch., patt. 15 h.tr.; turn.

4th row: 2 ch., miss 1 st., patt. 7 h.tr.; turn.

5th row: 2 ch., patt. 7 h.tr.

Fasten off.

Miss centre 22 (24, 26) sts. and rejoin yarn to next st., 2 ch., 15 h.tr.; turn.

Next row: 2 ch., patt. 15 h.tr.; turn.

Next row: 2 ch., miss 1 st., 7 h.tr.; turn.

Next row: 2 ch., 7 h.tr.

Fasten off.

FRONT

Work as Back until 2 h.tr. rows have been completed. Now beg. patt.

1st row: 2 ch., 1 h.tr. into each of next 20 (21, 22) sts., * (2 ch., miss 2 sts., 1 h.tr. into each of next 2 sts.) 3 times, 2 ch., miss 2 sts., 1 h.tr. into each of next 8 (10, 12) sts.; rep. from * once, (2 ch., miss 2 sts., 1 h.tr. into each of next 2 sts.) 3 times, 2 ch., miss 2 sts., 1 h.tr. into each of next 20 (21, 22) sts.

2nd row: 2 ch., 1 h.tr. into each of next 20 (21, 22) sts., * (2 h.tr. into next 2-ch.sp., 2 ch.) 3 times, 2 h.tr. into next 2-ch.sp., 1 h.tr. into each of next 8 (10, 12) sts.; rep. from * once, (2 h.tr. into next 2-ch.sp., 2 ch.) 3 times, 2 h.tr. into next 2-ch.sp., 1 h.tr. into each of next 20 (21, 22) sts.

3rd row: 2 ch., 1 h.tr. into each of next 20 (21, 22) sts., * (2 ch., miss 2 sts., 1 h.tr. into next 2-ch.sp.) 3 times, 2 ch., miss 2 sts., 1 h.tr. into each of next 8 (10, 12) sts.; rep. from * once, (2 ch., miss 2 sts., 1 h.tr. into next 2-ch.sp.) 3 times, 2 ch., miss 2 sts., 1 h.tr. into each of next 20 (21, 22) sts.

The last 2 rows form the patt. Cont. in patt. Work straight until Front measures same as Back to beg. of armholes.

Shape Armholes

Work as Back, keeping the 3 panels correct: 70 (72, 74) sts.

Cont. straight in patt. until Front measures 22 (22½, 23) in.

Shape Neck

Next row: 2 ch., patt. to within 2 sts. of centre panel, miss 1 st., 1 h.tr. into next st.; turn.

Working on this set of sts. only, and turning with 2 ch., miss 1 st. at neck edge on every row until 24 sts. remain, then on next 2 alt. rows: 22 sts.

Cont. straight until work measures same as Back to beg. of shoulder shaping, ending at neck edge.

Shape Shoulder

1st row: 2 ch., patt. 14; turn.

2nd row: 2 ch., patt. 14.

3rd row: 2 ch., patt. 7; turn.

4th row: 2 ch., patt. 7.

Fasten off.

Return to rem. sts., miss 14 sts., of centre panel, rejoin yarn to next st., then work 2 ch., miss 1 st., patt. to end.

Complete 2nd side of neck to match first, reversing shapings.

TO COMPLETE

Pin out to correct measurements and press lightly with a warm iron and damp cloth.

Join shoulder and side seams. Press seams.

Neck Border

Work 2 rounds of d.c. round neck edge.

Next round: * 3 ch., sl.st. to last d.c., 1 d.c. into each of next 3 d.c.; rep. from * to end.

Fasten off.

Lower Border

Work 2 rounds of d.c. round lower edge.

Armhole Borders

Work as Neck Border.

Press borders.

Sleeveless top and skirt

illustrated on following page

MATERIALS

For top: 12 (13, 13, 14, 14, 15) 25-gr. balls Twilleys Cortina Super Crochet Wool. Crochet hooks International Standard Sizes 3.00 and 2.50.

For skirt: 15 (15, 16, 16, 17, 17) 25-gr. balls Twilleys Cortina Super Crochet Wool. Crochet hooks International Standard Sizes 3.00 and 2.50. A 6-in. zip fastener.

MEASUREMENTS

To fit bust size 32 (34, 36, 38, 40, 42) in. and hip size 34 (36, 38, 40, 42, 44) in.; length of top 20 (20, 21, 21, 22, 22) in.; length of skirt 19 in. (adjustable).

TENSION

6 sts. and 5 rows to 1 in. with No. 2.50 hook.

ABBREVIATIONS

See page 19.

TOP BACK AND FRONT (make 2 pieces alike)

With No. 2.50 hook commence with 94 (100, 106, 112, 118, 124) ch.

Next row: 1 d.c. into 2nd ch. from hook, 1 d.c. into each ch. to end.

Work 4 rows in d.c.

Now work in patt.

1st row (right side): 2 ch., 1 tr. into 2nd d.c., 1 tr. into each d.c. to end.

2nd row: 1 ch., 1 d.c. into next st., 1 d.c. into each st. to end.

3rd row: 2 ch., miss first d.c., * y.o.h., insert hook into sp. before next tr. on first patt. row then out through centre bottom of this tr., y.o.h. and draw through long loop, y.o.h. and draw through 3 loops, 1 tr. into next d.c.; rep. from * to end.

4th row: as 2nd row.

These 4 rows form patt. Work 4 in. in patt.

Change to No. 3.00 hook and cont. in patt. until work measures 13½ (13½, 14, 14, 14½, 14½) in., ending with a 3rd patt. row.

63

SKIRT BACK AND FRONT (make 2 pieces alike)

With No. 2.50 hook commence with 67 (71, 75, 79, 83, 87) ch.
Next row: 1 d.c. into 2nd ch. from hook, 1 d.c. into each ch. to end.
Next row: 1 ch., 1 d.c. into next st., 1 d.c. into each st. to end. Rep. last row 5 times.
Next row: 1 ch., * 2 d.c. into next st., 1 d.c. into next st.; rep. from * to end: 99 (105, 111, 117, 123, 129) sts. Change to No. 3.00 hook and work 4 patt. rows as for Top.
Cont. in patt., inc. 1 st. at each end of 4th and every foll. 8th row until there have been 8 incs. made at each side, working extra sts. in tr. on first and 3rd patt. rows and in d.c. on 2nd and 4th patt. rows until there are 2 more sts. at each side, then take them into patt.
Cont. straight in patt. until work measures 19 in., ending with a 4th patt. row (adjust length here if required). Fasten off.

TO COMPLETE

Press lightly. Join side seams, leaving 6 in. open at top of left side seam. Sew zip in this opening. Press seams.

White lacy-patterned dress
illustrated opposite

MATERIALS

17 (18) oz. Lister Lavenda 4-ply Wool. Crochet hooks International Standard Sizes 2.50 and 3.00 (3.00 and 3.50). Six medium buttons.

MEASUREMENTS

To fit bust size 32/34 (36/38) in.; hip size 34/36 (38/40) in.; length from top of shoulder 36 (38) in. (adjustable).

TENSION

1 patt. to 2¼ in., and 6 tr. to 1 in. on No. 3.00 hook.
1 patt. to 2½ in., and 11 tr. to 2 in. on No. 3.50 hook.

Shape Armholes

Next row: sl.st. over first 14 (14, 16, 16, 18, 18) sts., d.c. to last 14 (14, 16, 16, 18, 18) sts.; turn: 65 (71, 73, 79, 81, 87) sts.
Cont. in patt. until work measures 18½ (18½, 19½, 19½, 20½, 20½) in., ending with a 3rd patt. row.

Shape Neck

Next row: 1 ch., miss first st., work 14 (16, 16, 18, 18, 20) d.c.; turn.
Work on these sts. only. Patt. 1 row.
Next row: 1 ch., d.c. to last 2 sts.; turn.
Rep. last 2 rows twice. Work 1 row straight. Fasten off. Leave centre 35 (37, 39, 41, 43, 45) sts., then rejoin yarn to next st. and d.c. across rem. 15 (17, 17, 19, 19, 21) sts. Work 1 row straight.
Next row: sl.st. over first 2 sts., d.c. to end.
Rep. last 2 rows twice. Work 1 row straight.
Fasten off.

TO COMPLETE

Join shoulder and side seams. With No. 2.50 hook work 3 rows d.c. around neck and each armhole. Fasten off. Press seams and top lightly.

ABBREVIATIONS
See page 19; dec. 1 tr., decrease 1 treble, by working next 2 tr., leaving last loop on hook each time, y.o.h., and draw through 3 loops tog., thus dec. 1 tr.

BACK
With No. 2.50 (3.00) hook make 132 ch.
1st row (right side): 1 d.c. in 2nd ch. from hook, 1 d.c. in each remaining ch.: 131 d.c.
2nd row: 1 d.c. in each d.c.
Repeat 2nd row twice.
Change to No. 3.00 (3.50) hook and commence patt.
1st patt. row: 3 ch., miss first 2 d.c., 1 tr. in next d.c., * miss 1 d.c., 1 ch., 1 tr. in next d.c.; rep. from * to end, 3 ch., turn (these to count as first tr. and ch.).
2nd patt. row: miss first tr. and ch., 1 tr. in next tr., * miss 1 tr., 5 ch., 1 d.tr. in next tr., 1 d.tr. in each of next 3 tr., miss 1 tr., 5 ch., 1 tr. in next tr., 1 ch., 1 tr. in next tr.; rep. from * to end, 3 ch., turn.
3rd row: miss first tr. and ch., 1 tr. in next tr., * 5 ch., 1 d.c. in d.tr., 1 d.c. in each of next 3 d.tr., 5 ch., 1 tr. in next tr., 1 ch., 1 tr. in next tr.; rep. from * to end, 3 ch., turn.
4th row: miss first tr. and ch., 1 tr. in next tr., * 5 ch., 1 d.c., 1 d.c. in each of next 3 d.c., 5 ch., 1 tr. in next tr., 1 ch., 1 tr. in next tr.; rep. from * to end, 3 ch., turn.
5th row: as 4th row.
6th row: miss first tr. and ch., 1 tr. in next tr., * 3 ch., 1 d.tr. in next d.c., 1 ch., 1 d.tr. in each of next 3 d.c., 3 ch., 1 tr. in next tr., 1 ch., 1 tr. in next tr.; rep. from * to end, 3 ch., turn.
7th row: miss first tr. and ch., 1 tr. in next tr., * 1 ch., 1 tr. in 2nd of 3 ch., (1 ch., 1 tr. in next d.tr.) 4 times, 1 ch., 1 tr. in 2nd of 3 ch., (1 ch., 1 tr. in next tr.) twice; rep. from * to end.
The 2nd-7th rows inclusive form the patt. Cont. until 10 patts. are complete, ending with a 7th row. (Skirt length may be adjusted at this point but must finish on a 7th row of patt.) Work a 2 ch. turn at end of last row.

Commence Bodice
1st row (wrong side facing): (working into front loop only, leaving back loop to form a ridge on right side) miss first tr. and ch., * (1 tr. in next tr., 1 tr. in ch., 1 tr. in next tr., miss next ch.) 3 times, (1 tr. in next tr., 1 tr. in next ch.) twice; rep. from * to end, 2 ch., turn: 105 tr.
2nd row: 1 tr. in each tr. to end, 2 ch., turn.
The 2nd row forms the patt. Cont. in patt. until bodice measures 9 (10) in.

Shape Armhole
1st row (right side facing): sl.st. over 6 tr., patt. to last 6 tr., 2 ch., turn.
2nd row: (dec. 1 tr.) twice (see Abbreviations), patt. to last 5 tr., (dec. 1 tr.) twice, 1 tr. in end tr.
Repeat 2nd row 3 times: 77 tr.
Cont. without shaping until bodice measures 15 (16½) in.

Shape Neck
1st row: patt. 15, dec. 1 tr. in next tr., 2 ch., turn.
2nd row: dec. 1 tr., patt. to end. Fasten off.
Miss centre 41 tr., and rejoin yarn to next tr.
1st row: 1 tr. in this tr., dec. 1 tr., patt. to end.
2nd row: patt. to last 3 tr., dec. 1 tr., 1 tr. in end tr. Fasten off.

FRONT
Work Skirt section exactly as given for Back, ending with a 7th row of patt.

Commence Bodice
1st row (wrong side facing): (working into front loop only) miss first tr. and ch., * (1 tr. in next tr., 1 tr. in ch., 1 tr. in next tr., miss next ch.) 3 times, (1 tr. in next tr., 1 tr. in next ch.) twice; rep. from * 3 times more, 2 ch., turn: 53 tr.
2nd row: 1 tr. in each tr. to end, 2 ch., turn.
Cont. in patt. until bodice measures 9 (10) in.

Shape Armhole
1st row (right side facing): sl.st. over 6 tr., patt. to end, 2 ch., turn.
2nd row: patt. to last 5 tr., (dec. 1 tr.) twice, 1 tr. in end tr., 2 ch., turn.
3rd row: (dec. 1 tr.) twice, patt. to end.
Rep. 2nd and 3rd rows once: 39 tr.
Cont. without shaping until Bodice measures 11½ (13) in.

Shape Neck
1st row (right side facing): patt. to last 15 tr., dec. 1 tr., 1 tr. in next tr., 2 ch., turn.
2nd row: dec. 1 tr., patt. to end, 2 ch., turn.
3rd row: patt. to last 3 tr., dec. 1 tr., 1 tr. in end tr.
Rep. 2nd and 3rd rows until 16 tr. remain.
Cont. without shaping until work measures same as Back to shoulders. Fasten off.
Rejoin yarn to centre.
1st row: 1 tr. in ch., * (1 tr. in next tr., 1 tr. in ch., 1 tr. in next tr., miss next ch.) 3 times, (1 tr. in next tr., 1 tr. in next ch.) twice; rep. from * 3 times, 2 ch., turn: 53 tr.
2nd row: 1 tr. in each tr. to end, 2 ch., turn.
Cont. in patt. until bodice measures 9 (10) in.

Shape Armhole
1st row (right side facing): patt. to last 6 tr., 2 ch., turn.
2nd row: (dec. 1 tr.) twice, patt. to end, 2 ch., turn.
3rd row: patt. to last 5 tr., (dec. 1 tr.) twice, 1 tr. in end tr., 2 ch., turn.
Rep. 2nd and 3rd rows once: 39 tr. Cont. without shaping until bodice measures 11½ (13) in.

Shape Neck
1st row (right side facing): sl.st. over 12 tr., 1 tr. in next tr., dec. 1 tr., patt. to end.
2nd row: patt. to last 3 tr., dec. 1 tr., 1 tr. in end tr., 2 ch., turn.
3rd row: dec. 1 tr., patt. to end, 2 ch., turn.
Rep. 2nd and 3rd rows until 16 tr. remain.
Cont. without shaping until work measures same as Back to shoulders.
Fasten off.

SLEEVES (make 2 alike)
With No. 2.50 (3.00) hook make 84 ch.
1st row: 1 d.c. in 2nd ch. from hook, 1 d.c. in each rem. ch.: 83 d.c.
2nd row: 1 d.c. in each d.c.
Change to No. 3.00 (3.50) hook and work 2 patts. as for Back ending with a 6th patt. row.

Shape Top
1st row: sl.st. over 6 sts., patt. to last 6 sts., 3 ch., turn. Cont. in patt., dec. 2 sts. at each end of every row until 10 sts. rem. Fasten off.

TO COMPLETE
Press each piece carefully. Sew side and shoulder seams. Sew in sleeves.
Edging
With No. 3.00 hook and commencing at lower edge of right front work 2 rows d.c. along front edge, working 6 buttonholes evenly along 2nd row. For each buttonhole work 2 ch., miss 2 d.c., 1 d.c. in next d.c. Break off yarn.
Now commencing at right side seam work 1 row d.c. all round edge of bodice — i.e. work into loops on right side across right front edge, up right front, round neck, down left front edge, across loops at left front and across loops at back.
2nd round: * 1 d.c. in first d.c., miss 2 d.c., 6 tr. in next d.c., miss 2 d.c.; rep. from * all round, sl.st. into first d.c. to complete round. Fasten off.
Press all seams. Sew on buttons to correspond with buttonholes.

Shell-patterned cardigan

MATERIALS
32 (32, 33) balls (1 oz.) Twilleys Crysette cotton yarn. One crochet hook International Standard Size 2.50. Seven medium buttons, or $\frac{1}{2}$-in. button moulds.

MEASUREMENTS
To fit bust size 34 (36, 38) in.; sleeve seam $18\frac{1}{2}$ in.

TENSION
7 ch. to 1 in. measured along the top of row, and 2 rows to 1 in.

ABBREVIATIONS
See page 19; l.tr., long treble: y.o.h., hook into ch. and pull through yarn, y.o.h. and pull through 1 loop, y.o.h. and pull through 2 loops, y.o.h. and pull through 2 loops (to leave 1 loop on hook).

RIGHT FRONT
Make 50 (57, 64) ch.

1st row: 5 l.tr. into 4th ch. from hook, * miss 2 ch., 1 l.tr. into next ch., 1 ch., 1 l.tr. into next ch., miss 2 ch., 5 l.tr. into next ch.; rep. from * ending with miss 2 ch., 1 l.tr. into next ch., 1 ch., 1 l.tr. into next ch., 3 ch. to turn.

2nd row: * 5 l.tr. into 1 ch. between the 2 l.tr., 1 l.tr., 1 ch., 1 l.tr. into top of 3rd tr. of block of 5; rep. from * to end.

Rep. the last row always working the 5 l.tr. into the ch. between the 2 l.tr. Work straight for $14\frac{1}{2}$ ($14\frac{3}{4}$, 15) in.

continued on page 70

Above: *gold bathing costume (see page 98).*

Opposite: *button-through dress (see page 70).*

Shape Armhole

Sl.st. over 7 ch. at side edge, work to end, work back to within ½ patt. of end, turn and work straight until armhole measures 4 in.

Shape Neck

Starting from centre front edge, sl.st. over 12 ch., work to end. Work to within ½ (1, 1) patt. at neck edge, turn.
Sl.st. over ½ patt., work to end.
Work as for Right Front, reversing all shapings.
Cont. straight until the armhole measures 6½ in. without stretching, then starting from the armhole edge, sl.st. over 7 ch., work to end, turn, and work to within 7 sts. of first dec. Break yarn. Fasten off.

LEFT FRONT

Work as for Right Front, reversing all shapings.

BACK

Make 100 (107, 114) ch. and work in patt. for 14½ (14¾, 15) in.

Shape Armholes

Sl.st. over 7 ch., work to within 7 ch. of the other end, turn and sl.st. over ½ patt., work to within ½ patt. of end, rep. this dec. for sizes 36 and 38 only.
Cont. until the armhole measures 6½ in.

Shape Shoulders

Sl.st. over 7 sts., work to within 7 sts. of end. Rep. this row once. Fasten off.

SLEEVES (make 2 alike)

Make 50 ch. and work in patt. for 4 in., then inc. 1 l.tr. at the beg. and end of each row working the incs. into the patt. When there are 10 (11, 11) patts. in the row and work measures 16½ (17, 17) in., shape the top as follows: sl.st. over 7 ch., work to within 7 ch. of end, and then dec. 2 l.tr. at beg. and end of next 10 rows (i.e. when you have 1 l.tr., 1 ch., 1 tr. at beg. of row dec. it, and when 5 l.tr., dec. 2 the first time, and 3 the next, and always end rows with 1 l.tr. into the edge to give a sewing edge for making up the garment afterwards).

TO COMPLETE

Sew the shoulder seams, matching the back with the fronts. Sew the side and sleeve seams, set the sleeves into the armholes. Work 3 rows of d.c. round the lower edges of the sleeves. Mark off positions for buttons on the left front. Work round the edge of cardigan in d.c., starting from side seam at lower edge and working to centre front, inc. by working 3 d.c. into corner, work up front, and inc. at corner, work round neck and down other front, and along the edge to side seam. Turn, and work another row of d.c. and make the buttonholes opposite the marks made for buttons. To make a buttonhole work 4 ch., miss 4 ch. along edge, cont. in d.c. to the next mark, and repeat.
Work 1 more row of d.c. working d.c. into each of ch. for buttonholes. Press the edges carefully, and sew on the buttons to match the buttonholes.

If you are using button moulds, then cover each mould with crochet as follows:
Wind yarn round finger to form a ring.
1st round: 1 d.c. into ring; draw commencing ring tight.
Now work in continuous rounds, working * 2 d.c. into next d.c., 1 d.c. into next d.c.; rep. from * until work is large enough to cover button mould. Fasten off. Attach cover to mould.

Button-through dress

illustrated in colour on previous page

MATERIALS

25 (27, 29) oz. Emu Double Knitting Crochet Wool. Crochet hooks International Standard Sizes 3.00, 3.50, 4.00 and 4.50. Eight medium buttons.

MEASUREMENTS

To fit bust size 34 (36, 38) in.; length 41 in. approx.

TENSION

9 tr. to 2 in.

ABBREVIATIONS

See page 19.

WAISTBAND

With No. 4.00 hook make 13 ch. and work 1 d.c. into 2nd ch. from hook, then 1 d.c. to end: 12 d.c.; 1 ch., turn.
Next row: work 1 d.c. into back loop of each d.c. to end, 1 ch., turn.
Rep. this row 119 (130, 141) times.

BODICE

Change to No. 3.00 hook and work 1 d.c. into top edge of each row along the waistband: 120 (131, 142) d.c., then 3 ch., turn.
Cont. as follows:
** **1st row:** 1 tr. into each of next 2 d.c., * miss 2 d.c., 1 ch., 2 tr., 1 ch., 2 tr. into next st., miss 2 d.c., 1 ch., then 1 tr. into each of next 5 (6, 7) d.c.; rep. from * to end, finishing 3 tr. instead of 5 (6, 7) tr., 3 ch., turn.
2nd row: 1 tr. into each of next 2 tr., * 1 ch., 2 tr., 1 ch., 2 tr. into centre ch. of gr., 1 ch., then 1 tr. into each of next 5 (6, 7) tr.; rep. from * to end, finishing 3 tr. instead of 5 (6, 7) tr., 3 ch., turn.
3rd row: 1 tr. into each of next 2 tr., * 1 ch., 1 d.c. loosely into the sp. 2 rows below, 3 ch., 2 tr., 1 ch., 2 tr. into next centre ch. of 3 ch., 1 d.c. loosely into the sp. 2 rows below, 1 ch., 1 tr. into each of next 5 (6, 7) tr.; rep. from * to end, finishing with 3 tr. instead of 5 (6, 7) tr., 3 ch., turn. **
Next row: as 2nd row.
Next row: as 2nd row.
Next row: as 3rd row.
Change to No. 3.50 hook and work last 3 rows twice. Change to No. 4.00 hook and work last 3 rows twice.
Next 2 rows: as 2nd row.

Shape Armholes and Divide for Fronts and Back

Next row: 1 tr. into each of next 2 tr., * 1 ch., 1 d.c. loosely into the sp. 2 rows below, 3 ch., 2 tr., 1 ch., 2 tr. into next gr., 3 ch., 1 d.c. loosely into the sp. 2 rows below, 1 ch., 1 tr. into each of next 5 (6, 7) tr.; rep. from * once, 1 ch., 1 d.c. loosely into sp. 2 rows below, 3 ch., 2 tr. into gr., 1 ch., turn.
Next row: 1 tr. into each of next 5 (6, 7) tr., patt. as 2nd row to end.
Next row: as 2nd row, but with 5 (6, 7) tr. instead of 3 tr. at armhole edge.
Work 3 rows in patt. with extra tr. at armhole edge. Rep. last 3 rows twice, then 2nd row once omitting 3 ch. on last row.

Shape Neck

Next row: sl.st. to first gr., 3 ch., 1 tr. in gr., 1 ch., patt. to end, turn.

Next row: patt. to last tr. panel, 1 tr. into each of 5 (6, 7) tr., 1 ch., 1 d.c. loosely into 2 rows below, turn.

Next row: sl.st. into first tr., patt. to end.

Next row: patt. to end, 3 ch., turn.

Next row: sl.st. over next 2 tr., patt. to end. Fasten off.

Rejoin yarn to work across back bodice by missing the 5 (6, 7) tr. panel, and join yarn at next gr., 3 ch., 1 tr. into same sp., 3 ch., 1 d.c. loosely into sp. 2 rows below, 1 ch., patt. to 4th gr. from other edge and work 2 tr. into this gr., 1 ch., turn.

Next row: as 2nd row of front armhole shaping, ending with 1 tr. into each of next 5 (6, 7) tr., 1 ch., sl.st. into first tr. of 2 tr. gr. of previous row, 3 ch., turn.

Work 17 rows in patt. with tr. blocks each side of armhole.

Next row: sl.st. over first 5 (6, 7) tr., * 3 ch., 1 d.c. in next gr., 3 ch., 1 tr. into next 5 (6, 7) tr.; rep. from * twice, 3 ch., 1 d.c. into next gr., 3 ch., sl.st. to next tr. Fasten off.

Work other side to match first side, reversing shapings. Join shoulders.

SKIRT

With No. 3.00 hook and wrong side of work facing, rejoin yarn at lower edge of waistband and work 1 d.c. into each row along the waistband: 120 (131, 142) d.c.

Rep. from ** to ** of bodice patt. once. Change to No. 3.50 hook and work 3 rows in patt.

Inc. row: as 2nd row but work 2 tr. into the first and last tr. of each 5 (6, 7) tr. panel and 2 tr. into the 3rd tr. from front edge and 2 tr. into the first tr. of the last 3 tr. in row at opposite edge. There are now 4 tr. in panel at each edge, and 7 (8, 9) in other panels.

Work 5 rows in patt. with extra tr. in panels.

Change to No. 4.00 hook. *** Work 3 more rows.

Inc. row: inc. as before so that there are now 5 tr. at each edge and 9 (10, 11) tr. in each panel. Work 5 rows in the new patt. ***

Work from *** to *** twice, then change to No. 4.50 hook and work from *** to *** once, then work 3 more rows in patt.

Next row: work an inc. row as before so that there are now 9 tr. at each edge and 17 (18, 19) in each panel. Work 2 more rows in patt.

Next row: * 1 tr. into each tr. of panel, 3 ch., 1 d.c. into centre ch. of gr., 3 ch.; rep. from * to end, finishing 1 tr. into each of last 9 tr. Now work a row of d.c. into each tr. and ch. to end, then work 4 rows of d.c. on d.c. working into back of loops. Fasten off.

TO COMPLETE
Neck Edging

With right side of work facing, and No. 3.50 hook, join yarn at neck edge and work 56 (60, 65) d.c. evenly round neck, 1 ch., turn. Work 5 rows of d.c. on d.c. working into back of loops. Fasten off.

Left Front Border

With No. 4.00 hook make 8 ch. and work in d.c. working into back of loops, with 1 ch. to turn each row, until border is long enough when slightly stretched to reach up left front. Fasten off. Place pins on border as a guide for buttonholes, the first one about 1 in. from top, the 2nd about 12 in. from lower edge, and 6 more at equal intervals between.

Right Front Border

Work to match Left Front Border, working buttonholes at pin positions as follows: 3 d.c., miss 2 d.c., 2 ch., d.c. to next buttonhole position. In the following row work in d.c. over d.c. and ch.

Armhole Borders

Make 2 more strips in a similar way as for Left Front Border. Sew borders in position. Sew on buttons to correspond with buttonholes. Lightly press.

Striped sports sweater
illustrated in colour overleaf

MATERIALS

9 (10, 10) balls Lister Lavenda Double Knitting in red, and 9 (10, 10) balls in white. Crochet hooks International Standard Sizes 5.00 and 4.50.

MEASUREMENTS

To fit bust size 34 (36, 38) in.

TENSION

4 sts. and 2 rows of tr. to 1 in.

ABBREVIATIONS

See page 19; tr. 2 tog., treble next 2 sts. together as follows: * y.o.h., insert hook into next st., y.o.h., pull loop through, y.o.h., pull through 2 loops, rep. from * into next st., ending y.o.h., pull through all loops; tr. 3 tog., as tr. 2 tog., but work rep. into 3rd st. before ending; R., red; W., white.

Note. Turning ch. counts as 1 stitch.

BACK

With No. 5.00 hook and W., make 60 (62, 64) ch.

Foundation row: 1 d.c. into 2nd ch. from hook, 1 d.c. into each ch. to end, turn.

1st row: 2 ch. Before proceeding with W., lay R. yarn along top of last row. Now work 1 tr. (with W.) into each of next 9 sts., encasing R. yarn; work the last of these as follows: y.o.h. (W.), insert hook in st., y.o.h. (W.), pull through 2 loops, drop W., pick up R., y.o.h. (R.), pull through 2 loops. Lay W. yarn along top of previous row. Now work 1 tr. with R. into next st. in the same way as last tr.

Lay R. yarn along row. Work 1 tr. with W. into next 6 sts., changing back from W. to R. on the last of these. Now cont. in this way working 1 tr. into each st. to end as follows: R. 2 tr., W. 5 tr., R. 3 tr., W. 4 tr., R. 4 tr., W. 3 tr., R. 5 tr., W. 2 tr., R. 6 tr., W. 1 tr., R. 10 tr., turn.

2nd row: as first row but reversing colours so that each st. worked is the same colour as the st. into which it is being worked, so that vertical stripes emerge.

3rd row: 2 ch., tr. 2 tog., cont. in patt. until 3 sts. rem., tr. 2 tog., tr. in last st., turn.

Repeat 1st-3rd rows twice more then work 3 rows straight: 54 (56, 58) sts.

13th row: 2 ch., 2 tr. into next st., patt. until 2 sts. rem., 2 tr. in next st., tr. in last st., turn.

14th row: work in patt.

15th row: as 13th row. continued on page 74

Striped sports sweater (see previous page).

Tunic sweater (see overleaf).

Shape Armholes

16th row: sl.st. across 2 sts., 2 ch., tr. 3 tog., patt. until 6 sts. rem., tr. 3 tog., tr. in next st., turn.

17th row: 2 ch., tr. 2 tog., patt. until 3 sts. rem., tr. 2 tog., tr. in next st., turn.

Now work 22 rows straight: 48 (50, 52) sts.

Shape Shoulders

1st row: 1 ch., d.c. in next st., h.tr. in next st., tr. in next st., tr. 3 tog., patt. until 7 sts. remain, tr. 3 tog., tr. in next st., h.tr. in next st., d.c. in next st., sl.st. in last st., turn.

2nd row (side 1): sl.st. across 4 sts., 2 ch., tr. 3 tog., tr. into each of next 5 sts., tr. 2 tog., tr. in next st., turn.

3rd row: 2 ch., tr. 3 tog., tr. in next st., tr. 3 tog. Fasten off. Rejoin yarn into 17th tr. from end of last complete row worked.

2nd row (side 2): 2 ch., tr. 2 tog., tr. into each of next 5 sts., tr. 3 tog., tr. in last st., turn.

3rd row: 2 ch., tr. 3 tog., tr. in next st., tr. 3 tog. Fasten off.

FRONT

Work as for Back to last d.c. of foundation row; join in R. with this st. and then cont. as for Back but reversing colours (i.e. first patt. row starts with tr. in R. etc.) until 38 tr. rows have been completed.

Shape Neck and Shoulders

1st row (side 1): 2 ch., tr. into each of next 15 tr., tr. 3 tog., tr. in next st., turn.

2nd row: 2 ch., tr. 3 tog., tr. in each st. to end, turn.

3rd row: 1 ch., d.c. in next st., h.tr. in next st., tr. in next st., tr. 3 tog., tr. in each of next 6 sts., tr. 2 tog., tr. in next st., turn.

4th row: 2 ch., tr. 2 tog., tr. in each of next 2 sts., tr. 3 tog., tr. in next st., turn.

5th row: 2 ch., tr. 3 tog., tr. in each of next 2 sts. Fasten off. Turn and rejoin yarn in 20th st. from end of last complete row worked.

1st row (side 2): 2 ch., tr. 3 tog., tr. in each st. to end, turn.

2nd row: 2 ch., tr. in each of next 13 sts., tr. 3 tog., tr. in next st., turn.

3rd row: 2 ch., tr. 2 tog., tr. in each of next 6 sts., tr. 3 tog., tr. in next st., h.tr. in next st., d.c. in next st., sl.st. in last st., turn.

4th row: sl.st. across 4 sts., 2 ch., tr. 3 tog., tr. in each of next 2 sts., tr. 2 tog., tr. in next st., turn.

5th row: 2 ch., tr. in next st., tr. 3 tog., tr. in last st. Fasten off.

UPPER SLEEVES (make 2 alike, 1 in R., 1 in W.)

With No. 5.00 hook make 3 ch., then work 3 tr. into first ch., turn with 3 ch., 1 tr. into base of turning ch., 2 tr. in each of next 3 sts.: 8 sts. Fasten off. Make a second triangle by repeating from beg.

Next row (2nd triangle): 3 ch., 1 tr. in base of turning ch., (1 tr. in next st., 2 tr. in next st.) 3 times, ending 1 tr. in last st., 26 ch., take up first triangle and work 1 tr. into last st. worked before fastening off, (2 tr. in next st., 1 tr. in next st.) 3 times ending 2 tr. in last st., turn.

Next row (whole upper sleeve): 3 ch., 3 tr. in next st., 1 tr. in each st. until 2 sts. remain (working 1 tr. into each of 26 ch. connecting triangles), ending 3 tr. in next st., tr. in last st., turn. Repeat last row 11 more times.

Shape Top

1st row: sl.st. across 3 sts., 2 ch., tr. 3 tog., tr. in each st. until 7 sts. remain, tr. 3 tog., tr. in next st., turn.

2nd row: sl.st. across 2 sts., 2 ch., tr. 3 tog., tr. into each st. until 6 sts. remain, tr. 3 tog., tr. in next st., turn. Repeat last row 9 more times. Fasten off.

TO COMPLETE

Pin out and press each piece on wrong side under a damp cloth. Join shoulder seams, set in upper sleeves and join side and sleeve seams.

Lower sleeves (make 2 alike, 1 in R., and 1 in W. to match upper sleeves)

With No. 5.00 hook, rejoin yarn at seam of upper sleeve (right side facing).

1st row: 2 ch., work round sleeve edge in tr. — 2 tr. per row and 1 tr. per st. — join into beg. with sl.st.: approx. 40 sts. Now cont. in tr., turning between rows and dec. 1 st. at join on alt. rows until 32 sts. rem., then work straight until a total of 24 rows have been worked. Change to No. 4.50 hook and work 2 rows in d.c. ending with 1 row picot edging as follows:

With right side facing, d.c. in same place as last sl.st., * 3 ch., sl.st. in same st. as last d.c., miss next st., d.c. in next st.; rep. from * ending 3 ch., sl.st. in same st. as last d.c., miss next st., sl.st. in first d.c. of row. Fasten off.

Edgings

With No. 4.50 hook and right side facing, join R. into neck edge and work 1 round in d.c. — 1 d.c. per st. and 2 d.c. per row — joining into beg. with sl.st. and making sure there are an even number of sts. in round.

Turn with 1 ch. and work a second round. Turn again and work 1 round picot edging as for lower sleeve.

Work edging around lower edge of garment as for neck edging but use W. instead of R.

Press seams and edgings.

Tunic sweater
illustrated in colour on previous page

MATERIALS

30 (31, 31) oz. Lee Target Loch Isle Double Knitting wool. One crochet hook International Standard Size 3.50. A 9-in. zip fastener. A 2-in. buckle.

MEASUREMENTS

To fit bust size 36 (38, 40) in.; length 29 in.; sleeve seam 17 in.

TENSION

6 sts. and 5½ rows to 1 in. over Pattern A, with No. 3.50 hook.

ABBREVIATIONS

See page 19.

PATTERN A (all main parts are worked in this patt.)

1st row: 1 d.c. in the first st. of last row, * 1 ch., miss 1 st., 1 d.c. in foll. st.; rep. from * to end.

2nd row: 1 ch. to turn; in every d.c. of row below, work 1 d.c., 1 ch. between each d.c.

The 2nd row forms the patt. Repeat it throughout.

PATTERN B (pocket, neckband and sleeve welts are worked in this patt.)

1st row: miss 1 ch., 1 d.c. in 2nd and 3rd ch., * 1 tr. in next ch., 1 tr. in next ch., 1 d.c. in next ch., 1 d.c. in next ch.; rep. from * to end.

2nd row: 1 ch. to turn; on the d.c. of last row work d.c., for every tr. work a ch. and miss the tr.

3rd row: 1 ch. to turn; on the d.c. of last row work d.c., round each tr. of first row work as follows in sculptured tr.: (always keeping the 2 ch. of the previous row at back of the work) y.o.h. and insert hook from front round the back of the tr. below, y.o.h. and pull through and work the tr. in the usual way.

4th row: as 2nd row.

5th row: as 3rd row, working the sculptured tr. round the sculptured tr. of the 3rd row.

The 4th and 5th rows form Pattern B.

BACK

Make 115 (121, 127) ch. and begin Pattern A. Work straight for 4 in. Dec. 1 st. at both ends of next and every foll. 30th row until 109 (115, 121) sts. remain. Work straight until Back measures 21½ in. from beg.

Divide for Zip

Next row: work across 54 (57, 60) sts. to centre back, turn and work this side first.

**Shape Armhole

Sl.st. across 4 (5, 6) sts. at armhole edge once, work to centre.

Next row: work to armhole.

Next row: sl.st. across 2 sts. at armhole edge, work to centre.

Next row: work to armhole.

Rep. last 2 rows 3 times more. Work on 42 (44, 46) sts. until armhole measures 7 (7½, 8) in. from beg., ending at armhole edge.

Shape Shoulder

Next row: sl.st. across 8 (8, 9) sts., work to neck edge.

Next row: work to end.

Next row: sl.st. across 8 (9, 9) sts., work to end.

Next row: work to end.

Next row: sl.st. across 9 sts., work 17 (18, 19) sts. for half of back of neck. Fasten off. **

Rejoin yarn at inner edge and work from ** to **, reversing all shapings.

FRONT

Work as for Back until 109 (115, 121) sts. remain. Work straight until Front matches Back to beg. of armhole.

Shape Armholes

Next row: sl.st. across 4 (5, 6) sts., work to last 4 (5, 6) sts., turn, leaving them unworked.

Next row: work across in patt.

3rd row: sl.st. across 2 sts., work to last 2 sts., turn, leaving them unworked.

4th row: work to end.

Rep. last 2 rows 3 times more. Work on 84 (88, 92) sts. until armhole measure 5 (5½, 6) in. from beg. of shaping.

Shape Neck

Next row: work across 36 (37, 38) sts., turn and work this side first.

***Dec. 1 st. at neck edge (by either sl.st. across or leaving it unworked) on foll. 11 rows. At the same time when armhole

matches Back to shoulder, shape shoulder as follows:
Sl.st. on alt. rows beg. at armhole edge across 8 (8, 9) sts. once, 8 (9, 9) sts. once, and 9 sts. once. Fasten off. ***

Count centre 12 (14, 16) sts. and leave them unworked. Rejoin yarn next to them and work from *** to ***, reversing shapings.

POCKET

Make 31 ch. and work in Pattern B for 5½ in. Fasten off.

SLEEVES (make 2 alike)

Make 43 ch. and work in Pattern B for 5½ in. Begin Pattern A and inc. 23 sts. evenly across first row of pattern to 65 sts. Cont. in Pattern B, inc. 1 st. at both ends of every 5th (5th, 4th) row until there are 85 (87, 89) sts. on the sleeve. Work straight until sleeve measure 17 in. from beg.

Shape Top

Next row: sl.st. across 4 (5, 6) sts., work to last 4 (5, 6) sts., turn, leaving them unworked. **Next row:** work to end.

3rd row: sl.st. across 3 sts., work to last 3 sts., turn, leaving them unworked.

4th row: work to end.

Rep. 3rd and 4th rows 7 times more.

19th row: sl.st. across 4 sts., work to last 4 sts., turn.

20th row: work to end.

21st row: sl.st. across 5 sts., work to last 5 sts.

Fasten off, leaving 11 sts. at top of sleeve.

BELT

Make 13 ch. and work in Pattern A for 38 (40, 42) in. Fasten off.

TO COMPLETE

Join shoulder seams.

Neckband

With right side of work facing, work 58 (63, 68) d.c. around neck.

Next row: 1 ch. to turn; work d.c., then beg. Pattern B as follows: * 3 d.c., 2 sculptured tr.; rep from * to last 3 sts., 3 d.c. Work in this way for 3 rows. Now work 4 rows and work 2 d.c. only between the 2 sculptured tr. Work 1 row d.c. up and down the zip opening. Fasten off.

To Make Up

Press pieces on wrong side under a damp cloth, using a moderate iron. Join side and sleeve seams. Set in sleeves. Sew pocket to right half of front, 2½ in. above lower edge. Set in zip. Sew buckle to belt. Press all seams.

Suit and beret

illustrated in colour overleaf

MATERIALS

20 (22) oz. Emu Scotch 4-ply in green, 3 (4) oz. in dark green, 2 oz. in white. Crochet hooks International Standard Sizes 3.00, 4.50 and 5.00. A waist length of elastic, 1 in. wide. Five small buttons.

MEASUREMENTS

To fit bust size 32/34 (36/38) in.; hip size 34/36 (38/40) in.; centre back length of jacket 21 (22½) in.; sleeve seam 18 (18½) in.; skirt length at side seam 19 (20) in.

TENSION

15 rows and 12 sts. to 3 in. on No. 5.00 hook.

ABBREVIATIONS

See page 19; G., green; D.G., dark green; W., white.

JACKET LEFT FRONT

With No. 5.00 hook and G., make 38 (42) ch.
1st row: miss first 2 ch., d.c. into next ch., d.c. to end: 36 (40) sts.
Cont. to work in d.c. on these sts., dec. 1 st. on side edge only every 5th (6th) row 4 times in all: 32 (36) sts.
Work 24 rows in d.c. without shaping.
Next row: inc. 1 st. at side edge.
Inc. 1 st. at side edge on every foll. 10th row twice, then cont. straight for another 5 (7) rows: 35 (39) sts.

Shape Armhole and Neck

Next row: sl.st. across 5 sts., d.c. to 3rd st. from end, d.c. 2 sts. tog., d.c. in last st. Place coloured thread on this last st. to mark it.
Next row: work in patt., dec. 1 st. at armhole edge.
Work 1 row in patt.

continued on page 78

Blue bikini (see page 87).

Next row: dec. 1 st. on neck and armhole edges.
Cont. to dec. 1 st. every alt. row on armhole, and 1 st. every 3rd row on neck edge until 10 rows have been worked from start of armhole and neck shaping. **
No further shaping for armhole is now required, but cont. to dec. at neck edge as before 11 (13) more times.
Work 1 row straight: 10 (12) sts.

Shape Shoulder
Next row: sl.st. across 2 (3) sts., d.c. to end, turn, d.c. 6, turn, sl.st. across 2 sts., d.c. 4. Fasten off.

JACKET RIGHT FRONT
Work as for Jacket Left Front, reversing all shapings.

JACKET BACK
With No. 5.00 hook and G., make 78 (86) ch. Work as for Jacket Left Front as far as armhole and neck shaping, but shaping on both side edges (instead of just one): 74 (82) sts.

Shape Armhole
*** Work armhole shaping as given for Jacket Left Front as far as **, working shaping at both ends of work, and omitting the neck shaping given for Front. *** Work straight for 30 (36) rows: 54 (62) sts.

Shape Neck
Next row: d.c. 20 (22), turn, sl.st. across 2 sts., d.c. to end.
Next row: d.c. 16 (18), turn, sl.st. across 2 sts., d.c. to end.
Next row: shape shoulders as given for Front, and cont. to dec. 2 sts. each row on neck edge.
Last 2 rows: sl.st. across 2 sts. on neck, d.c. 6, turn, sl.st. 2, d.c. 4. Fasten off.
Fasten yarn to 20th (22nd) st. from end of row and complete second shoulder to match first, reversing shapings.

JACKET SLEEVES (make 2 alike)
With No. 4.50 hook and D.G., make 34 (42) ch.
1st row: miss 2 ch., d.c. to end.
Work 8 more rows in d.c. Change to W., and work 2 rows.
Change to No. 5.00 hook and G., and cont. in patt., inc. 1 st. at each end of next and every foll. 10th row 7 times.
Work 4 (10) more rows straight: 48 (56) sts.

Shape Top
Work shaping as given for Jacket Back, from *** to ***: 28 (36) sts. Dec. 1 st. each end of every 3rd row 6 times, then dec. 1 st. each end of every alt. row 3 (5) times: 10 (14) sts. Fasten off.

TO COMPLETE JACKET
Sew shoulder and side seams. Sew sleeve seams.

Sleeve Edgings
With No. 4.50 hook and W., work 2 rows of d.c. round lower edge of each sleeve.

Front Borders
With No. 4.50 hook and W., join yarn to lower edge of centre front edge on jacket left front, 3 d.c. on st. at this corner edge, working up centre front, miss 1 st., * d.c. into each of next 2 d.c., miss 1 st.; rep. from * to coloured thread marker: 50 (55) sts. worked. Continuing up shaped edge of front neck, d.c. into each row end: 48 (50) sts. worked on shaped neck edge. Continuing round back neck, d.c. into each row end or st.: 34 (38) sts. worked on back neck edge. Work d.c. down shaped edge of right front, as for left front, and down straight centre front edge of right front, work 2 d.c. into corner st. at lower edge. Work 148 (164) d.c. evenly across lower edge of jacket, to beg. of round. Work 2 d.c. into last st. to turn corner, sl.st. to first st. of first round.
Next round: with W., work as for first round to first marker, work 2 d.c. into next st., work in d.c. to 2nd marker, and work 2 d.c. into next st., work to end of round, working 2 d.c. into corner sts. at centre fronts as before.
Rep. this shaping at marker points every alt. round, thus inc. 1 st. at each hem corner on every round and 1 st. at each marker point every alt. round.
Next round: change to D.G., and patt. right round.
Next round: still working in patt., and shaping at corner and marker points, shape neck as follows: work to marker, d.c. into each of next 12 (16) sts., then dec. 10 sts. in next 100 sts. as follows: d.c. 4, d.c. 2 tog., (d.c. 8, d.c. 2 tog.) 9 times, d.c. 4, d.c. 12 (16) to next marker, work in patt. to end of round. In the 4th round of D.G., work to first marker, d.c. 8 (12), dec. 10 sts. in next 100 as before, d.c. 8 (12) to second marker; now form buttonholes: 2 ch., miss 2 sts., (d.c. 10 (11), 2 ch., miss 2 sts.) 4 times, d.c. 3 (4).
In the 5th round of D.G., work d.c. into each of ch. worked for buttonholes in previous round.
In the 6th round of D.G., work neck shaping between markers as follows: d.c. 4 (8), dec. 10 sts. in next 100 as before, d.c. 4 (8).
8th round of D.G.: d.c. 0 (4), dec. 10 sts. in 100 sts. between markers as before, d.c. 0 (4).
Work 1 more row of D.G. without shaping.
Next row: change to W., and work as 2nd row of W. before.
Next row: in W., d.c. all round, with no extra sts.

To Make Up
Sew sleeves into armholes. Sew on buttons to left front to correspond with buttonholes worked in right front. If wished, make crochet covered buttons, with D.G., following instructions on page 60.

SKIRT FRONT AND BACK (make 2 pieces alike)
With No. 4.50 hook and D.G., make 82 (98) ch.
Work border in D.G. and W. as given for Sleeves.
Change to No. 5.00 hook and G., and work 13 rows in patt., dec. 1 st. at each end of next and every foll. 14 rows 4 times. Then dec. 1 st. each end of every foll. 4th row 5 (7) times: 62 (70) sts. Fasten off.

TO COMPLETE SKIRT
Join side seams, matching rows carefully.
With No. 4.50 hook and W., work 2 rows of d.c. round hem edge. Fasten off.

Waistband
With No. 4.50 hook and G., work 5 rows of d.c., then work 2 rounds of tr. Turn band of tr. to inside of skirt and sl.st. each tr. st. to first d.c. row of waistband to form a casing. Fasten off, and thread elastic through this casing, joining ends of elastic together.

BERET
With No. 4.50 hook and G., make a ch. of 4, and join into a ring with sl.st.
1st round: work 2 d.c. into each ch. on ring, sl.st. to join.
Next round: work 2 d.c. into each d.c. of previous round, sl.st. to join.

Next round: 1 d.c. into each d.c., sl.st. to join.
Next round: * 2 d.c. into first d.c., 1 d.c. into next d.c.; rep. from * to end, sl.st. to join.
Next round: 1 d.c. into each d.c., sl.st. to join.
Rep. last 2 rounds 3 times for first size. For second size, rep. last 2 rounds 3 times, then on next round inc. 1 st. every 9 sts., and then work 1 more round without inc.
Both sizes. D.c. 22 (26) rounds on 81 (90) sts.

Border

With No. 4.50 hook and W., work in d.c. for 2 rounds, then change to D.G. and work 7 rounds of d.c.
Next round: dec. 1 st. every 9 sts.
Next round: d.c. 72 (81) sts.
Change to W., and work 2 rounds d.c. fairly tightly. Fasten off.

TO COMPLETE BERET

Darn in all ends. Press very lightly over a damp cloth on the wrong side. Fill beret with crumpled tissue paper while still damp to obtain rounded shape.

Sleeveless blouse

MATERIALS

7 (7, 8) oz. Emu 4-ply crochet wool. One crochet hook International Standard Size 4.00.

MEASUREMENTS

To fit bust size 34 (36, 38) in.; length 23 (23½, 24) in.

TENSION

6 sts. to 1 in.

ABBREVIATIONS

See page 19.

BACK

Make 112 (118, 124) ch. to measure 18½ (19½, 20½) in.

continued on page 82

Cotton jumper with lacy-patterned sleeves and neckband (see page 82).

Circular shawl in dramatic stripes of black and white (see page 91).

Foundation row: 1 tr. into 6th ch. from hook, * 1 ch., miss next ch., 1 tr. into next ch.; rep. from * to end; turn: 54 (57, 60) 1-ch.sps.

Patt. row: 4 ch., miss first tr., * 1 tr. into next tr., 1 ch.; rep. from * ending with 1 tr. into 5th of 6 ch. on first patt. row and 3rd of 4 ch. on subsequent patt. rows; turn.

Rep. last row until work measures 16 in.

Shape Armholes

1st row: sl.st. over 6 sts., 4 ch., work rep. of patt. row to last four 1-ch.sps., 1 tr. into next tr.; turn.

2nd row: sl.st. over first 2 sts., 4 ch., work rep. of patt. row to last 2 sps., 1 tr. into last tr.; turn.

Rep. last row 5 (5, 6) times, then rep. patt. row until armholes measure 6½ (7, 7½) in. Fasten off.

FRONT

Work as Back until armholes measure 4 (4½, 4½) in.

Shape Neck

1st row: patt. until eleven 1-ch.sps. have been worked; turn.

2nd row: miss first st., sl.st. over next 2 sts., 4 ch., work rep. and ending of patt. row; turn.

3rd row: patt. to last 2 sps., 1 tr. into last tr.; turn.

Rep. 2nd row once then rep. patt. row until 1 more row has been worked from beg. of armhole shaping than for Back. Fasten off.

Count 11 ch.sps. from other side edge, attach yarn to next tr. and patt back to side; turn.

Work 3rd, 2nd and 3rd rows of first side of neck shaping, then complete as for first side. Fasten off.

TO COMPLETE

Join shoulder and side seams.

Lower Edging

With right side facing, attach yarn to lower edge, then work d.c. evenly round, having a multiple of 3, 1 d.c. into first d.c.

Next round: * 3 ch., sl.st. into last d.c. made, 1 d.c. into each of next 3 d.c.; rep. from *, sl.st. into first d.c.

Fasten off.

Neck and Armhole Edgings

Work as lower edging.

Cotton jumper – in six sizes

illustrated in colour on page 80

MATERIALS

9 (10, 10, 11, 12, 12) oz. Twilleys Lyscordet cotton yarn. One crochet hook International Standard Size 3.00. A 4-in. zip fastener.

MEASUREMENTS

To fit bust size 32 (34, 36, 38, 40, 42) in.; length 21 (21, 22, 22, 23, 23) in.; sleeve seam 2 in.

TENSION

6 tr. to 1 in.

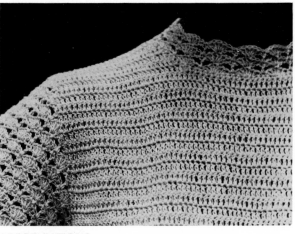

ABBREVIATIONS

See page 19.

FRONT

Make 85 (91, 97, 103, 109, 115) ch.

1st row: 1 tr. in 3rd ch. from hook, (1 tr. in next ch.) to end: 84 (90, 96, 102, 108, 114) sts.

Next row: 2 ch., 1 tr. in 2nd tr., (1 tr. in next tr.) to end. Working in tr. in this way, inc. 1 tr. each end of every 5th row until there are 8 incs. at each side: 100 (106, 112, 118, 124, 130) sts. Cont. until work measures 14 (14, 14½, 14½, 15, 15) in. from beg.

Armhole Shaping

Next row: sl.st. across first 8 (9, 10, 11, 12, 13) tr., 2 ch., 1 tr. in 2nd tr., 1 tr. in each tr. to last 8 (9, 10, 11, 12, 13) sts., turn.

Next row: sl.st. across first tr., 2 ch., 1 tr. in 2nd tr., 1 tr. in each tr. to last st., turn.

Work 1 row. Rep. last 2 rows twice more: 78 (82, 86, 90, 94, 98) sts. Cont. straight in tr. until work measures 19½ (19½, 20½, 20½, 21½, 21½) in. from beg.

Neck Shaping

Next row: work 28 (30, 32, 34, 36, 38), turn. Work on these sts. only.

Next row: sl.st. across first 2 tr., 2 ch., 1 tr. in 2nd tr., tr. to end.

Work 1 row straight. Rep. last 2 rows once more then dec. row again. Fasten off. Leave centre 22 sts., rejoin yarn to rem. 28 (30, 32, 34, 36, 38) sts. and tr. to end.

Next row: tr. to last 2 sts., turn.

Work 1 row. Rep. last 2 rows once more then dec. row again. Fasten off.

BACK

Work as Front until work measures 18 (18, 19, 19, 20, 20) in. from beg.

Back dividing row: work 39 (41, 43, 45, 47, 49), turn. Work on these sts. only until work measures 21 (21, 22, 22, 23, 23) in. from beg. Fasten off. Complete other side to match.

SLEEVES (make 2 alike)

Make 76 (76, 81, 81, 85, 85) ch.

1st row: 1 d.c. in 2nd ch. from hook, (1 d.c. in next ch.) to end: 75 (75, 80, 80, 84, 84) sts.

Next row: 1 ch., 1 d.c. in each d.c. to end.

Rep. last row twice more.

Next row: 1 ch., 1 d.c. in each of first 3 (3, 5, 5, 3, 3) d.c., (2 d.c. in next d.c., 1 d.c. in each of next 2 d.c.) to end: 99 (99, 105, 105, 111, 111) sts.

Now patt. thus:

Foundation row: 1 ch., 1 d.c. in each of first 2 d.c., (miss 2 d.c., 5 tr. in next d.c., miss 2 d.c., 1 d.c. in next d.c.) to last st., 1 d.c. in last d.c.

1st patt. row: 2 ch., 1 tr. in 2nd d.c., (2 ch., 1 d.c. in centre of 5 tr., 2 ch., 1 tr. in next d.c.) to last st., 1 tr. in last d.c.

2nd patt. row: 1 ch., 1 d.c. in each of first 2 d.c., (5 tr. in next d.c., 1 d.c. in next tr.) to last st., 1 d.c. in last tr.

These 2 rows form the patt.

Work 6 rows more in patt.

Next row: sl.st. across first complete patt. (6 sts.), patt. to last complete patt., turn. Work 1 row straight. Rep. last 2 rows 5 (5, 6, 6, 7, 7) times more. Fasten off.

TO COMPLETE

Join shoulders. Work across 17 sts. in d.c. at left side of back neck, work 13 d.c. down left side of front neck, work in d.c. across 22 sts. at centre front, 12 d.c. up right side of front neck then work in d.c. across 17 sts. at right side of back neck: 81 sts. Now work foundation patt. row as for Sleeves, then rep. first and 2nd patt. rows of Sleeves twice. Fasten off. Do not press. Set in sleeves. Join side and sleeve seams. Work 1 row d.c. round back opening, then sew in zip fastener. Press seams.

Lacy overpull

also illustrated on page 86

MATERIALS

7 (7, 8, 8, 9) 20-gr. balls Twilleys Mohair. Crochet hooks International Standard Sizes 3.00 and 2.50.

MEASUREMENTS

To fit bust size 32 (34, 36, 38, 40) in.; length 19 in.; sleeve seam 4 in.

TENSION

8 sts. and 2 rows to 1 in. with No. 3.00 hook.

ABBREVIATIONS

See page 19.

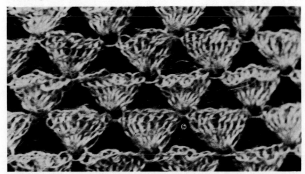

BACK

With No. 2.50 hook and 2 strands of yarn, make 120 (128, 136, 144, 152) ch.

Continue with 1 strand of yarn only.

Next row: 2 ch. to turn, h.tr. in 3rd ch. from hook, h.tr. in every ch. to end: 120 (128, 136, 144, 152) h.tr. altogether.

Next row: 2 ch. to turn, h.tr. in 2nd st., h.tr. in every foll. h.tr. to end of row. Change to No. 3.00 hook and begin patt.

1st patt. row: 1 sl.st. on each of next 3 h.tr. of previous row, 4 ch., (3 d.tr., 1 ch., 4 d.tr., 1 ch.) all into next st., * miss 7 sts., work (4 d.tr., 1 ch., 4 d.tr., 1 ch.) in next st.; rep. from * to last 5 sts., work (4 d.tr., 1 ch., 4 d.tr.) in next st., miss 3 sts., 1 d.c. in last st.

2nd patt. row: sl.st. as far as the first d.tr. of first gr., in the 1 ch. between the d.tr. of last row work: 4 ch., 3 d.tr., 1 ch., 4 d.tr., * in the next ch. between the 2 gr. of d.tr. work: 1 ch., 4 d.tr., 1 ch., 4 d.tr.; rep. from * to end finishing with 1 d.tr. in ch. at end of row.

The 2nd row forms the patt. Repeat this row throughout.

Work straight in patt. until Back measures 10½–11 in. from beg.

Shape Armholes

There are 15 (16, 17, 18, 19) gr. on Back.

Next row: sl.st. across 1 gr., patt. to last gr., turn, leaving this gr. unworked.

Next row: patt. to end.

Next row: sl.st. across 1 gr., patt. to last gr., turn, leaving this gr. unworked.

Sizes 32, 34 and 36 only. Work straight on 11 (12, 13) gr. until armhole measures 8½ in. from beg., measured on the straight.

Sizes 38 and 40 only. Sl.st. across ½ gr., work to within ½ gr., turn, leaving this ½ gr. unworked. Work straight on 13 (14) gr. until armhole measures 8½ in. from beg., measured on the straight.

Shape Shoulders (all sizes)

Next row: sl.st. across 2 gr., patt. to within last 2 gr., turn, leaving them unworked.

Next row: patt. to end.

Next row: sl.st. across 1½ (1½, 2, 2, 2½) gr., patt. to last 1½ (1½, 2, 2, 2½) gr., turn, leaving them unworked. Fasten off. Leave 4 (5, 5, 5, 5) gr. for back of neck.

FRONT

Work as for Back until Front measures 9 in. from beg.

Shape Neck

Next row: work across 6½ (6½, 7, 7½, 8) gr., turn and work this side first.

** Now dec. ½ a gr. at neck edge on 2 alt. rows beg. at neck edge. At the same time when Front matches Back to armhole begin to shape armhole as follows:

Sl.st. across 1 gr. at armhole edge on alt. rows twice, then sl.st. across 0 (0, 0, ½, ½) gr. on next alt. row. Work straight on rem. 3½ (3½, 4, 4½, 4½) gr. until armhole matches Back to shoulder.

Shape Shoulder

Next row: sl.st. across 2 gr. at armhole edge, patt. 1½ (1½, 2, 2, 2½) gr. to end.

Next row: patt. to armhole. Fasten off. **

Count 2 (3, 3, 3, 3) gr. at centre front and leave them free. Rejoin yarn next to these sts. and patt. across 6½ (6½, 7, 7½, 8) gr. to end. Now work from ** to ** reversing all shapings.

continued on page 86

Above and left: *tank top with optional flower motif trimming (see page 91).*

84

Multicoloured pullover worked in vivid shades of blue, red and yellow (see page 90).

SLEEVES (make 2 alike)

With No. 3.00 hook, and 2 strands of yarn, make 88 (88, 88, 96, 96) ch. Cont. with 1 strand of yarn only.

Work as for Back until 2 patt. rows have been worked. Inc. by ½ a gr. at both ends of next row. Work on 12 (12, 12, 13, 13) gr. until sleeve measures 4 in. from beg.

Shape Top

Next row: sl.st. across ½ a gr., patt. to within ½ a gr., turn, leaving it unworked. Rep. this last row 8 times more. Fasten off, leaving 3 (3, 3, 4, 4) gr. for top of sleeve.

TO COMPLETE

Press pieces on wrong side under a damp cloth, using a moderate iron. Join shoulder, side and sleeve seams. Set in sleeves.

With No. 2.50 hook, work round lower edges as follows: working into st. containing a gr. (upside down) 4 d.tr., 1 ch., 4 d.tr., 1 ch.; miss intervening sts. and work the same gr. into st. containing next gr. Work all round lower edges, ending with a sl.st. into first ch.

Fasten off.

Now leave 4 (5, 5, 5, 5) gr. at back of neck undisturbed, and rejoin work at shoulder seam and with No. 2.50 hook work 21 gr. as on lower edge round neck edge, ending at other shoulder seam and holding neck edge in well to get a nice rounded outline. Fasten off. Press all edges, shrinking lower edges in a little to get a neat edge.

Chapter six
JUST FOR FUN
colourful play
clothes for high days
and holidays

Blue bikini
illustrated in colour on page 77

MATERIALS
3 balls (2 oz. each) Twilleys Stalite cotton yarn in main shade, one ball in each of two contrasting colours. Crochet hooks International Standard Sizes 3.00 and 4.00. 2½ yd. elastic, ½ in. wide. 2 large hooks and eyes.

MEASUREMENTS
To fit bust size 32 (34, 36) in.; hip size 34 (36, 38) in.

TENSION
9 tr. and 6 rows to 2 in.

ABBREVIATIONS
See page 19; K., kingfisher (main shade); O., orange; W. white.

TOP
With No. 3.00 hook and K., make 126 (136, 146) ch.
1st row: 1 d.c. in 2nd ch. from hook, 1 d.c. in each ch. to end: 125 (135, 145) sts.
2nd row: 1 ch., 1 d.c. in each d.c. to end.
Rep. 2nd row 6 times more.
Break yarn. Change to No. 4.00 hook.
Rejoin K to 33rd (35th, 37th) st. (leaving 32 (34, 36) sts. for left back strap), 1 ch., 1 d.c. in same d.c., 1 d.c. in each of next 2 d.c., (2 d.c. in next d.c., 1 d.c. in each of next 2 d.c.) 8 (9,10) times, turn.
Work on these 35 (39, 43) sts. only for left side of top.
** **Next row**: 3 ch. (for first tr.), 1 tr. in 2nd d.c., 1 tr. in each d.c. to end.
Next row: sl.st. over first st., 3 ch., 1 tr. in 2nd tr., 1 tr. in each tr. to last st., turn.
Rep. this last row, thus dec. 1 st. each end of every row, until 3 sts. remain.
Next row: sl.st. over first st., 1 d.c. in next st.
Fasten off. **
With right side facing rejoin K. to 8th d.c. from end of left side (leaving 7 sts. at centre front), 1 ch., 1 d.c. in same d.c., 1 d.c. in each of next 2 d.c., (2 d.c. in next d.c., 1 d.c. in each of next 2 d.c.) 8 (9, 10) times, turn (leaving 32 (34, 36) sts. for right back strap). Now work right side as left from ** to **

Front and Shoulder Straps (make 2 alike)
With No. 3.00 hook and W., make 88 (94, 100) ch.
*** **1st row**: 1 d.c. in 2nd ch. from hook, 1 d.c. in each ch. to end.
2nd row: 1 ch., 1 d.c. in each d.c. to end. Join O.
With O. rep. 2nd row twice. Break off O. With W. rep. 2nd row twice. Fasten off. ***

Side Borders
With No. 3.00 hook and K., work 1 row d.c. along outer edges of top.

TO COMPLETE
Sew one end of each front and shoulder strap to centre front edge of top, lapping left strap over right. Stitch each strap in place along inner edge of top. Sew other end of straps to back bands, 4 in. from ends of back straps. Cut a piece of elastic 26 (28, 30) in. long. Sew ends to wrong side ends of back straps and herringbone remainder to wrong side of lower edge of top. Sew hooks and eyes to ends of back straps. Press top lightly.

PANTS
Back
With No. 3.00 hook and K., make 77 (81, 87) ch.
1st row: 1 d.c. in 2nd ch. from hook, 1 d.c. in each ch. to end.
2nd row: 1 ch., 1 d.c. in each d.c. to end.
Rep 2nd row 6 times more.
Change to No. 4.00 hook.
Next row: 3 ch. (for first tr.), 1 tr. in 2nd st., 1 tr. in each st. to end.
Rep. last row until work measures 3 in. from beg. ****
Next row: sl.st. over first 3 (5, 8) sts., 3 ch., 1 tr. in 2nd tr., 1 tr. in each tr. to last 3 (5, 8) sts., turn.
Next row: sl.st. over first 2 sts., 3 ch., 1 tr. in 2nd tr., 1 tr. in each tr. to last 2 sts., turn.
Rep. last row until 18 (18, 18) sts. remain.
Continue until work measures 9¼ in. from the beg. Fasten off.

Front
Work as Back to ****.
Next row: sl.st. over first 18 (20, 23) sts., 3 ch., 1 tr. in 2nd tr., 1 tr. in each tr. to last 18 (20, 23) sts., turn.
Next row: sl.st. over first st., 3 ch., 1 tr. in 2nd tr., 1 tr. in each tr. to last st., turn.
Rep. this last row until 18 (18, 18) sts. remain. Cont. until work measures 9¼ in. from the beg. Fasten off.

Side Bands (make 2 alike)
With No. 3.00 hook and W., make 20 ch. Work as for Front and Shoulder Straps of top from *** to ***

Leg Borders
Join side and crutch seams. With No. 3.00 hook and K., work 2 rows of d.c. evenly round leg edges. Fasten off.

TO COMPLETE
Sew side bands to sides of front, turning in ½ in. at each end. Cut a piece of elastic 32 (34, 36) in. long and join in a ring, then herringbone st. to wrong side of top of pants. Press pants lightly.

Lace-up motif waistcoat (see page 95).

Evening skirt and blouse (see page 103).

Multicoloured pullover
illustrated in colour on page 85

MATERIALS
Of Twilleys Stalite cotton yarn – 2 balls (2 oz. per ball) each in red, gold and dark blue, 1 ball in light blue. One crochet hook International Standard Size 3.50.

MEASUREMENTS
To fit bust size 36 in.; length 18 in.

TENSION
$3\frac{1}{4}$ in. across at the end of 2nd round of D.B.

ABBREVIATIONS
See page 19; D.B., dark blue; R., red; G., gold; L.B., light blue.

BACK AND FRONT (make 2 pieces alike)
With R., make 4 ch., and join with sl.st. into ring.
1st round: 2 ch., 8 h.tr. into ring, sl.st. to top of 2 ch.
2nd round: 2 ch., 1 h.tr. into same st. as sl.st., 2 h.tr. into each h.tr. to end, sl.st. to top of 2 ch.
3rd round: as 2nd round.
4th round: 2 ch., 1 h.tr. into each h.tr. to end, sl.st. to top of 2 ch.: 36 h.tr.
Change to D.B.
5th round: 1 d.c. into each h.tr. to end, join with sl.st.
6th round: 2 d.c. into each d.c. to end, join with sl.st.
Change to R.
7th row: 2 ch., 1 h.tr. into each of the next 49 d.c., 2 ch., turn.
8th row: * 1 h.tr. into next 11 h.tr., 3 h.tr. into next h.tr.; rep. from * twice, 1 h.tr. into next 12 h.tr., 2 ch., turn.
9th row: 1 h.tr. into next 12 h.tr., * 3 d.tr. into next h.tr., 1 h.tr. into next 13 h.tr.; rep. from * twice.
10th row: working as 9th row, work extra h.tr. between inc.
11th round: as previous row to end, 3 h.tr. into corner, 6 h.tr. along sides of R., 22 h.tr. across D.B., 6 h.tr. along R., 3 h.tr. into corner, join with sl.st., 2 ch., turn.

12th round: 3 h.tr. into next h.tr., * 1 h.tr. into each h.tr. to next inc., h.tr., 3 h.tr. into centre h.tr.; rep. from * to end, finishing with 3 h.tr., join with sl.st. Break yarn. Change to G.
13th round: with right side facing, join yarn into side edge, 1 d.c. into each h.tr., join with sl.st.
14th round: d.c. into each d.c.

Points
15th row: 2 ch., 1 h.tr. into each of the next 19 d.c., turn.
16th row: sl.st. into next h.tr., 2 ch., 1 h.tr. into next 17 h.tr.
Cont. in this way until there are 2 ch., 1 h.tr. Fasten off.
To work second point, miss 1 d.c., join yarn into next d.c., work as for first point.
Work 3rd and 4th points in a similar way.
Cont. with G., with right side of work facing, join yarn at bottom edge of first point.
1st round: * work 1 d.c. to point, 3 d.c. into point, d.c. to bottom of point, miss 1 d.c. between points; rep. from * to end of points, 1 d.c. into each d.c. along bottom edge, sl.st. into first d.c. Join R.
2nd round: working from the bottom of the first point, 1 h.tr. into each d.c. round points, missing 1 d.c. between points, finish at the bottom of last point. Join L.B., 1 h.tr. into each d.c. along the bottom, join with sl.st. Join R.
3rd round: as 2nd round, working 2 h.tr. into 3 h.tr. along top of points, 1 h.tr. into each h.tr. until 2 remain between points, miss 1 h.tr., 1 h.tr. into next h.tr., miss 1 h.tr.; cont. to end of round, working h.tr. along bottom with L.B. as before.
4th row: with L.B., rep. 3rd round to end of R., sl.st. at end of points, turn.
5th and 6th rows: join D.B. and rep. 4th row.
7th row: join L.B. at the bottom of first point, * 1 h.tr. into each h.tr. until 3 h.tr. remain from point, 2 h.tr. into each of the next 6 h.tr.; rep. from * to end, 1 h.tr. into each h.tr. to end of last point.
8th row: working from first point (bottom edge) R. 2 ch., 3 tr., L.B. 4 tr., (R. 4 tr., L.B. 4 tr.) 5 times, R. 4 tr., L.B. 2 tr., miss 1 h.tr. between points, 2 tr., (R. 4 tr., L.B. 4 tr.) 4 times, R. 4 h.tr., 7 d.c., miss 1 d.c. between points, 7 d.c., 4 h.tr., (L.B. 4 tr., R. 4 tr.) 4 times, L.B. 2 tr., miss 1 h.tr. between points, 2 tr., (R. 4 tr., L.B. 4 tr.) 6 times, R. 4 tr.
9th row: join L.B. as before, (L.B. on R., R. on L.B.) 3 times, 3 h.tr. L.B., 1 d.c. into next tr. Break yarn, join L.B. at the beg. of 4th R. from end, 1 d.c., 3 h.tr. Cont. working alt. colours to the end.
10th row: as 9th row, alt. colours as before and only working patt. twice.
11th row: with G., join at the beg. edge and work 1 d.c. into each tr. all round to bottom edge.

Strap
Join L.B. at the centre of first point.
1st row: 1 h.tr. into each d.c. until 2 d.c. remain at the bottom of point, miss 2 d.c., 1 h.tr. into 14 d.c., 1 tr. into each of the next 15 d.c., turn.
2nd row: with R., 3 ch., 9 tr.
3rd row: with D.B., rep. 2nd row.
4th row: with L.B., rep. 2nd row.
5th row: with G. rep. 2nd row.
Rep. last 4 rows once. Rep. R. row.
To make second strap, join L.B. into d.c. over 4th R. tr. at next point, 3 ch., 14 tr., 14 h.tr., miss 2 d.c., 1 h.tr. into each d.c. to 4th R. tr. at point. Fasten off.
With wrong side facing join R. into 10th L.B. tr. from end.
Work 2nd–5th rows as for first strap.
Join D.B. at the beg. of L.B. across the bottom edge. Inc. each end of each row, work 4 rows h.tr.
With G., inc. each end, work 2 rows h.tr.
With D.B., work 4 rows without inc.
With right side of work facing, work along bottom edge of point. With D.B., 2 ch., 13 h.tr., turn. Rep. last row for $3\frac{1}{4}$ in.
With G., join into the bottom of inside edge, and work 2 rows d.c.

With D.B., work 2 rows d.c.
With G., work 1 row d.c., 3 d.c. into corner, 2 d.c. along the top, turn, 1 ch., 1 d.c. into each d.c. to end.
Work second side to correspond with first inside edge.

TO COMPLETE
Sew flap to each side of centre piece. Join shoulder and side seams.

Neck Edging
With L.B., work 1 round d.c. round neck edge. With G., rep. last round.

Armholes (make both alike)
Join L.B. into L.B. tr. at the bottom of strap and work d.c. to end of strap. Join with sl.st. into L.B. tr.
With G., join into beg. of strap, 1 d.c. into each d.c. to end of strap, * miss 1 st., 1 d.c. into each of the next 6 sts.; rep. from * to end of armhole, sl.st. into first d.c.

To Make Up
Press on the wrong side with a hot iron over a damp cloth.

Circular shawl
illustrated in colour on page 81

MATERIALS
16 balls (25 gr. each) Twilleys Cortina Super Crochet Wool in white, 11 balls in black. One crochet hook International Standard Size 3.50

MEASUREMENTS
Finished shawl has a diameter of approx. 60 in.

TENSION
6 sts. and 2 rows to 1 in.

ABBREVIATIONS
See page 19; W., white; B., black.

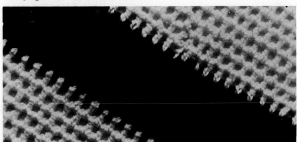

TO MAKE
With W., make 6 ch., sl.st. into first ch. to form a ring.
1st round: 4 ch., (1 tr., 1 ch.) into ring 13 times, sl.st. into 3rd of 4 ch.: 14 sps.
2nd round: sl.st. into first sp., 4 ch., 1 tr., 1 ch. into same sp. as sl.st., * (1 tr., 1 ch., 1 tr., 1 ch.) all into next sp.; rep. from * to end, sl.st. into 3rd of 4 ch.
3rd round: sl.st. into first sp., 4 ch., 1 tr., 1 ch. into same sp., * 1 tr., 1 ch. into next sp., (1 tr., 1 ch., 1 tr., 1 ch.) all into next sp.; rep. from * to end, sl.st. to 3rd of 4 ch.
4th round: sl.st. into first sp., 4 ch., 1 tr., 1 ch. into same sp. as sl.st., * (1 tr., 1 ch. into next sp.) twice, (1 tr., 1 ch., 1 tr., 1 ch.) all into next sp.; rep. from * to end, sl.st. into 3rd of 4 ch.
5th round: sl.st. into first sp., 4 ch., 1 tr., 1 ch. into same sp., * (1 tr., 1 ch. into next sp.) 3 times, (1 tr., 1 ch., 1 tr., 1 ch.) all into next sp.; rep. from * to end, sl.st. into 3rd of 4 ch.
6th round: sl.st. into first sp., draw loop up on hook about $\frac{1}{4}$ in., (y.o.h., hook into same sp. as sl.st.) 3 times, y.o.h. and pull

through all loops on hook: a puff st. worked; 1 ch., (y.o.h., hook into same sp. as last puff st.) 4 times, y.o.h. and pull through all loops on hook, 1 ch., * (1 tr., 1 ch.) 4 times, work 2 puff sts. into next sp.; rep. from * to end, sl.st. into 3rd of 4 ch.
Rep. last round, but working 2 puff sts. into 1 ch.sp between puff sts. and extra (1 tr., 1 ch.) between sets of puff sts. When 12 rounds have been worked, break off W., and cont. in patt., work stripes as follows:
6 rounds B., 8 rounds W., 6 rounds B., 8 rounds W., 6 rounds B., 8 rounds W., 6 rounds B., 8 rounds W.

Picot Edging
With B., * 1 d.c. into next sp., 3 ch., sl.st. into 3rd ch. from hook: a picot formed; 1 d.c. into top of tr.; rep. from * to end, sl.st. into first d.c.
Fasten off.

Tank top
illustrated in colour on page 84

MATERIALS
5 (6, 7, 8) 25-gr. balls Twilleys Afghan Wool. Oddments of same yarn in two contrasting colours (for flower motifs, if made). Crochet hooks International Standard Sizes 4.00 and 4.50. A Flower Loom to make flower motifs, if required.

MEASUREMENTS
To fit bust size 32 (34, 36, 38) in.; length 12 (12, $12\frac{1}{4}$, $12\frac{1}{4}$) in.

TENSION
2 sp. and 2 rows to 1 in. on No. 4.50 hook.

ABBREVIATIONS
See page 19.

BACK AND FRONT (make 2 pieces alike)
With No. 4.50 hook make a ch. of 68 (72, 76, 80) loosely, and work in patt. thus:
1st row: into the 4th ch. from hook, work 1 tr., * 1 ch., miss 1 ch., 1 tr. into next ch.; rep. from * to end, 3 ch., turn: 33 (35, 37, 39) sps.
2nd row: * 1 tr. over next tr., 1 ch.; rep. from * ending with 1 tr. into 2nd of starting ch. of previous row, 3 ch., turn.
Rep. 2nd row 5 times.

Shape Armholes
Next row: sl.st. over 2 sps., 2 ch., * 1 tr., 1 ch.; rep. from * ending 3 sps. from the other side, 1 tr. into the next tr., 2 ch.
Next row: * 1 tr. over next tr., 1 ch.; rep. from * ending with 1 tr. over the last tr., 3 ch.
Next row: * 1 tr. over next tr., 1 ch.; rep. from * ending with 1 tr. over last tr., 3 ch.
11th row: * 1 tr. over next tr., 1 ch.; rep. from * ending with 1 tr. into 2nd of starting ch., 3 ch. Rep. last row until the armholes measure 8 (8, $8\frac{1}{4}$, $8\frac{1}{4}$) in. Fasten off.

TO COMPLETE
Press out to correct measurements. Press work firmly but carefully with a warm iron over a damp cloth. Join shoulder, and side seams. With No. 4.00 hook, work 2 rows d.c. around edges of armholes, and around bottom edge of work and neck edge. Fasten off.

Fringe
Cut yarn into 8-in. lengths. Using 4 strands tog. make a fringe by drawing strands through every other d.c. around bottom edge. Trim fringe.
If wished make 18 flower motifs with a Flower Loom, in colours as wished, and sew to Tank Top, as indicated in photograph on page 84.

Striped waistcoat (see page 97).

White waistcoat (see page 95) and purple waistcoat (see page 94).

Purple waistcoat
illustrated in colour on previous page

MATERIALS
8 (9) oz. Robin Vogue Double Knitting. Crochet hooks International Standard Sizes 6.00, 5.00 and 4.00.

MEASUREMENTS
To fit bust size 34 (36) in.; length 29 (30½) in.

TENSION
3 patts. to 5 in. in width and 1 patt. to 3 in. in depth with No. 5.00 hook.

ABBREVIATIONS
See page 19.

MAIN PIECE
With No. 6.00 hook commence with 134 (146) ch. made loosely.
Foundation row: 1 d.c. into 2nd ch. from hook, * 10 ch., miss 5 foundation ch., 1 d.c. into next ch.; rep. from * to end; turn: 22 (24) loops.
Next row: 10 ch., * 1 d.c. into next loop, 6 ch.; rep. from * to last loop, 1 d.c. into loop, 3 ch., 1 tr.tr. into first d.c. of previous row; turn.
Beg. patt.
1st row: 4 ch., * 1 d.c. into next d.c., 6 ch.; rep. from * to last d.c., 1 d.c. into d.c., 3 ch., 1 d.c. into loop; turn.
2nd row: * 10 ch., 1 d.c. into next 10-ch. loop working below and over the d.c. of previous 2 rows (now called d.c. under); rep. from * to last d.c., 10 ch., 1 d.c. under, 5 ch., 1 tr.tr. into first ch. of previous row; turn.
3rd row: 1 ch., * 6 ch., 1 d.c. into next 10-ch. loop; rep. from * to end; turn.
4th row: 7 ch., * 1 d.c. into d.c., 6 ch.; rep. from * ending with 1 d.c. into first ch. of previous row; turn.
5th row: * 10 ch., 1 d.c. under; rep. from * ending with 10 ch., 1 d.c. into first ch. of previous row; turn.
6th row: 10 ch., * 1 d.c. into next loop, 6 ch.; rep. from * to last loop, 1 d.c. into loop, 3 ch., 1 tr.tr. into first ch. of previous row; turn.
These 6 rows form the patt. Rep. patt. rows 3 times.
Change to No. 5.00 hook and rep. patt. rows twice more then first to 4th rows again.

Shape Front Slope
Next row: as 5th patt. row until last d.c. under has been worked, 5 ch., 1 tr.tr. into first ch. of previous row; turn.
Work 3rd and 4th patt. rows.
Size 36 only. Rep. last 3 rows once.
Both sizes. Next row: (10 ch., 1 d.c. under) 4 times, 5 ch., 1 tr.tr. under next loop (in the same way as d.c. under); turn.

1st Front
Work 3rd and 4th patt. rows.
Next row: (10 ch., 1 d.c. under) 3 times, 5 ch., 1 tr.tr. under last loop; turn.
Work 3rd and 4th patt. rows.
Next row: (10 ch., 1 d.c. under) twice, 10 ch., 1 d.c. into first ch. of previous row; turn.
Next row: 10 ch., (1 d.c. into loop, 6 ch.) twice, 1 d.c. into last loop; turn.
Next row: 1 ch., (6 ch., 1 d.c. into next d.c.) twice, 3 ch., 1 d.c. into last loop; turn.
Next row: (10 ch., 1 d.c. under) twice, 5 ch., 1 tr.tr. into first ch. of previous row; turn.
Next row: 7 ch., 1 d.c. into next loop, 6 ch., 1 d.c. into last loop; turn.
Next row: 7 ch., 1 d.c. into next d.c., 6 ch., 1 d.c. into first ch. of previous row; turn.
Next row: (10 ch., 1 d.c. under) twice; turn.
Next row: 10 ch., 1 d.c. into first loop, 6 ch., 1 d.c. into last loop. Fasten off.

Back
Rejoin yarn at armhole at same place as tr.tr.
Next row: (10 ch., 1 d.c. under) 11 (12) times, 5 ch., 1 tr.tr. under next loop; turn.
Work 3rd and 4th patt. rows.
Next row: (10 ch., 1 d.c. under) 9 (10) times, 5 ch., 1 tr.tr. into first ch. of previous row; turn.
Now work 3rd to 6th patt. rows then first to 4th patt. rows.

Shape Shoulders
Next row: 10 ch., 1 d.c. under, 5 ch., 1 tr.tr. under next loop; turn.
Next row: 7 ch., 1 d.c. into loop, 3 ch., 1 tr.tr. into loop.
Fasten off.
Miss 4 (5) loops and rejoin yarn to next d.c.
Next row: 1 d.c. under same loop, 10 ch., 1 d.c. under, 10 ch., 1 d.c. into first ch.; turn.
Next row: 4 ch., 1 d.c. into loop, 6 ch., 1 d.c. into loop of previous row.
Fasten off.

Second Front
Rejoin yarn at armhole at same place as tr.tr.
Next row: (10 ch., 1 d.c. under) 4 times, 5 ch., 1 tr.tr. into first ch. of previous row; turn.
Work 3rd and 4th patt. rows.
Next row: (10 ch., 1 d.c. under) 3 times, 5 ch., 1 tr.tr. into first ch. of previous row; turn.
Work 3rd and 4th patt. rows.
Next row: (10 ch., 1 d.c. under) twice, 5 ch., 1 tr.tr. into first ch. of previous row; turn.
Next row: 7 ch., 1 d.c. into next loop, 6 ch. 1 d.c. into next loop, 3 ch., 1 tr.tr. into first ch. of previous row; turn.
Next row: 4 ch., (1 d.c. into next d.c., 6 ch.) twice, 1 d.c. into first ch. of previous row; turn.
Next row: (10 ch., 1 d.c. under) twice, 10 ch., 1 d.c. into first ch. of previous row; turn.
Next row: 7 ch., 1 d.c. into next loop, 6 ch., 1 d.c. into next loop; turn.
Next row: 7 ch., 1 d.c. into next d.c., 6 ch., 1 d.c. into first ch. of previous row; turn.
Next row: 10 ch., 1 d.c. under, 5 ch., 1 tr.tr. into first ch. of previous row; turn.
Next row: 7 ch., 1 d.c. into next loop, 3 ch., 1 tr.tr. into first ch. of previous row.
Fasten off.

TO COMPLETE
Pin out work on wrong side to foll. measurements: width across lower edge 37 (39) in.; width at armhole 35 (37) in.; length from shoulder to armhole 7 (7½) in.; length from armhole to lower edge 22 (23) in.
Press work with a warm iron over a damp cloth. Leave to dry before removing pins.
Join shoulder seams.

Armbands
With No. 4.00 hook rejoin yarn to bottom of one armhole.
1st round: 2 ch., work 8 d.c. into each end loop and 1 d.c. between loops all round armhole, sl.st. to top of 2 ch. Work 2 more rounds in d.c. Fasten off.
Work round other armhole in same way.

Front and Lower Edging
With No. 4.00 hook rejoin yarn at left shoulder, and working as for armbands, work down left front, along lower edge, up right front and round back neck, working 3 d.c. into each corner.

Ties (make 2 alike)
With No. 5.00 hook and 2 strands yarn, make a ch. length of approx. 24 in.
Fasten off. Sew ties at neck.

White waistcoat
illustrated in colour on page 93

MATERIALS
10 balls (25 gr. each) Hayfield Diane in white. One crochet hook International Standard Size 4.50.

MEASUREMENTS
To fit bust size 30 to 32 in.; length 33 in.

TENSION
1 motif is 4 in. square.

ABBREVIATIONS
See page 19.

SQUARES (make 62 alike)
Commence with 5 ch. and sl.st. to form a ring.
1st round: 3 ch. (to stand as first tr.), 11 tr. into ring, sl.st. to 2nd of 3 ch.
2nd round: 3 ch., 2 tr. into each sp. between tr. to end, 1 tr. into last st., sl.st. into starting ch.: 24 sts.
3rd round: 8 ch., miss 5 sts., * work 6 tr. into next st., 5 ch.; rep. from * twice, miss 5 sts., 5 tr. into last st., sl.st. into 3rd of 8 ch.
4th round: 3 ch., work 5 tr. into ch. loop, * work 8 tr. between 3rd and 4th tr. of 6-tr.gr., work 5 tr. into next ch. loop; rep. from * twice, 8 tr. between 3rd and 4th tr. of next gr., sl.st. into first ch.
5th round: 3 ch., * 1 tr. into each of next 5 sps. between tr., 6 ch., 1 tr. into 4th tr., 1 ch., 1 tr. into next tr., 6 ch.; rep. from * 3 times, sl.st. into first ch. Fasten off.

1 square = 1 motif

TO COMPLETE
Join Squares as shown in diagram, above.
Work 1 round of tr. round each armhole, and round outer edge.

Lace-up motif waistcoat
illustrated in colour on page 88

MATERIALS
5 (5, 6) oz. Hayfield Gaylon Double Knitting in main shade, 1 (2, 2) oz. in each of four contrasting shades. One crochet hook International Standard Size 4.00 (4.50, 5.00).

MEASUREMENTS
To fit bust size 34 (36, 38) in.

TENSION
One motif measures $4\frac{1}{2}$ in. square.

ABBREVIATIONS
See page 19; M., main shade; C., contrast shade.

TO MAKE
Motif
With 1st C., make 8 ch., and join into a ring with sl.st.
1st round: 6 ch., work (1 tr., 3 ch.) 7 times into ring, sl.st. to join.
2nd round: join in 2nd C. and work 2 ch., 3 tr., 2 ch. into first sp., * 4 tr., 2 ch. into next sp.; rep. from * to end of round, sl.st. to join.
3rd round: with 1st C., 2 ch., 5 tr., 1 ch. into first sp., * 6 tr., 3 ch. into next sp., 6 tr., 1 ch. into next sp.; rep. from * to end, sl.st. to join.
4th round: with 2nd C., 2 ch., 1 tr., 3 ch., 2 tr. into 3 ch.sp. at corner, * 3 ch., 1 d.c. between 3rd and 4th tr. of next gr., 3 ch., 1 d.c. into 1 ch.sp., 3 ch., 1 d.c. between 3rd and 4th tr. of next gr., 3 ch., (2 tr., 3 ch., 2 tr.) into 3 ch.sp. at corner; rep. from * 3 times and from * excluding instructions in brackets once more, sl.st. to join.
Fasten off.
Make 7 more motifs in 1st and 2nd C., then make 8 more using 3rd and 4th C., then make 7 more using M. only.

TO COMPLETE
Join alternate C. squares to make 2 strips each with 8 squares, then join 2 strips of 2 squares each in M., and one strip of 3 squares in M.
Take the strip of 3 M. squares (this will form centre back of waistcoat), rejoin yarn and work 19 tr. across one short edge (this will be top edge), 3 ch., turn.
1st row: 1 tr. in next 2 tr., * 1 ch., miss next tr., 1 tr. in next 3 tr.; rep. from * to end of row, 4 ch., turn.
2nd row: miss next tr., * 1 tr. in next tr., 1 tr. in ch.sp., 1 tr. in next tr., 1 ch.; rep. from * to end of row ending with 1 tr. in 3rd of the 4 turning ch., 3 ch., turn.
3rd row: as first row. Fasten off. This completes the centre back panel.

continued on page 97

Fold one strip of C. motifs in half, and join one strip of 2 M. motifs to the 2 bottom squares at each end, thus giving the effect of side, back and front with armhole shaping.

Join the other strip of C. motifs to the other strip of 2 M. motifs in a similar way.

Round the long side of the C. strips work 1 row in tr. then the first row of the 3 tr., 1 ch. patt. as for centre back panel.

Join both side pieces to the centre back panel. The waistcoat is now assembled.

With M., rejoin yarn at bottom of front opening and working up centre front, work the 2 rows of 3 tr., 1 ch. as far as top of 2nd square (counting from lower edge). Fasten off. Repeat along other centre front edge.

Work 1 row of tr., then 1 row of d.c. all round outer edges and armholes. With 3 strands of yarn in 3 different C. shades, make a chain 2 yd. long. Lace up front of waistcoat, then curl each end of ch. round and stitch in place to make a flat circle approx. 1 in. in diameter. Stitch firmly to hold circle in place.

Long fringed cover-up
illustrated opposite

MATERIALS
18 oz. Hayfield Gaylon Double Knitting in main shade, 1 oz. each in seven contrasting shades for fringe. Crochet hooks International Standard Sizes 4.50 and 4.00.

MEASUREMENTS
The cover-up is loose fitting so should comfortably fit any average size up to 38 in. bust; length 46 in.

TENSION
4 tr. and 2 rows measure 1 in.

ABBREVIATIONS
See page 19; M., main shade.

BACK
With No. 4.50 hook and M., make 73 ch.
1st row: 1 tr. into 3rd ch. from hook (this stands for first tr. of every row); work 1 tr. into each ch. to end of row.
2nd row: 1 tr. into each tr. of previous row.
Work 46 rows straight in tr.
Next 4 rows: dec. 1 st. at each end of the row for waist.
Work straight until work measures 33 in.

Shape for Armholes
Next row: sl.st. over 4 sts., work to last 4 tr., turn with 3 ch. Cont. to dec. 1 st. at each end of every alt. row until there are 43 tr. Cont. straight until 20 rows have been worked from beg. of armhole. Fasten off.

FRONTS (as work is reversible, make 2 pieces alike – i.e. no need to reverse shapings for second piece)
With No. 4.50 hook and M., make 39 ch.
1st row: 1 tr. into 3rd ch. from hook (this stands for first tr. of every row), work 1 tr. into each ch. to end of row.
2nd row: 1 tr. into each tr. of previous row.
Work 46 rows straight in tr.
Next 4 rows: dec. 1 st. at one end of each row for waist. Work straight until work measures same as Back to start of armhole shaping.

Shape for Armhole and Neck
Next row: sl.st. over 4 tr. at armhole edge, work to end of row. Dec. 1 st. at armhole edge on every alt. row, making 6 decs. in all. At the same time dec. at centre front edge on every row until you have 12 tr.
Cont. on these 12 tr. till you have worked 20 rows from beg. of armhole shaping. Fasten off.

TO COMPLETE
Press with slightly damp cloth. Join shoulder and underarm seams.

Borders
With No. 4.00 hook and M., and starting at lower corner of centre front edge, work 4 rows of d.c. round all edges. Work a similar border round each armhole.

To Make Fringe
To make each individual tassel in the fringe, cut 1 strand in each of the 7 contrast shades, each strand 8 in. long. Place the strands together, double them, and working on right side of garment pull loop end of strands through the crochet fabric, take cut ends of strands down through the loop and pull tight. Work tassels on each front as follows: start tassels on the 4th row of tr. up from lower edge, and make first tassel on first tr. at centre front edge; make another tassel on every 4th tr. across row, until 7 tassels in all have been worked.

Work similar rows of tassels on every 3rd row of tr. up front of garment. Gradually reduce number of tassels at edge nearest side seam until you have only 3 tassels in the row at waist level. Increase tassels gradually after this point so that at top of fronts entire area of crocheted fabric is filled with tassels.

Work 5 rows of tassels across back yoke of garment, working rows of tassels on every 3rd row of tr. patt. as before.

Striped waistcoat
illustrated in colour on page 92

MATERIALS
5 (6, 6) oz. Robin Vogue Double Knitting in maroon, 4 (5, 5) oz. each of yellow, orange and pink. Crochet hooks International Standard Sizes 5.00 and 4.00.

MEASUREMENTS
To fit bust size 34 (36, 38) in.; length from shoulder 32 in.

TENSION
1 shell measures $1\frac{1}{4}$ in. in width, and 3 stripes measure 2 in. in depth on No. 5.00 hook.

ABBREVIATIONS
See page 19; sh., shell (work 5 tr. all in the same place); M., maroon; Y., yellow; O., orange; P., pink.

BACK
With No. 5.00 hook and M., beg. at right shoulder, work as follows: Make 6 ch.
1st row (wrong side): 1 d.c. into 2nd ch. from hook, 2 ch., miss 2 ch., 1 d.c. into each of last 2 ch., turn.
2nd row: 2 ch., 1 sh. in sp. (see Abbreviations), 1 d.c. in last st., turn.
3rd row: break M., join in P., 4 ch., 1 d.c. in each of centre 3 tr. of sh., 2 ch., 1 d.c. in last st. Break yarn and fasten off.

Left Shoulder
Make another piece exactly the same but do not break yarn.
4th row: 3 ch., 2 tr. in sp., 1 d.c. in centre d.c., 1 sh. in last sp., make 35 (40, 45) ch. for back neck, now work across first piece, 1 sh. in first sp., 1 d.c. in centre d.c., 3 tr. in last sp., turn.
5th row: break P. Join in O., 2 ch., 1 d.c. in next tr., 2 ch., miss 3 sts., 1 d.c. in each of centre 3 tr. of sh., 2 ch., miss 3 sts., (1 d.c. in each of next 3 ch., 2 ch., miss 2 ch.) 6 (7, 8) times, 1 d.c. in next 3 ch., 2 ch., 1 d.c. in each of centre 3 tr. of sh., miss 3 sts., 2 ch., 1 d.c. in each of last 2 sts., turn.
6th row: 2 ch., * 1 sh. in next sp., 1 d.c. in centre d.c.; rep. from * ending 1 d.c. in last st., turn.

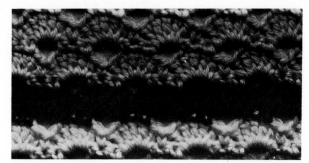

7th row: break O. Join in Y., 4 ch., * 1 d.c. in centre 3 tr. of sh., 2 ch., miss 3 sts.; rep. from * ending 1 d.c. in last st., turn.
8th row: 3 ch., 2 tr. in first sp., * d.c. in centre d.c., 1 sh. in sp.; rep. from * ending 1 d.c. in centre d.c., 3 tr. in last sp., turn.
9th row: break Y. Join in M., 2 ch., 1 d.c. in next tr., * 2 ch., miss 3 sts., 1 d.c. in each of centre 3 tr. of sh.; rep. from * ending 2 ch., miss 3 sts., 1 d.c. in each of last 2 sts., turn.
10th row: as 6th row.
7th-10th rows form the 4-row patt.
Now working throughout in a stripe sequence of 2 rows each M., P., O. and Y., rep. the 4 patt. rows once more.

Shape Armhole
15th row: as 7th row.
16th row: 3 ch., 4 tr. in sp., * 1 d.c. in centre d.c., 1 sh. in sp.; rep. from * to end, turn.
Rep. the last 2 rows 3 times more. This completes the armhole shaping, the 3rd O. stripe is completed: 14 (15, 16) sh.
Beg. with the 7th row, cont. in patt. until the 6th M. stripe has been worked. Now commence side shaping as follows:
** **Next row:** as 7th row.
Next row: as 8th row but working 3 tr. in the first sp. and 4 tr. in the last sp.
Next row: 2 ch., 1 d.c. in next 2 tr., cont. as 9th row from * ending 1 d.c. in each of last 3 sts.
Next row: 2 ch., 1 d.c. in next d.c., cont. as 6th row from * ending 1 d.c. in each of last 2 sts.
Rep. the last 4 rows.
Next row: as 7th row.
Next row: as 8th row but working 4 tr. in first sp. and 5 tr. in the last sp.
Next row: 2 ch., 1 d.c. in each of next 3 tr., then cont. as 9th row from * ending 1 d.c. in each of last 4 sts.
Next row: 3 ch., 1 d.c. in next d.c., cont. as 6th row from * ending miss 1 d.c., 1 d.c. in next d.c., miss 1 d.c., 1 tr. in last st., turn. Rep. the last 4 rows once more.
Next row: as 7th row.
Next row: 2 ch., * 1 sh. in sp., 1 d.c. in centre d.c.; rep. from * ending 1 sh., 1 d.c. in last sp., turn.
Next row: as 7th row.
Next row: as 8th row but working 1 tr. only into first sp., and 2 tr. into last st.
Next row: as 9th row but beg. with 4 ch. not 2, and ending with 2 ch., 1 d.c. in last st.
Next row: as 10th row. **
Rep. 7th-10th rows once, then work from ** to **.
The 12th M. stripe has been completed: 16 (17, 18) sh. Fasten off.

LEFT FRONT
With No. 5.00 hook and M., make 6 ch.
1st row: 1 d.c. in 2nd ch. from hook, 2 ch., miss 2 ch., 1 d.c. in each of last 2 ch., turn.
2nd row: 2 ch., 1 sh. into sp., 1 d.c. in last st., turn.
Change to P. and cont. in colour sequence as for Back.
3rd row: 4 ch., miss 1 tr., 1 d.c. in each of next 3 tr., 2 ch., miss 2 tr., 1 d.c. in last st., turn.
4th row: 3 ch., 2 tr. in sp., 1 d.c. in centre d.c., 3 tr. in sp., turn.
5th row: 2 ch., 1 d.c. in next tr., 2 ch., miss 3 sts., 1 d.c. in each of last 2 sts., turn.

Cont. in patt. as set by 2nd-5th rows until second O. stripe has been worked.

Neck and Armhole Shaping
Next row: as 3rd row.
Next row: 3 ch., 4 tr. in first sp., 1 d.c. in centre d.c., 1 sh. in sp., turn.
Rep. 15th and 16th rows of Back 3 times: 5 sh. in the row. ***
Sizes 34 and 38 only Next row: as 15th row of Back.
Next row: make 12 (18) ch. loosely, 2 tr. in 3rd ch. from hook, (miss 2 ch., 1 d.c. in next ch., miss 2 ch., 1 sh. in next ch.) once (twice), miss 2 ch., 1 d.c. in next ch., (1 sh. in next sp., 1 d.c. in centre d.c.) 5 times, 3 tr. in last sp., turn.
Size 36 only. Next row: as 15th row of Back.
Next row: make 16 ch. loosely, 1 d.c. in 4th ch. from hook, (miss 2 ch., 1 sh. in next ch., miss 2 ch., 1 d.c. in next ch.) twice, (1 sh. in next sp., 1 d.c. in centre d.c.) 5 times, 3 tr. in last sp., turn.
All sizes. This completes neck and armhole shaping: 7 (7½, 8) sh.
Size 36 only. Work in the foll. 4-row patt.
**** **1st row:** 2 ch., 1 d.c. in next tr., * 2 ch., miss 3 sts., 1 d.c. in each of next 3 tr.; rep. from * ending 2 ch., 1 d.c. in last st., turn.
2nd row: 3 ch., 2 tr. in sp., * 1 d.c. in centre d.c., 1 sh. in sp.; rep. from * ending 1 d.c. in last st., turn.
3rd row: 4 ch., * 1 d.c. in centre 3 tr. of sh., 2 ch., miss 3 sts.; rep. from * ending 1 d.c. in each of last 2 sts., turn.
4th row: 2 ch., * 1 sh. in sp., 1 d.c. in centre d.c.; rep. from * ending 3 tr. in last sp. ****
Sizes 34 and 38 only. Rep. 9th, 6th, 7th and 8th rows of Back. *****
All sizes. Cont. in patt. as set until the 6th M. stripe has been completed. Now shape at side edge only as on Back, keeping the front edge straight until the 12th M. stripe has been worked and there are 8 (8½, 9) sh. in the row. Fasten off.

RIGHT FRONT
Work exactly as Left Front to ***.
Next row: with Y., make 13 (16, 19) ch. loosely, sl.st. to first st. of row, then work across in patt. beg. with 1 d.c. in centre 3 tr.
Next row: 3 ch., 2 tr. in first sp., (1 d.c. in centre d.c., 1 sh. in next sp.) 4 times, 1 d.c. in centre d.c., miss last d.c. and sl.st., (1 sh. in next ch., miss 2 ch., 1 d.c. in next ch., miss 2 ch.) 2 (2, 3) times, 3 tr. (5 tr., 3 tr.) in last (next, last) ch. **(Size 36 only.** Miss 2 ch., 1 d.c. in last ch.): 7 (7½, 8) sh. in row.
Work in 4-row patt. as follows:
Sizes 34 and 38 only. Work 9th, 6th, 7th and 8th rows of Back.
Size 36 only. Work from **** to **** on Left Front, beg. with the 3rd row.
All sizes. Complete as Left Front from *****.

TO COMPLETE
Press pieces on wrong side using a warm iron over a damp cloth. Join shoulder seams. Rejoin M. yarn at bottom of Right Front. With No. 4.00 hook work 3 rows of d.c. round fronts and neck edges, working 3 d.c. into each row, 1 d.c. in each ch. and 3 d.c. into each corner st.
Work 3 rows d.c. in a similar way round each armhole. Join underarm seams. Press seams.

Gold bathing costume
illustrated in colour on page 68

MATERIALS
5 oz. Twilleys Goldfingering. One crochet hook International Standard Size 2.50.

MEASUREMENTS
To fit bust size 34/36 in.

TENSION
6 tr. to 1 in.

ABBREVIATIONS
See page 19.

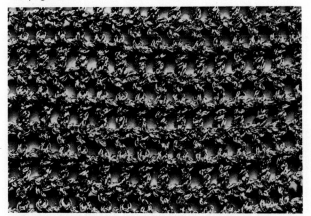

PANTS
Commence with yarn round finger to form a ring.
1st round: 3 ch., 15 tr. into ring, sl.st. into 3rd of 3 ch.
2nd round: 4 ch., * 1 tr. into next tr., 1 ch.; rep. from * sl.st. into 3rd of 4 ch.
3rd round: 3 ch., * 2 tr. into next sp., 1 tr. into next tr., into next sp. work 1 tr., 1 ch., 1 tr. (a 'V' st. formed), 1 tr. into next tr., 2 tr. into next sp., 1 tr. into next tr., 1 ch., 1 tr. into next tr.; rep. from * omitting last tr. of last rep., sl.st. into 3rd of 3 ch.
4th round: 3 ch., * 1 tr. into each of next 4 tr., a V st. into next V st., 1 tr. into each of next 5 ch., 2 ch., 1 tr. into next tr.; rep. from * omitting last tr. of last rep., sl.st. into 3rd of 3 ch.
5th round: 3 ch., * 1 tr. into each of next 5 tr., a V st. into next V st., 1 tr. into each of next 6 tr., 3 ch., 1 tr. into next tr.; rep. from * omitting last tr. of last rep., sl.st. into 3rd of 3 ch.
6th round: 4 ch., miss next tr., * 1 tr. into each of next 5 tr., a V st. into next V st., 1 tr. into next 5 tr., 1 ch., miss next tr., 1 tr. into next tr., (1 ch., 1 tr.) twice into next sp., 1 ch., 1 tr. into next tr., 1 ch., miss next tr.; rep. from * omitting last tr. and ch. at end of last rep., sl.st. into 3rd of 4 ch.
7th round: 4 ch., * 1 tr. into next tr., 1 ch., miss next tr., 1 tr. into next tr., 1 ch., 1 tr. into each of next 3 tr., a V st. into next V st., 1 tr. into each of next 3 tr., 1 ch., 1 tr. into next tr., 1 ch., miss next tr., (1 tr. into next tr., 1 ch) 5 times, miss next tr.; rep. from * omitting last tr. and ch. at end of last rep., sl.st. into 3rd of 4 ch., fasten off.
8th round: attach thread to a V st., 3 ch., * 1 tr. into next tr., 1 ch., 1 tr. into next tr., 1 ch., miss next tr., (1 tr. into next tr., 1 ch.) 10 times, miss next tr., 1 tr. into next tr., 1 ch., 1 tr. into next tr., a V st. into next V st.: rep. from * twice omitting last tr. at end of last rep., turn.
9th row: 3 ch., miss first tr., (1 tr. into next tr., 1 ch.) 12 times, miss next tr., 1 tr. into next tr., 1 ch., 6 tr. into next V st., 1 ch., 1 tr. into next tr., 1 ch., miss next tr., (1 tr. into next tr., 1 ch.) 3 times, (1 d.c. into next tr., 1 ch.) 6 times, (1 tr. into next tr., 1 ch.) 3 times, miss next tr., 1 tr. into next tr., 1 ch., 6 tr. into next V st., 1 ch., 1 tr. into next tr., miss next tr., 1 ch., into each tr. work 1 tr., 1 ch. to within last V. st., 1 tr. into V st., turn.
** 10th row: 3 ch., into each tr. work 1 tr., 1 ch. until 6 tr. group is reached, 1 tr. into centre sp. of next 6 tr. group, miss 2 tr., 1 d.tr. into next tr., turn.
11th row: 3 ch., miss first tr., into each tr. work 1 tr., 1 ch. to within last 2 sp., 1 tr. into next tr., turn.
12th row: 4 ch., into each tr. work 1 tr., 1 ch., 1 tr. into 3rd of 4 ch., turn.
13th row: 4 ch., miss first tr., into each tr. work 1 tr., 1 ch. to within last 3 sp., 1 tr., into next tr., 1 ch., 1 tr. into next tr., turn.
Rep. last 2 rows until only six 1 ch.sp. remain, then work 12th row twice more. Fasten off. ******

Second Side
Work to correspond with first side attaching yarn to 3rd of 4 ch. and working from ** to ** of first side.

Crutch
1st row: mark centre of sp. of crutch, attach yarn to 4th tr. before marked sp., 4 ch., (1 tr. into next tr., 1 ch.) 6 times, 1 tr. into next tr., turn.
Work 12th row 4 times. Fasten off.
Make a 2nd piece the same, and then join side and crutch seams.

BRA
Yarn round finger to form a ring.
1st round: 3 ch., 11 tr. into ring.
2nd-5th rounds: same as for 2nd to 5th rounds of pants.
6th row: 4 ch., miss first tr., 1 tr. into each of next 5 tr., 1 V st. into next V st., patt. to within last V st., 1 V st. into last V st., 1 tr. into each of next 5 tr., miss next tr., 1 tr. into next tr., turn.
7th row: 1 sl.st. into first tr., 3 ch., (miss next tr., 1 tr. into next tr., 1 ch.) twice, 1 V st. into next V st., patt. to within last V st., 1 V st. into next V st., (1 ch., miss next tr., 1 tr. into next tr.) twice, miss next tr., 1 tr. into next tr., turn.
8th row: 3 ch., miss first 2 tr., 1 tr. into next tr., 1 ch., 1 tr. into next V st., patt. to within last V st., 1 tr. into next V st., 1 ch., miss next tr., 1 tr. into each of next 2 tr., turn.
9th row: 3 ch., miss first 2 tr., 1 tr. into next tr., 1 ch., patt. to within turning ch., turn.

Strap
1st row: 4 ch., miss first tr., (1 tr. into next tr., 1 ch.) twice, 1 tr. into next tr., turn.
Rep. 12th row of pants 11 times. Fasten off.

Second Half
Work as first half until strap is reached. Fasten off.

Strap
1st row: with right side facing attach yarn to 4th tr. from beg. of last rep., then work as first row of first strap, turn.
Complete as first strap. Fasten off.
Join 2 halves by sewing three 1 ch.sp. together.

BODY SECTION
1st round: with right side facing attach yarn to first tr. from centre back of pants, 4 ch., 1 tr., 1 ch. into each row-end all round, 1 tr. into same place as join, turn: 109 sp. altogether. Work 12th row of pants 11 times (adjust length here if necessary).
13th row: 1 sl.st. into each of first 10 sts., patt. to within last 5 sp., turn.
14th row: 1 sl.st. into each of first 6 sts., patt. to within last 3 sp., turn.
Rep. last row twice more.
17th row: 1 sl.st. into each of first 2 sts., patt. to within last sp., turn.
Rep. last row 7 times more, then work 12th row of pants 6 times. Fasten off.

TO COMPLETE
Sew bra to top of body section.

Edging
1st round: with right side facing attach yarn to centre back, then work d.c. evenly round, 1 d.c. into first d.c.
2nd round: work d.c. evenly round making 3 d.c. into corners and missing 2 d.c. where the 2 halves of the bra were joined together.

Straps
Using double thickness of yarn attach yarn to top of bra and work 18 in. of chain, sl.st. into top of other bra cup. Fasten off.
Attach yarn to top corner of back and work a chain 10 in. long. Fasten off. Repeat at other side.

Chapter seven
EVENING ELEGANCE
dresses, skirts and tops for parties and special occasions

Party tunic

MATERIALS

20 (21, 23) balls (20 gr. each) Coats Chain Mercer-Crochet No. 20. One steel crochet hook International Standard Size 1.25. Three hooks and eyes. Ribbon and beads for lining and decorating Border Motifs (optional).

MEASUREMENTS

To fit bust size 34 (36, 38) in.; length 29 in. (adjustable); length of sleeve seam 17 in. (adjustable).

TENSION

4 rows to $\frac{3}{4}$ in. and 1 rep. of patt. to $\frac{1}{2}$ in.; each motif $1\frac{3}{4}$ in. in diameter.

ABBREVIATIONS

See page 19.

BACK

Commence with 267 (279, 291) ch.

1st row: 1 tr. into 4th ch. from hook, 1 tr. into each ch., 1 ch.; turn.

2nd row: 1 d.c. into first tr., * miss 2 tr., 5 tr. into next tr. (1 sh. made), miss 2 tr., 1 d.c. into next tr.; rep. from * working last d.c. into next ch., 4 ch.; turn: 44 (46, 48) sh.

3rd row: * into centre tr. of next sh. work 1 tr., 3 ch. and 1 tr. (1 V st. made over a sh.), 1 ch.; rep. from * omitting 1 ch. at end of last rep., 1 d.tr. into next d.c., 3 ch.; turn.

4th row: 1 tr. into next tr., * 3 tr. into next sp., 1 tr. into each of next 3 sts.; rep. from * omitting 1 tr. at end of last rep., 3 ch.; turn.

5th row: 2 tr. into first tr. (1 sh. made at beg. of row), * miss 2 tr., 1 d.c. into next tr., miss 2 tr., 1 sh. over next tr.; rep. from * to within last 6 sts., miss 2 tr., 1 d.c. into next tr., miss 2 tr., 3 tr. into 3rd of 3 ch. (1 sh. made at end of row), 4 ch.; turn.

6th row: 1 tr. into first tr., * 1 ch., 1 V st. over next sh.; rep. from * ending with 1 ch. into 3rd of 3 ch. work 1 tr., 1 ch. and 1 tr., 3 ch.; turn.

7th row: 1 tr. into first sp., * 1 tr. into each of next 3 sts., 3 tr. into next sp.; rep. from * omitting 2 tr. at end of last rep., 1 tr. into 3rd of 4 ch., 1 ch.; turn.

The 2nd to 7th rows form the patt.

Rep. 2nd row once.

1st dec. row: patt. until 7 (8, 9) 1-ch. sps. have been completed, 1 V st. over each of next 3 sh. (2 sts. dec.), 1 ch., * patt. to within last 10 (11, 12) shs., 1 ch., 1 V st. over each of next 3 shs. (another 2 sts. dec.), 1 ch., patt. to end.

2nd dec. row: * patt. to within tr. before next dec., leaving the last loop of each on hook work 1 tr. into each of next 2 tr., y.o.h. and draw through all loops on hook (a joint tr. made), 3 tr. into next sp., a joint tr. over next 2 tr. **, rep. from * once more, patt. to end: 4 sts. dec.

3rd dec. row: * patt. to within tr. before next join tr., miss 3 sts., 1 sh. into next tr., miss 3 sts., 1 d.c. into next tr., miss 2 tr. **; rep. from * once more, patt. to end.

Work 6 more rows in patt.

Rep. from first dec. row twice.

*** Rep. first to 3rd dec. row once.

Work 3 more rows in patt.

Rep. from *** 5 times.

Work 1 more row in patt.

1st inc. row: patt. until 39 (45, 51) tr. have been completed, * (2 tr. into next tr., 3 tr. into next sp., 2 tr. into next tr., 1 tr. into next ch.) twice *, patt. to within last 9 (10, 11) 1-ch. sps. between V sts., 1 tr. into next ch.; rep. from * to * once more, patt. to end: 8 sts. inc.

2nd inc. row: patt. to within first inc., miss 2 tr., 1 d.c. into next tr., * miss 1 tr., 1 sh. into next tr., miss 1 tr., 1 d.c. into next tr., miss 2 tr. *, patt. to within last 46 (52, 58) sts.; rep. from * to * once more, patt. to end.

Work 4 more rows in patt.

Rep. from first inc. row 4 times more.

Work 12 more rows in patt., or length required ending with a 6th patt. row, omitting turning ch. at end of last row.

Shape Armholes

1st row: sl.st. into each of first 13 sts., 2 ch., 1 tr. into next tr., 1 tr. into next ch., patt. to within last 3 1-ch.sps. between V sts., 1 tr. into next ch., a joint tr. over next tr. and centre ch. of next sp., 1 ch.; turn.

2nd row: miss first st., sl.st. into next tr., 3 ch., 2 tr. into same place as sl.st., miss 2 tr., 1 d.c. into next tr., patt. to within last 4 tr., miss 2 tr., 1 tr. into next tr., 4 ch.; turn.

3rd row: miss first d.c., a V st. over next sh., 1 ch., patt. to within last d.c., 1 d.tr. into 3rd of 3 ch., 1 ch.; turn.

4th row: miss first st., sl.st. into each of next 3 sts., 2 ch., 1 tr. into next tr., 1 tr. into next ch., patt. to within last 1-ch.sp., 1 tr. into next ch., a joint tr. over next tr. and centre ch. of next sp., 1 ch.; turn.

Rep. last 3 rows once more, then 2nd and 3rd rows again, ending last row with 3 ch.; turn.

10th row: miss first st., 1 tr. into next tr., patt. ending with 1 tr. into 4th of 4 ch., 3 ch.; turn.

Work 8 more rows in patt.

Shape Neck

1st row: patt. until 39 (45, 51) tr. have been worked, a joint tr. over next tr. and centre ch. of next sp., 1 ch.; turn.

2nd row: miss first st., sl.st. into next tr., 3 ch., 2 tr. into same place as sl.st., miss 2 tr., 1 d.c. into next tr., patt. to end.

3rd row: patt. to within last d.c., 1 d.tr. into 3rd of 3 ch., 1 ch.; turn.

4th row: miss first st., sl.st. into each of next 3 sts., 2 ch., 1 tr. into next tr., 1 tr. into next ch., patt. to end.

5th row: patt. to within last 4 tr., miss 2 tr., 3 tr. into next tr., 4 ch.; turn.

6th row: miss first d.c. a V st. over next sh., 1 ch., patt. to end.

7th row: patt. to within last 1-ch. sp., 1 tr. into next ch., a joint tr. over next tr. and centre ch. of next sp., 1 ch.; turn.

Rep. 2nd to 5th rows of neck shaping.

12th row: 1 tr. into first tr., 1 ch., patt. to end. Work 4 (4, 7) rows in patt. omitting turning ch. at end of last row. Fasten off. Miss 9 V sts. at centre, attach thread to centre ch. of next V st. 2 ch., 1 tr. into next tr., 1 tr. into next ch., complete to correspond with first side of neck.

LEFT FRONT

Commence with 117 (123, 129) ch. and work as Back for 8 rows.

1st dec. row: as first dec. row of Back to *, patt. to end.

2nd dec. row: as 2nd dec. row of Back to **, patt. to end.

3rd dec. row: as 3rd dec. row of Back to **, patt. to end.

Work 6 more rows in patt.

Next dec. row: patt. until 9 1-ch.sps. have been worked, a V st. over each of next 3 shs. (2 sts. dec.), 1 ch., patt. to end.

Next dec. row: as 2nd dec. row of Left Front.

Next dec. row: as 3rd dec. row of Left Front.

Work 6 more rows in patt.

Rep. first to 3rd dec. rows.

Work 6 more rows in patt.

Next dec. row: patt. until 7 1-ch. sps. have been worked, a V st. over each of next 3 sh. (2 sts. dec.) 1 ch., patt. to end.

Next 2 dec. rows: as 2nd and 3rd dec. rows of Left Front. Work 3 more rows in patt.

Rep. last 6 rows 5 times more working decs. over decs. to correspond with Back.

Work 1 more row in patt.

1st inc. row: as first inc. row of Back to 2nd *, patt. to end.

2nd inc. row: as 2nd inc. row of Back to 2nd *, patt. to end.

Work 4 more rows in patt.

Rep. from first inc. row 4 times more.

Work 12 more rows in patt., or as Back to armholes, omitting turning ch. at end of last row.

Shape Armhole

1st row: sl.st. into each of first 13 sts., 2 ch., 1 tr. into next tr., 1 tr. into next ch., patt. to end.

2nd to 4th rows: as 5th to 7th rows of Back neck shaping.

Rep. 2nd to 6th rows of Back neck shaping ending last row with 1 ch.; turn.

Shape Neck

1st row: miss first st., sl.st. into each of next 3 sts., 2 ch., 1 tr. into next tr., 1 tr. into next ch., patt. ending with 1 tr. into 4th of 4 ch., 3 ch.; turn.

Rep. 5th to 7th rows of Back neck shaping.

Rep. 2nd to 7th rows of Back neck shaping, then 2nd to 5th rows again.

Next row: 1 tr. into first tr., patt. to end. Work 10 (10, 13) rows more in patt. omitting turning ch. at end of last row. Fasten off.

RIGHT FRONT

Work as Left Front reversing all shapings.

SLEEVES (make 2 alike)

Commence with 141 (141, 147) ch. and work as Back for 7 rows.

Work in patt. until work measures approximately 14½ in. or approx. 1½ in. less than length required for sleeve seam ending with a 6th patt. row, omitting turning ch. at end of last row.

Shape Top

Work as Back armhole shaping for 3 rows ending last row with 3 ch.; turn.

Work in patt. for 2 rows more.

6th row: as 3rd row of Back armhole shaping ending with 3 ch.; turn.

Rep. last 3 rows 6 (6, 7) times more ending last row 1 ch.; turn.

Next row: as 4th row of Back armhole shaping. Rep. 2nd and 3rd rows of Back armhole shaping omitting turning ch. at end of last row. Fasten off.

TO COMPLETE

Sew shoulder, side and sleeve seams. Set in Sleeves. With right side facing, attach thread to lower edge of Right Front and work a row of d.c. evenly along lower edge ending at lower edge of Left Front. Fasten off.

Sleeve Motifs

1st Motif 1st row: commence by winding thread 10 times round forefinger, remove from finger and work 32 d.c. into ring, sl.st. into first d.c.

2nd row: 1 d.c. into same place as sl.st., * 5 ch., miss 3 d.c., 1 d.c. into next d.c.; rep. from * ending with 5 ch., sl.st. into first d.c.

3rd row: * into next loop work 1 d.c., 1 h.tr. and 2 tr., 3 ch., sl.st. into last tr., into same loop work 1 tr., 1 h.tr. and 1 d.c.; rep. from * ending with sl.st. into first d.c.

4th row: 1 ch., inserting hook from the back of previous row work 1 d.c. into first d.c. made on 2nd row, * 6 ch., 1 d.c. into next d.c. on 2nd row; rep. from * ending with 6 ch., sl.st. into first d.c.

5th row: 3 ch., * into next loop work 3 tr., 3 ch. and 3 tr., 1 tr. into next d.c.; rep. from * omitting 1 tr. at end of last rep., sl.st. into 3rd of 3 ch. Fasten off.

2nd Motif. Work as first motif for 4 rows.

5th row: 3 ch., * 3 tr. into next loop, 1 ch., 1 d.c. into corresponding loop on first motif, 1 ch., 3 tr. into same loop on 2nd motif, 1 tr. into next d.c.; rep. from * once, complete as first motif.

Make 6 more motifs joining each as 2nd motif was joined to first, leaving 2 loops free on each side between joinings and joining last motif to first motif as well. Work and join 8 more motifs for 2nd Sleeve.

Sleeve Edging

1st row: with right side of motifs facing, attach thread to first free loop to left of any joining, 1 d.c. into same place as join, * 7 ch., 1 d.c. into next loop, 5 ch., miss 3 tr., a joint d.tr. working 1 d.tr. into next st., miss 3 tr. on next motif, 1 d.tr. into next st. (a joint d.tr. made over joining), 5 ch., 1 d.c. into next loop *, rep. from * to * omitting 1 d.c. at end of last rep., sl.st. into first d.c.

2nd row: 1 d.c. into same place as join, * 7 d.c. into next loop, 1 d.c. into next d.c., 5 d.c. into next loop, 1 d.c. into sp. between 2 d.tr., 5 d.c. into next loop, 1 d.c. into next d.c.; rep. from * omitting 1 d.c. at end of last rep., sl.st. into first d.c. Fasten off. Working edging on opposite side to correspond, then work both edges of motifs for 2nd Sleeve. Line and decorate with beads if desired.

Front Motifs

Make 15 motifs (or number required for straight edge of Right Front) in same way as for Sleeves, joining each as before.

Corner Motif

Work as first sleeve motif for 4 rows.

5th row: 3 ch., 3 tr. into next loop, 1 ch., miss 2 free loops on right of previous motif, 1 d.c. into next loop, 1 ch., 3 tr. into same loop on corner motif, * 1 tr. into next d.c., into next loop work 3 tr., 3 ch. and 3 tr.; rep. from * ending with sl.st. into 3rd of 3 ch.

Fasten off. Mark corner motif with a coloured thread. Make 1 more motif joining as 2nd sleeve motif was joined to first leaving 2 loops free on inner edge of corner motif and 3 loops free on outer edge. Make 15 more motifs or number required for neck edge joining each as 2nd sleeve motif was joined to first.

Work corner motif as before, then complete motifs to correspond with Right Front edge.

Front Edging

1st row: with right side of motifs facing, attach thread to first free loop to left of joining on first motif worked, 1 d.c. into same place as join, (7 ch., 1 d.c. into next loop, 9 ch., 1 d.c. into next loop) twice; rep. from * to * on first row of sleeve edging working last d.c. into first free loop of motif before next corner motif, (7 ch., 1 d.c. into next loop) twice, 5 ch., a joint d.tr. over next joining, 5 ch., 1 d.c. into next loop, 7 ch., 1 d.c. into next loop; rep. from * to * on first row of sleeve edging working last d.c. into first free loop on motif after next shoulder, ** 5 ch., 1 d.c. into next loop, 3 ch., a joint d.tr. over next joining, 3 ch., 1 d.c. into next loop; rep. from ** working last d.c. into first loop on motif before next shoulder, 5 ch., 1 d.c. into next loop, 5 ch., a joint d.tr. over next joining, 5 ch., 1 d.c. into next loop; rep. from * to * of first row of sleeve edging along outer edge working next corner and opposite end of strip to correspond, cont. along inner edge working last d.c. into first loop of next corner motif, 7 ch., 1 d.c. into next loop, 1 ch., a joint d.tr. over next joining, 1 ch., 1 d.c. into next loop; rep. from * to * on first row of sleeve edging working next corner to correspond and omitting 1 d.c. at end of last rep., sl.st. into first d.c.

2nd row: 1 d.c. into same place as sl.st., cont. to work a row of d.c. evenly all round in the same manner as 2nd row of sleeve edging, working 1 d.c. for each ch. on loops and ending with sl.st. into first d.c. Fasten off.

Line motifs if desired and attach beads.
Sew sleeve and front motifs in position.
With right side facing, attach thread to any side seam at lower edge and work a row of d.c. neatly all round working 3 d.c. into centre d.c. on each lower corner and ending with sl.st. into first d.c.
Fasten off.
With right side facing, attach thread to any d.c. on lower edge of Sleeve and work a row of d.c. neatly all round ending with sl.st. into first d.c.
Fasten off. Work other Sleeve to correspond.
Sew hooks and eyes to top of front edge to fasten (see photograph on page 100).
Damp and press.

Evening skirt and blouse
illustrated in colour on page 89

MATERIALS
For blouse: 16 (17, 18, 19) balls Robin Tricel-Nylon Double Knitting. Twelve medium buttons.
For skirt: 15 (16, 17, 18) balls Robin Tricel-Nylon Double Knitting and 16 (17, 18, 19) balls Robin Camilla Crêpe Double Knitting in a contrasting colour. A waist length of elastic, 1 in. wide.
For both: crochet hooks International Standard Sizes 3.00, 4.00, 4.50 and 5.00.

MEASUREMENTS
To fit bust size 32 (34, 36, 38) in.; hip size 34 (36, 38, 40) in.; skirt length 39½ in.

TENSION
9 tr. to 2 in. and 6 rows to 2½ in. on No. 4.00 hook with Tricel-Nylon Double Knitting; 6 tr. and 3 rows to 2 in. on No. 5.00 hook with Tricel-Nylon and Camilla Crêpe together.

ABBREVIATIONS
See page 19; dec. 1, decrease 1 tr. by inserting hook into next st., draw through loop, insert hook into next st. and draw through loop, insert hook into next st. and draw through loop, (y.r.h., draw through 2 loops) twice.

BLOUSE BACK
With No. 4.00 hook and Tricel-Nylon Double Knitting make 80 (84, 90, 94) ch.
Foundation row: work 1 tr. into 3rd ch. from hook, 1 tr. into each ch. to end, 2 ch., turn.
Work 1 tr. into each tr. and turn each row with 2 ch. until work measures 15 in. from beg.; do not work ch. to turn on last row.

Shape Armholes
Next row: sl. st. over 4 (5, 5, 6) sts., 1 d.c., work in tr. to last 5 (6, 6, 7) sts., 1 d.c., no ch. to turn.
Next row: sl.st. over 2 sts., 1 d.c., work in tr. to last 3 sts., 1 d.c., no ch. to turn.
Rep. the last row 2 (2, 3, 3) times more, 2 ch. to turn on last row.
Now work straight until armhole measures 7 (7½, 8, 8½) in., no ch. to turn.

Shape Shoulder
Next row: sl.st. over 9 sts., 1 d.c., work to last 10 sts., 1 d.c., no ch. to turn.
Next row: sl.st. over 9 (9, 10, 10) sts., 1 d.c., work to last 10 (10, 11, 11) sts., 1 d.c. Fasten off.

BLOUSE LEFT FRONT
With No. 4.00 hook and Tricel-Nylon Double Knitting make 73 (77, 83, 87) ch. Work foundation row and 1 row of treble as Back.

Shape Front
Dec. 1 tr. at front edge on every row until the same number of rows as Back to armhole have been worked ending at side edge.

Shape Armhole
1st row: sl.st. over 4 (5, 5, 6) sts., 1 d.c., work in tr., dec., last st.
2nd row: dec. 1, work to last 3 sts., 1 d.c., no ch. to turn.
3rd row: sl.st. over 2 sts., 1 d.c., work to end, dec. last st.
1st and 2nd sizes. Work 2nd row again.
3rd and 4th sizes. Work 2nd and 3rd rows again.
All sizes. 2 ch., turn.
Keeping side edge straight, dec. 1 st. at front edge on every row to 18 (18, 19, 19) sts. Then work straight until the same number of rows as Back to shoulder have been worked ending at side edge, no ch. to turn on last row.

Shape Shoulder
Sl.st. over 9 sts., 1 d.c., work to end. Fasten off.

BLOUSE RIGHT FRONT
Work to match Left Front reversing shapings.

BLOUSE SLEEVES (make 2 alike)
With No. 4.00 hook and Tricel-Nylon Double Knitting make 62 (64, 66, 68) ch. and work as back to 18 in. from beg.

Shape Armholes
Next row: sl.st. over 4 (5, 5, 6) sts., 1 d.c., work to last 5 (6, 6, 7) sts., 1 d.c., no ch. to turn.
Next row: sl.st. over 2 sts., 1 d.c., work to last 3 sts., 1 d.c., no ch. to turn.
Rep. the last row 4 times more.
Dec. 1 st. at each end of the next 4 (4, 5, 5) rows.
Fasten off.

BLOUSE CUFFS (make 2 alike)
With No. 3.00 hook and Tricel-Nylon Double Knitting make 40 (40, 42, 42) ch.
Work 1 d.c. into 2nd ch. from hook, 1 d.c. into each ch. to end, 1 ch., turn.
Now work in d.c. to 4½ in. from beg. Now work 2 rows d.c. all round cuff but on the 2nd row make loops on side edge for 6 buttons.

BLOUSE TIE
With No. 3.00 hook and Tricel-Nylon Double Knitting make 254 (275, 292, 309) ch. and work in patt. as cuff to 2 in. from beg. Fasten off.
With 63 ch. make another tie in the same way.

TO COMPLETE BLOUSE
Lightly press all parts on wrong side using a warm iron over a damp cloth.
Join shoulder, side and sleeve seams.
With No. 3.00 hook work 2 rows d.c. evenly on each front edge and round back neck. Easing fullness round back and sides, pin long tie to lower edge of blouse beg. at edge of left front and ending at right front edge with 11 in. of tie free for fastening. Sew tie into place. Sew short tie to left front about 2 in. from side edge. Beg. at centre of sleeve edge and sew cuff to edge of sleeve easing fullness. Set sleeves into armhole gathering fullness at shoulder. Press seams as before, sew on buttons.

SKIRT BACK AND FRONT (make 2 pieces alike)
With No. 5.00 hook and using one strand of Tricel-Nylon Double Knitting and one strand of Camilla Crêpe tog., make 66 (70, 72, 76) ch.
Foundation row: 1 tr. into 3rd ch. from hook, 1 tr. into each ch. to end, 2 ch., turn.
Now work 5 in. in tr., turning each row with 2 ch. Cont. in tr. dec. 1 tr. at each end of the next row and at 5-in. intervals to 52 (56, 58, 62) tr. Change to No. 4.50 hook and work straight to 34 in. from beg.

Work 6 rows dec. 1 st. at each end of the first, 3rd and 5th rows. Change to No. 4.00 hook and work straight to 39 in. from beg. Fasten off.

TO COMPLETE SKIRT

Press work lightly on wrong side using cool iron over a dry cloth. Join side seams. Press as before. Join elastic and sew inside waist using a herringbone casing stitch.

Golden party sweater
illustrated in colour on page 121

MATERIALS

10 balls Lister Bel Air Starspun 4-ply Knitting. Crochet hooks International Standard Sizes 3.00, 2.50 and 4.00.

MEASUREMENTS

To fit bust size 34/36 (38/40) in.; length 21 in.; sleeve seam 3 in.

TENSION

1 rep. (of 18 sts.) to 3 in. and 9 rows to 3 in.

ABBREVIATIONS

See page 19; 1 bobble, make bobble as follows: 1 tr. around tr. 4 times, y.o.h. and pull yarn through, yarn over hook and pull through all 9 loops, 1 chain on top of bobble to close it; gr., group (of 3 tr. together).

THE PATTERN

1st row: 3 ch. to turn, in 4th ch. work 1 tr., miss 2 ch., 3 tr. in next ch., miss 2 ch., 3 tr. in next ch., miss 2 ch., * 1 bobble in next ch., (miss 2 ch., 3 tr. in next ch.) 5 times, miss 2 ch.; rep. from * to end, finishing with 1 bobble in next ch., (miss 2 ch., 3 tr. in next ch.) twice, miss 2 ch., 2 tr. in last ch.
2nd row: 3 ch. to turn, 3 tr. between the first 2 tr. of row and next gr. of 3 tr., 3 tr. between next 2 groups, 1 bobble between group and bobble, * 1 bobble between bobble and group, (1 group between 2 groups) 4 times, 1 bobble between last group and bobble; rep. from * to end, finishing with 2 groups, work 1 single tr. in turning ch. of row below.
3rd row: 3 ch. to turn, 1 tr. in 3rd ch. from hook, 1 group between the 2 groups below, 1 bobble between group and bobble, * 1 group between 2 bobbles, 1 bobble between bobble and group, (1 group between groups) 3 times, 1 bobble between group and bobble; rep. from * to end, finishing with 1 group, then 2 tr. into turning ch.
4th row: 3 ch. to turn, 1 group between 2 tr. and first group, * 1 bobble, 2 groups, 1 bobble, 2 groups; rep. from * to end, finishing with 1 bobble, 1 group, 1 tr. in turning ch. of last row.
5th row: 3 ch. to turn, 1 tr. in 3rd ch. from hook, 1 bobble between first group and bobble, * 3 groups, 1 bobble, 1 group, 1 bobble; rep. from * to end, finishing with 3 groups, 1 bobble, 2 tr. in turning ch.
6th row: 3 ch. to turn, 1 bobble between 2 tr. and bobble, *

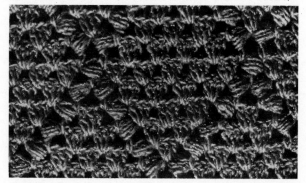

4 groups, 1 bobble, 1 bobble; rep. from * to end, finishing with 4 groups, 1 bobble, 1 tr. in turning ch.
7th row: 1 bobble on single tr., * 5 groups, 1 bobble; rep. from * to end.
8th row: as 6th row.
9th row: as 5th row.
10th row: as 4th row.
11th row: as 3rd row.
12th row: as 2nd row.
13th row: 3 ch. to turn, 1 tr. in 3rd ch. from hook, 2 groups, * 1 bobble, 5 groups; rep. from * to end, finishing with 1 bobble, 2 groups, 2 tr. in turning ch.
The 2nd-13th rows inclusive form the patt.

BACK

With No. 2.50 hook, make 108 ch. and begin patt.
Work straight for 3 in. Change to No. 3.00 hook and work straight for 6 in. more.
Size 38/40 only. Change to No. 3.50 hook and cont. until Back measures 14½ in. from beg.
Size 34/36 only. Cont. with No. 3.00 hook until Back measures 14½ in. from beg.

Shape Armholes (all sizes)

Sl.st. across 2 groups (or bobbles), work to last 2 groups, turn and leave them unworked.
Next row: work to end.
Next row: sl.st. across 1 group (or bobble), work to within 1 group, turn.
Next row: work to end.
Repeat last 2 rows twice more. Work straight on 26 groups (or bobbles) remaining until armhole measures 7 (7½) in. from beg.

Shape Shoulders

Next row: sl.st. across 3 groups, work to last 3 groups, turn and work 1 row straight.
3rd row: sl.st. across 4 groups, work to last 4 groups, sl.st. to end across 4 groups, leaving 12 groups for back of neck.

FRONT

Work as for Back until first row of armhole shaping has been worked (there are 32 groups, or bobbles, on work).

Shape Neck

Next row: work across 13 groups, turn and work this side first.
** Now dec. (by leaving unworked or sl.st. across) 1 group (or bobble) at neck edge on next 3 rows, at the same time dec. 1 group at armhole edge on alt. rows 3 times. Work on 7 groups until armhole matches back to shoulder.

Shape Shoulder

Sl.st. across 3 groups at armhole edge, work to end.
Next row: work to armhole.
Next row: sl.st. across 4 groups.
Fasten off. **
Leave 6 groups (or bobbles) at centre front free.
Rejoin yarn next to them and work across 13 groups to end. Now work from ** to **, reversing all shapings.

SLEEVES (make 2 alike)

With No. 3.00 hook make 72 ch. and work in patt. on these 4 patt. repeats for approx. 3 in., ending with same patt. row as Back to armhole.

Shape Top

1st row: sl.st. across 1 group (or bobble), work to last group, turn.
2nd row: work to end across 22 groups.
3rd row: sl.st. across 1 group, work to within 1 group, turn.
4th row: work to end.
Repeat last 2 rows 3 times more until 14 groups (or bobbles) remain.

11th row: sl.st. across 1 group, work to within 1 group, turn, leaving it unworked. Repeat 11th row 3 times more.
Fasten off, leaving 6 groups (or bobbles) for top of sleeves.

TO COMPLETE
Join shoulder seams.

Neck Edging
With right side of work facing, work 1 row of d.c. around neck edge.
Next row: 3 ch. to turn, * 1 bobble on 3rd st. from hook, miss 2 sts.; rep. from * all round neck. Work 1 row d.c. holding neck in and missing a few sts. Fasten off.

To Make Up
Join sleeve and side seams. Sew in sleeves. Work around sleeve and lower edge as follows:
1st row: d.c.
Next row: 3 ch., * 1 bobble on 3rd st. from hook, miss 2 sts.; rep. from * to end.
Work 1 more row d.c.
Fasten off. Press seams on wrong side under a damp cloth, using a cool iron.

Blue top and long skirt
illustrated in colour on page 116

MATERIALS
For top: 13 (14, 15) balls Emu Tricel. Crochet hook International Standard Size 3.50 (4.00, 4.00). **For skirt:** 21 (23) balls Emu Filigree. A 7-in. zip fastener. Crochet hooks International Standard Sizes 3.50, 4.00, 4.50, 5.00, 5.50 (4.00, 4.50, 5.00, 5.50 and 6.00).

MEASUREMENTS
Top: to fit bust size 34 (36, 38) in. **Skirt:** to fit waist size 25/26 (27/28) in.; length 45 in.

TENSION
1 patt. repeat measures 1 in. deep on No. 3.50 hook with Tricel yarn.

ABBREVIATIONS
See page 19.

SKIRT (made all in one piece)
With No. 4.00 (4.50) hook make 122 ch.
Foundation row: 1 tr. in 5th ch. from hook, * miss 2 sts., 1 tr.

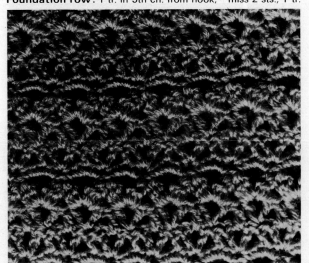

in next ch., miss 2 sts., (1 tr., 2 ch., 1 tr.) in next ch.; rep. from * to last 3 ch., miss 2 sts., 1 tr. in last ch., 4 ch., turn.
1st row: 2 d.tr., 1 ch., 2 d.tr. in each 2 ch.sp. to end, 1 d.tr. in turning ch., 3 ch., turn.
2nd row: * (1 tr., 2 ch., 1 tr.) in 1 ch.sp., 1 tr. between (2 d.tr., 1 ch., 2 d.tr.) gr.; rep. from * to end, 1 tr. in turning ch., 4 ch., turn.
Next row: as first row. Change to No. 4.50 (5.00) hook.
Work 2nd row and first row once. Change to No. 5.00 (5.50) hook. Work 2nd row and first row once. Mark the sps. between the 3rd and 4th, 7th and 8th, 13th and 14th, 17th and 18th grs.
Next row (inc. row): ** work as 2nd row but when you come to the marked places work (1 tr., 2 ch., 1 tr.) instead of 1 tr.
Next row: as first row. **Next row:** as 2nd row.
Next row: as first row. **
Mark in between 3rd and 4th, 8th and 9th, 16th and 17th, 21st and 22nd grs.
Work from ** to ** once: 16 rows.
Mark between 4th and 5th, 10th and 11th, 18th and 19th, 24th and 25th grs.
Work from ** to ** once.
Mark 4th and 5th, 11th and 12th, 21st and 22nd, 28th and 29th grs. Work from ** to ** once.
Mark 5th and 6th, 13th and 14th, 23rd and 24th, 31st and 32nd grs. Work from ** to ** once.
Mark 5th and 6th, 14th and 15th, 26th and 27th, 35th and 36th grs.
Work from ** to ** once.
Mark 6th and 7th, 16th and 17th, 28th and 29th, 38th and 39th grs. Work from ** to ** once: 44 grs.
Change to No. 5.50 (6.00) hook.
Mark 6th and 7th, 17th and 18th, 31st and 32nd, 42nd and 43rd grs. Work from ** to ** once. Mark 7th and 8th, 19th and 20th, 33rd and 34th, 45th and 46th grs. Work from ** to ** once: 52 grs.
Last row: work 1 d.c. in each d.tr. and 1 d.c. in each 1 ch.sp. Fasten off.
Sew up back seam to within 7 in. of waist (for placket). With No. 3.50 hook work 6 rows of d.c. neatly around waist for waistband. Work 3 rows of d.c. along one side of placket. Work 1 row of d.c. along other side of placket. Sew in zip.

TOP BACK
** With No. 3.50 (4.00, 4.00) hook make 122 (122, 134) ch.
Foundation row: 1 tr. in 5th ch. from hook, * miss 2 sts., (1 tr., 2 ch., 1 tr.) in next ch.; rep. from * to last 3 ch., miss 2 ch., 1 tr. in last ch., 4 ch., turn.
1st row: 1 tr. in same first st., * 1 tr. in next 2 ch.sp., (1 tr., 2 ch., 1 tr.) in next tr.; rep. from * to end, 1 tr. in last 2 ch.sp., 3 ch.; turn.
2nd row: 3 tr. in next 2 ch.sp. but leave last loop of each tr. on hook, yarn round and draw loop through all 4 loops on hook (1 cluster worked), 3 ch., work another cluster in same 2 ch.sp., work (1 cluster, 3 ch., 1 cluster) in each 2 ch.sp. to end, 1 tr. in turning ch., 2 ch.; turn.
3rd row: * 5 d.c. in each 3 ch.sp.; rep. from * to end, 1 d.c. in turning ch., 4 ch.; turn.
4th row: * miss next 2 d.c., 1 tr. in next d.c., miss next d.c., (1 tr., 2 ch., 1 tr.) in next d.c.; rep. from * to last 5 sts., miss 2 d.c., 1 tr. in next d.c., miss 2 d.c., 1 tr. in turning ch., 3 ch.; turn.
5th row: * (1 tr., 2 ch., 1 tr.) in next tr., 1 tr. in 2 ch.sp.; rep. from * to end, ending with 1 tr. in turning ch., 3 ch.; turn.
Work 2nd, 3rd, 4th and 5th rows 3 times: 18 rows.
Work 2nd and 3rd rows once only.
Work from *** to *** as given for Sleeve (see below) twice: 36 rows. Fasten off.

To Shape Armholes
Rejoin yarn in the 11 d.c., 3 ch., * miss next 2 d.c., 1 tr. in next d.c., miss next d.c., (1 tr., 2 ch., 1 tr.) in next d.c.; rep. from * to last 13 d.c., miss next d.c., 1 tr. in next d.c., 3 ch.; turn.

Next row: * 1 tr. in 2 ch.sp., (1 tr., 2 ch., 1 tr.) in next tr.; rep. from * to end, ending 1 tr. in last 2 ch.sp., 1 tr. in turning ch., 3 ch.; turn. **
Work 2nd, 3rd, 4th and 5th rows 4 times.

To Shape Shoulder
Next row: (1 cluster, 3 ch., 1 cluster) in next 2 ch.sp.; rep. from * 3 times, 1 tr. in next 2 ch.sp., 2 ch.; turn.
Next row: as 3rd row.
Next row: as 4th row.
Next row: as 5th row.
Fasten off.
Miss next eight 2 ch.sps., rejoin yarn in next 2 ch.sp., 3 ch., (1 cluster, 3 ch., 1 cluster) in each 2 ch.sp. to end. Work to match first shoulder.

FRONT
Work as for Back from ** to **
Work 2nd, 3rd, 4th and 5th rows twice.

To Shape Shoulder
Next row: (1 cluster, 3 ch., 1 cluster) in next 2 ch. sp.; rep. from * 5 times, 1 tr. in next 2 ch.sp., 2 ch.; turn.
**** **Next row:** as 3rd row.
Next row: as 4th row.
Next row: 1 tr. in next 2 ch.sp.; work as 5th row to end. ****
Next row: * (1 cluster, 3 ch., 1 cluster) in next 2 ch.sp.; rep. from * 4 times, 1 tr. in next tr., 2 ch., turn.
Work from **** to **** once.
Next row: * (1 cluster, 3 ch., 1 cluster) in next 2 ch.sp.; rep. from * 3 times.
Work 3rd, 4th and 5th rows once. Fasten off.
Miss next four 2 ch.sp., rejoin yarn in next 2 ch.sp., 3 ch., (1 cluster, 3 ch., 1 cluster) into each 2 ch.sp. to end.
Work to match other shoulder.
Sew shoulder and side seams.
Join yarn at one shoulder seam and work (1 cluster, 3 ch., 1 cluster) evenly right round neck, sl.st. to first tr., 1 ch., turn.
Next round: 5 d.c. into each 3 ch.sp., sl.st. to first d.c.
Fasten off.
Work these 2 rows also round lower edge of garment.

TOP SLEEVES (make 2 alike)
With No. 3.50 (4.00, 4.00) hook, make 53 (53, 65) ch.
Foundation row: 1 tr. in 5th ch. from hook, * miss 2 sts., 1 tr. in next ch., miss 2 sts., (1 tr., 2 ch., 1 tr.) in next ch.; rep. from * to end, 3 ch.; turn.
1st row: * 1 tr. in 2 ch.sp., (1 tr., 2 ch., 1 tr.) in next tr.; rep. from * to end, 3 ch.; turn.
2nd row: (1 cluster, 3 ch., 1 cluster) into each 2 ch.sp. to end, 1 tr. in turning ch., 2 ch.; turn.
3rd row: 1 d.c. in first st., * 5 d.c. in each 3 ch.sp.; rep. from * to end, 2 d.c. in turning ch., 4 ch.; turn.
4th row: (1 tr., 2 ch., 1 tr.) in next d.c., * miss 2 d.c., 1 tr. in next d.c., miss next d.c., (1 tr., 2 ch., 1 tr.) in next d.c.; rep. from *, 1 tr. in turning ch., 4 ch.; turn.
5th row: 1 tr. in same place as 4 ch., * 1 tr. in 2 ch.sp., (1 tr., 2 ch., 1 tr.) in next tr.; rep. from * to end, 3 ch.; turn.
6th row: 1 cluster into first 2 ch.sp., (1 cluster, 3 ch., 1 cluster) into each 2 ch.sp. until last 2 ch.sp., work only 1 cluster into this last sp., 1 tr. into turning ch., 2 ch.; turn.
7th row: 1 d.c. in next d.c., 5 d.c. in each 3 ch.sp. to end, 1 d.c. in next d.c., 1 d.c. in turning ch., 3 ch.; turn.
*** **Next row:** as 4th row.
Next row: as 5th row.
Next row: (1 cluster, 3 ch., 1 cluster) into each 3 ch.sp. to end, 1 tr. in turning ch., 2 ch.; turn.
Next row: as 3rd row.
Next row: as 4th row.
Next row: as 5th row.
Next row: as 6th row.
Next row: as 7th row. ***
Work from *** to *** 4 times: 48 rows.

To Shape Armhole
Rejoin yarn in 8th d.c., 3 ch., * miss next 2 d.c., 1 tr. in next d.c., miss next d.c., (1 tr., 2 ch., 1 tr.) in next d.c.; rep. from * to last 9 d.c., miss next d.c., 1 tr in last d.c., 3 ch.; turn.
Next row: * 1 tr. in 2 ch.sp., (1 tr., 2 ch., 1 tr.) in next tr.; rep. from * to end, ending 1 tr. in last 2 ch.sp., 1 tr. in turning ch., 3 ch.; turn.
Next row: as 2nd row.
Next row: as 3rd row.
Next row: miss 3 d.c., * 1 tr. in next d.c., miss 1 d.c., (1 tr., 2 ch., 1 tr.) in next d.c., miss 2 d.c.; rep. from * ending 1 tr. in turning ch., 3 ch.; turn.
Next row: * 1 tr. in 2 ch.sp., (1 tr., 2 ch., 1 tr.) in next tr.; rep. from * to last 2 ch.sp., 1 tr. in this 2 ch.sp., 1 tr. in turning ch., 3 ch.; turn.
Work last 4 rows twice.
Next row: 1 cluster in first 2 ch.sp., * (1 cluster, 3 ch., 1 cluster) in next 2 ch.sp.; rep. from * to last 2 ch.sp., 1 cluster in this 2 ch.sp., 1 tr. in turning ch., 1 ch.; turn.
Next row: 5 d.c. in each 3 ch.sp. to end, 3 ch.; turn.
Next row: * miss 2 d.c., 1 tr. in next d.c., miss 1 d.c., (1 tr., 2 ch., 1 tr.) in next d.c.; rep. from * to end, 1 tr. in turning ch.; fasten off.
Sew sleeve seams, sew sleeves into position. Work 1 row of d.c. neatly around each sleeve edge.

Long pink dress
illustrated in colour on page 117

MATERIALS
31 (32, 33, 34) balls (23.25 gr. each) Wendy Courtelle Crêpe 4-ply. Crochet hooks International Standard Sizes 3.00, 3.50, and 2.50. Eighteen small buttons.

MEASUREMENTS
To fit bust size 34 (36, 38, 40) in.; sleeve seam 17½ in.; length from shoulder 56 in.

TENSION
4 patts. measure 4½ in.

ABBREVIATIONS
See page 19.
Note. This patt. is worked from the neckline downwards so can be adjusted to any length. Allow one ball of given yarn more or less for every 2 in. of adjustment required.

BACK

With No. 3.00 hook, make 80 (88, 96, 104) ch. plus 2 ch. to turn. Work 8 d.c., miss 3 ch., 3 h.tr., 2 ch., 3 h.tr. in next ch., miss 3 ch., 1 h.tr. in next ch.; * miss 3 ch., 3 tr., 2 ch., 3 tr. (1 group) in next ch., miss 3 ch., 1 tr. in next ch.; rep. from * 4 (5, 6, 7) times, miss 3 ch., 1 gr. in next ch., miss 3 ch., 1 h.tr. in next ch., miss 3 ch., 3 h.tr., 2 ch., 3 h.tr. in next ch., miss 3 ch., 9 d.c.

Next row: 3 ch., turn, miss 3 ch., 1 gr. in next st., miss 3 ch., 1 tr. in next st., * 1 gr. in next 2 ch.sp., 1 tr. in single tr.; rep. from * 7 (8, 9, 10) times, 1 gr. in next 2 ch.sp., 1 tr. in first d.c., miss 3 ch., 1 gr. in next st., miss 3 ch., 1 tr. in last st.

Pattern row: 3 ch., turn, * 1 gr. in next 2 ch.sp., 1 tr. in single tr.; rep. from * across row ending 1 tr. in last st.: 10 (11, 12, 13) patts.

Rep. this row 10 times.

Shape Armholes

1st row: 4 ch., turn, 3 tr. into st. at base of ch., patt. across row ending 3 tr. and 1 d.tr. into last st.

2nd row: 4 ch., turn, 1 gr. into first tr., patt. across row ending 1 gr. into last st., 1 d.tr. into same st.

Repeat these 2 rows once more: 14 (15, 16, 17) patts. Cont. in patt. till work measures 5½ in. from armhole.

1st waist row: 3 ch., turn, make grs. of 2 tr., 2 ch., 2 tr., 1 tr. into single tr. Rep. this row once.

2nd waist row: 3 ch., turn, make grs. of 2 tr., 1 ch., 2 tr., 1 tr. into single tr. Rep. this row 3 times.

3rd waist row: change to No. 2.50 hook and rep. 2nd waist row 4 times. Change to No. 3.00 hook and work 2nd waist row for 2 rows and first waist row for 2 rows. Then work main patt. for 4 rows.

1st inc. row: 4 ch., turn, * 1 gr. in next 2 ch.sp., 1 ch., 1 tr. into single tr., 1 ch.; rep. from * across row ending 1 ch., 1 tr. into last st.

Rep. this row 11 times.

2nd inc. row: 4 ch., turn, * 1 gr. into next 2 ch. sp., 1 ch., 2 tr. into single tr., 1 ch.; rep. from * across row.

Next row: 4 ch., turn, * 1 gr. into 2 ch.sp., 1 ch., 1 tr. into each tr., 1 ch.; rep. from * across row ending 1 ch., 1 tr. into last st. Rep. this row 10 times.

3rd inc. row: 4 ch., turn, * 1 gr. into next 2 ch.sp., 1 ch., 1 tr. into tr., 1 ch., 1 tr. into tr., 1 ch.; rep. from * across row ending 1 ch., 1 tr. into last st.

Rep. this row 11 times.

4th inc. row: 5 ch., turn, * 1 gr. in 2 ch.sp., 2 ch., 1 tr., 1 ch., 1 tr., 2 ch.; rep. from * across row ending 2 ch., 1 tr. into last st. Rep. this row 13 times.

5th inc. row: as before but work 2 ch. between the single tr. and 3 ch. in the centre of the groups.

6th inc. row: change to No. 3.50 hook and work the same row until work measures 56 in. (or desired length) from the shoulder. Fasten off.

LEFT FRONT

With No. 3.00 hook make 33 (33, 41, 41) ch.

1st row: into 5th ch. from hook, work 3 tr., miss 3 ch., * 1 tr. in next ch., miss 3 ch., 1 gr. in next ch., miss 3 ch.; rep. from * 0 (0, once, once), 1 tr. in next ch., miss 3 ch., 3 h.tr., 2 ch., 3 h.tr. in next ch., miss 3 ch., d.c. into each of next 9 ch.

2nd row: 3 ch., turn, miss 3 d.c., 1 gr. in next d.c., miss 3 ch., 1 tr. in next d.c., patt. across row ending 3 tr., 1 ch., 1 tr. in last sp.

Pattern row: 4 ch., turn, 3 tr. into first sp., patt. to end: 3½ (3½, 4½, 4½) patts.

** Shape Neck

Sizes 34 and 38 only. Working the extra sts. into the patt. inc. by 1 tr. at the end of next and every alt. row for 19 rows, and at the same time when 10 rows from ** have been worked, shape the armhole (see below).

Sizes 36 and 40 only. Working the extra sts. into the patt. inc. by 1 tr. at the end of next and every alt. row for 10 rows, then

every row for 9 rows, and at the same time when 10 rows from ** have been worked, shape the armhole.

Shape Armhole (all sizes)

1st row: 4 ch., turn, 3 tr. into st. at base of ch., patt. across row.

2nd row: patt. to end, into turning ch.sp. work 1 gr. then 1 d.tr. into 3rd of turning ch.

Rep. these 2 rows once.

Cont. straight at side edge and inc. as given at neck edge till there are 7 (7½, 8, 8½) patts.

When work measures 5½ in. from armhole, complete as given for Back.

RIGHT FRONT

With No. 3.00 hook make 30 (30, 38, 38) ch.

1st row: d.c. in 3rd ch. from hook, 1 d.c. in next 8 ch., miss 3 ch., 3 h.tr., 2 ch., 3 h.tr. in next ch., * miss 3 ch., 1 tr. in next ch., miss 3 ch., 1 gr. in next ch.; rep. from * 0 (0, once, once) miss 3 ch., 1 tr. in next ch., miss 3 ch., 3 tr., 1 ch., 1 tr. in last st.

2nd row: 4 ch., turn, 3 tr. in sp. under hook, patt. to 9 d.c., 1 gr. in first d.c., miss 3 ch., 1 gr. in next d.c., miss 3 ch., 1 tr. in last st.: 3½ (3½, 4½, 4½) patts.

Work 1 row.

** Shape Neck

At beg. of next row, work incs. as given for Left Front, and when 10 rows from ** have been worked, shape armhole as follows.

Shape Armhole

1st row: patt. to end of row, work 3 tr. and 1 d.tr. into top of turning ch.

2nd row: 4 ch., turn, work 1 gr. into top of d.tr., patt. to end. Rep. these 2 rows once.

Complete to match Left Front.

SLEEVES (make 2 alike)

With No. 3.00 hook make 27 ch.

Work 1 gr. into 7th ch. from hook, miss 3 ch., 1 tr. in next ch., * miss 3 ch., 1 gr. in next ch., miss 3 ch., 1 tr. into next ch.; rep. from *: 3 patts.

Work first and 2nd rows of back armhole shaping (making turning ch. and d.tr. quite loose) until 11 patts. have been completed.

Work 2 rows straight.

Now dec. by working 1 tr. less at both ends of every row for 9 rows: 7 patts. and 1 half gr. at each end.

Cont. straight till sleeve measures 7 in. from armhole. Change to patt. as for first waist row for 2 rows, with No. 2.50 hook work 2nd waist row for 2 rows.

With No. 3.00 hook work first waist row for 2 rows.

Work main patt. for 4 rows then work 2 rows each of the 6 inc. rows as given for the Back cont. the last row until sleeve measures 17½ in. from armhole.

TO COMPLETE

Sew shoulder seams.

Front and Neck Bands

With No. 3.00 hook and starting at lower edge of Right Front, join yarn to front and work 1 row of tr. along right front, around neck and along left front working 2 tr. to every row. Work another row of tr.

Starting at top of straight edge of right front, mark places for 9 pairs of buttonholes with 4 tr. between 2 holes then 10 tr. to next hole. Work 1 row d.c. working 1 ch. and missing 1 st. where marked. Work 2 more rows of tr. Fasten off.

To Make Up

Set in sleeves. Stitch side and sleeve seams matching patterns. Press lightly with a cool, dry iron.

Sew on buttons to correspond with buttonholes.

Bolero and skirt
illustrated in colour on page 117

MATERIALS
8 (9) 50-gr. balls Pingouin Classique Crylor in light blue, and 1 ball each in red, yellow, green and black. One crochet hook International Standard Size 4.00 (4.50). A waist length of elastic, ¾ in. wide.

MEASUREMENTS
To fit bust size 32/34 (36/38) in., and hip size 34/36 (38/40) in.; length of skirt 37½ (38) in.; length of bolero 16 (17) in.

TENSION
4 tr.gr. to approx. 2¾ in. with No. 4.00 hook, and 4 tr.gr. to approx. 3 in. with No. 4.50 hook.

ABBREVIATIONS
See page 19; B., blue; R., red; Y., yellow; G., green; Bl., black.

Note. For the first size use No. 4.00 hook throughout; for the second size use No. 4.50 hook throughout.

BOLERO
With B., make 109 ch. loosely.
Foundation row: 2 tr. into 4th ch. from hook, * 1 ch., miss 2 ch., 3 tr. into next ch.; rep. from * to end: 36 tr.gr.
1st patt. row: 4 ch., * 3 tr. into next sp., 1 ch.; rep. from * until 1 tr.gr. remains, 1 tr. into turning ch.
2nd patt. row: 3 ch., 2 tr. into first sp., * 1 ch., 3 tr. into next sp.; rep. from * working last 3 tr. into end sp.
These 2 rows form patt. Rep. them 5 times, then rep. first row again.

Divide for Armholes
Next row: 3 ch., 2 tr. into first sp., * 1 ch., 3 tr. into next sp., rep. from * 3 times more, turn and continue straight on these 5 tr.gr. until armhole measures approx. 7½ in.
Fasten off.
Leave the next 6 tr.gr. free for first armhole and rejoin yarn into next sp. (between 6th and 7th tr.gr.), 3 ch., 2 tr. into same sp., * 1 ch., 3 tr. into next sp.; rep. from * 14 times, turn and work on these 16 tr.gr. Cont. straight until armhole measures approx. 7½ in. Fasten off.
Leave the next 6 tr.gr. free for second armhole and rejoin yarn into next sp., 3 ch., 2 tr. into same sp., patt. to end. Cont. straight on these 5 tr.gr. until armhole measures 7½ in.
Fasten off.

Small Motifs
With G., make 5 ch., and join into ring with sl.st.
1st round: 3 ch., 2 tr. into ring, (1 ch., 3 tr. into ring) 3 times, 1 ch., sl.st. to top of 3rd ch. Fasten off.

2nd round: join R. into a 1 ch.sp., (3 ch., 2 tr., 2 ch., 3 tr.) all into same sp., * 1 ch., (3 tr., 2 ch., 3 tr.) all into next sp.; rep. from * twice more, 1 ch., sl.st. to top of 3rd ch. Fasten off.
3rd round: join Y. to a corner sp., 3 ch., in same sp. work 2 tr., 2 ch. and 3 tr., 1 ch., 3 tr. in next sp., * 1 ch., into next sp. work 3 tr., 2 ch. and 3 tr., 1 ch., 3 tr. in next sp.; rep. from * twice more, 1 ch., sl.st. to top of 3rd ch. Fasten off.
4th round: with Bl., work 1 row of d.c. all round motif, working 1 d.c. into every tr. and into every 1 ch.sp. and 2 d.c. into corner spaces. Fasten off.
Work another 8 motifs as above. Now work 8 motifs as follows: use Y. for making 5 ch. and first round, B. for 2nd round, R. for 3rd round, and Bl. for 4th round.

HALF MOTIF (make 2 alike)
With Y., make 5 ch. and join into a ring with sl.st.
1st row: with Y., 4 ch., 3 tr. into ring, 1 ch., 3 tr. into ring, 1 ch., 1 tr. into ring. Fasten off.
2nd row: join B. into top of 4th ch. at beg of last row, 4 ch., 3 tr. into same sp., 1 ch., (3 tr., 2 ch., 3 tr.) into next sp., 1 ch., 3 tr. into last sp., 1 ch., 1 tr. into same sp. Fasten off.
3rd row: join R. into top of 4th ch. at beg. of last row, 4 ch., 3 tr. into same sp., 1 ch., 3 tr. into next sp., 1 ch., (3 tr., 2 ch., 3 tr.) into next sp., (1 ch., 3 tr. into next sp.) twice, 1 ch., 1 tr. into same sp. Fasten off.
4th round: join Bl. into top of 3rd ch. and work a round of d.c. all round motif.
Fasten off.

SKIRT
Large Motif
With Y., make 5 ch., and join into ring with sl.st.
1st round: with Y., 3 ch. for first tr., 2 tr. into ring, (1 ch., 3 tr. into ring) 3 times, 1 ch., sl.st. to top of 3rd ch.
2nd round: with Y., sl.st. into next sp., (3 ch., 2 tr., 2 ch., 3 tr.) all into same sp., * 1 ch., (3 tr., 2 ch., 3 tr.) all into next sp.; rep. from * twice more, 1 ch., sl.st. to top of 3rd ch. Fasten off.
3rd round: join B. to a corner sp., 3 ch., in same sp. work (2 tr., 2 ch., 3 tr.), 1 ch., 3 tr. in next sp., * 1 ch., (3 tr., 2 ch., 3 tr.) all into next sp., 1 ch., 3 tr. in next sp.; rep. from * twice more, 1 ch., sl.st. to top of 3rd ch.
4th round: with B., sl.st. into next sp., 3 ch., in same sp. work (2 tr., 2 ch., 3 tr.), * 1 ch., (3 tr. in 1 ch.sp., 1 ch.) twice, (3 tr., 2 ch., 3 tr.) all into next sp.; rep. from * twice more, 1 ch., (3 tr. in 1 ch.sp., 1 ch.) twice, sl.st. to top of 3rd ch. Fasten off.
5th round: join R. to a corner sp. and work as for 4th round, but work the (3 tr. into 1 ch.sp., 1 ch.) 3 times instead of twice.
6th round: join Y. to a corner sp. and work as for 4th round, but work the (3tr. into 1 ch.sp., 1 ch.) 4 times.
7th round: join Bl. to a corner sp. and work as for 4th round, but work the (3 tr. into 1 ch.sp., 1 ch.) 5 times. Fasten off.
Work another 3 motifs as above. Now work 4 motifs thus: use G. for making 5 ch. and first 2 rounds, R. for 3rd and 4th rounds, Y. for 5th round, B. for 6th round, and Bl. for 7th round.

Fill-in Triangles (make 16 alike)
With B., make 5 ch., and join into a ring with sl.st.
1st row: 4 ch., 3 tr. into ring, 1 ch., 1 tr. into ring, turn.
2nd row: 4 ch., 3 tr. into first sp., 1 ch., 3 tr. into end sp., 1 ch., 1 tr. into same sp., turn.
3rd row: 4 ch., 3 tr. into first sp., 1 ch., 3 tr. into next sp., 1 ch., 3 tr. into end sp., 1 ch., 1 tr. into same sp., turn.
4th row: 4 ch., 3 tr. into first sp., (1 ch., 3 tr. into next sp.) twice, 1 ch., 3 tr. into end sp., 1 ch., 1 tr. into same sp., turn.
5th row: as 4th row, but rep. between brackets 3 times.
6th row: as 4th row, but rep. between brackets 4 times.
7th row: as 4th row, but rep. between brackets 5 times.
8th row: as 4th row, but rep. between brackets 6 times.
9th row: 3 ch., 2 tr. into first sp., (1 ch., 3 tr. into next sp.) 7 times, 3 tr. into end sp. Fasten off.
Join large motifs at corners as shown in diagram, alternating colours, to form a ring. Then sew in fill-in triangles at each side.

Next round: join B. into a 2-ch. sp. at top of one motif, 4 ch., * (3 tr. into next 1 ch.sp. of fill-in triangle, 1 ch.) 8 times, 3 tr. into 2 ch.sp. of next motif, 1 ch.; rep. from * twice, (3 tr. into next 1 ch.sp. of fill-in triangle, 1 ch.) 8 times, 1 tr. into 2 ch.sp. of next motif and mark this tr. with a thread (for side decreasings), work along second side of skirt in a similar way, ending with 1 ch., sl.st. into top of 3rd of 4 ch. and again mark this last st. with a thread as before. Now dec. thus:

1st round: sl.st. into first sp., 3 ch., 1 tr. into same sp., (1 ch., 3 tr. into next sp.) to within 1 sp. before first marked tr., 2 tr. into sp. before single tr., 2 tr. into sp. after single tr., (1 ch., 3 tr. into next sp.) to within 1 sp. before second marked tr., 2 tr. into sp. before single tr., sl.st. into top of 3rd ch.

2nd round: sl.st. into first sp., 3 ch., 2 tr. into same sp., (1 ch., 3 tr. into next sp.) to end, (working over the 4 tr. at side edge as over a tr.gr.), 1 ch., sl.st. into top of 3rd ch.

3rd round: turn and work a sl.st. into last sp. just worked, 4 ch., turn work again, (3 tr. into next sp., 1 ch.) to sp. above first marked tr., 1 tr. into sp. above marked tr., 1 ch., (3 tr. into next sp., 1 ch.) to end, sl.st. to top of 3rd of 4 ch.

Rep. last 3 rounds 16 times, then rep. first round again. For first size only, work 1 round straight.

Next row: work 1 d.c. into each tr. of previous round and 1 d.c. into each sp. Turn and work another 5 rows of d.c. Fasten off. Join ends of border.

Lower Border

With B., work 2 (1) rounds of patt., (3 tr. into each sp. and work 1 ch. between each tr.gr. as before) along lower edge of skirt. Fasten off. Join any two of the contrasting colours and work another 2 rounds of patt. Fasten off.

TO COMPLETE

Press very lightly with a cool iron.

Bolero. Join motifs as shown in diagram, alternating colours. Join shoulder seams, then sew border to main part ending about ½ (¾) in. below shoulder seams. With Bl., work a row of d.c. along lower, front and neck edges.

With B., work 2 rows of d.c. round armhole edges. Press seams and edgings very lightly.

Skirt. Join elastic into ring and sew inside waist with herring-bone casing stitch.

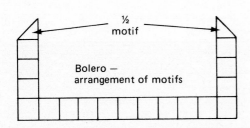

Bolero — arrangement of motifs

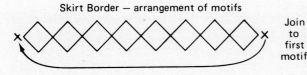

Skirt Border — arrangement of motifs

Join to first motif

Trimming for hostess skirt
also illustrated overleaf

MATERIALS

4 balls (20 gr. each) Coats Chain Mercer-Crochet No. 20. One steel crochet hook International Standard Size 1.25. Suitable plain-coloured evening skirt.

MEASUREMENTS

Depth of trimming including tassel 8½ in.

TENSION

1 motif 5 in. wide.

ABBREVIATIONS

See page 19; p., picot.

FIRST MOTIF

Commence with 30 ch., join with sl.st. to form a ring.

1st row: 13 ch., * 15 d.tr. into ring, 9 ch.; rep. from * once more, 14 d.tr. into ring, sl.st. into 4th of 13 ch.

2nd row: sl.st. into first ch., sl.st. into same loop, 6 ch., leaving last loop of each on hook work 4 qd.tr. into same loop, y.o.h. and draw through all loops on hook (a 4-qd.tr.cl. made), * 7 ch., into same loop work a 5-d.tr.cl., 7 ch. and a 5-qd.tr.cl., 10 ch., miss 7 d.tr. 1 d.c. into next d.tr., 10 ch., a 5-qd.tr.cl. into next loop; rep. from * omitting a 5-qd.tr.cl. at end of last rep., sl.st. into first cl.

3rd row: * 8 d.c. into next loop, 1 d.c. into next cl., 8 d.c. into next loop, 3 ch., 11 d.c. into next loop, 1 d.c. into next d.c., 11 d.c. into next loop, 3 ch.; rep. from * omitting 3 ch. at end of last rep., 1 ch., 1 h.tr. into first d.c.

4th row: 3 ch., 2 tr. into loop just made, 1 tr. into same place as last h.tr., * 1 tr. into each of next 16 d.c., 5 tr. into next loop, 1 tr. into each of next 9 d.c., miss 5 d.c., 1 tr. into each of next 9 d.c., 5 tr. into next loop, 1 tr. into next d.c.; rep. from * omitting 6 tr. at end of last rep., 2 tr. into same loop as first tr., sl.st. into 3rd of 3 ch.

5th row: 1 d.c. into same place as sl.st., * (12 ch., miss 10 tr., 1 d.c. into next tr.) twice, 14 ch., miss 11 tr., 1 d.c. into next sp., 14 ch., miss 11 tr., 1 d.c. into next tr.; rep. from * omitting 1 d.c. at end of last rep., sl.st. into first d.c.

6th row: 1 d.c. into same place as sl.st., 5 d.c. into next loop, 9 ch., 6 d.c. over last 9 ch. made, 3 ch., sl.st. into last d.c. (a p. made), 5 d.c. over same 9 ch. (a p. loop made), * sl.st. into last d.c. made before p. loop, (11 d.c. into same loop, 1 d.c. into next d.c., 5 d.c. into next loop, 9 ch., remove loop from hook, insert hook into 5th last d.c. made on previous loop and draw dropped loop through, into 9-ch. loop work 6 d.c. a p. and 5 d.c. (another p. loop made), (sl.st. into last d.c. made before p. loop) twice **, 11 d.c. into same loop, into next d.c. work 2 tr., a p. and 1 tr., 5 d.c. into next loop, a p. loop, sl.st. into last d.c. (another p. loop made), (sl.st. into last d.c. made before p. next d.c., 5 d.c. into next loop, a p. loop; rep. from * twice more ending last rep. at **, 13 d.c. into same loop, 1 d.c. into next d.c., 13 d.c. into next loop, place right side of first p. loop made to front of Motif, sl.st. into free end of first p. loop, inserting hook from the back of p. loop work 5 d.c. into same 14-ch. loop, sl.st. into first d.c.
Fasten off.

SECOND MOTIF

Work as First Motif to within p. on third p. loop, 1 ch., sl.st. into corresponding p. on First Motif, 1 ch., sl.st. into last d.c. made on Second Motif, complete as First Motif.

OTHER MOTIFS

Make 10 more motifs, or number required, joining each as Second Motif was joined to First, leaving 5 p. free on top edge between joinings, and joining last Motif to First Motif as well.

TASSELS (make 1 for each motif)

Wind thread 50 times round a piece of cardboard 5 in. in depth. Draw loops tog. and tie securely at top. Remove card and tie thread tightly round Tassel approximately ½ in. from top. Cut and trim bottom ends.

Top

Commence with 6 ch., join with sl.st. to form a ring.
1st row: 3 ch., 11 tr. into ring, inserting hook from right to left work 1 sl.st. over first 3 ch.
2nd row: 2 ch., * 1 tr. round stem of next tr.; rep. from * ending with 1 sl.st. round first 2 ch.
Rep. last row 5 times more. Cut thread leaving an end. Pull tassel through top and secure firmly at tied thread.

TO COMPLETE

Damp motifs and pin out to measurements. Place trimming in position approx. 7 in. from lower edge of skirt and sew on neatly. Attach one tassel at centre of lower edge of each motif.

Chapter eight
LITTLE THINGS
MEAN A LOT
fashion accessories and gift ideas

Striped scarf and hat in an openwork pattern (instructions start overleaf).

Striped scarf and hat

illustrated opposite and also on previous page

MATERIALS

For scarf: 7 balls (20 gr. each) Robin Super Crimp Bri-Nylon D.K. in main shade, and 5 balls in each of two contrasting shades plus 3 extra balls in main shade if fringe is required. **For hat:** 1 ball of same yarn in main shade, and 1 ball in each of two contrasting shades. **For both:** one crochet hook International Standard Size 4.00.

MEASUREMENTS

Scarf: width 18 in.; length (excluding fringe) 118 in.
Hat: to fit an average size head.

TENSION

2 patts. to $1\frac{1}{4}$ in. approx.

ABBREVIATIONS

See page 19; M., main shade; C., contrast shade.

SCARF

With No. 4.00 hook and M., commence with 122 ch.
Foundation row: 1 d.c. into 2nd ch. from hook, * 5 ch., miss 3 ch., 1 d.c. into next ch.; rep. from * to end, 3 ch., turn. Continue in patt.
1st row: 1 d.c. into centre ch. of first 5 ch. loop, * 5 ch., 1 d.c. into centre ch. of next 5 ch. loop; rep. from * ending 2 ch., 1 tr. into last d.c., 1 ch.; turn.
2nd row: 1 d.c. into tr., * 5 ch., 1 d.c. into centre ch. of next 5 ch. loop; rep. from * ending 5 ch., 1 d.c. into 3rd of 3 turning ch., 3 ch.; turn.
These 2 rows form the patt.
Work 4 more rows.
7th row: as first row; break M. and join 1st C. by drawing a ch. through loop on hook; turn.
Continue in stripes.
Work 6 rows in 1st C., 6 rows in 2nd C., and 8 rows in M., joining new colours as in 7th row. Rep. these 20 rows until Scarf measures 118 in. or required length, ending with an M. stripe, and working last row as follows:
Last row: 1 d.c. into centre ch. of first 5 ch. loop, * 3 ch., 1 d.c. into centre ch. of next 5 ch. loop; rep. from * ending 2 ch., 1 tr. into last d.c. Fasten off.
Sew in ends.

Fringe

Using 8 strands of M. yarn 14 in. long for each tassel work a fringe along narrow edges of scarf, working a tassel into each ch. loop as follows: insert hook into loop, double yarn strands and pull doubled end through loop then pull yarn ends through doubled end. Trim.

HAT

With No. 4.00 hook and 2nd C., commence with 6 ch. and join with sl.st. to form a ring.
1st round: * 5 ch., 1 d.c. into ring; rep. from * 4 times.
2nd round: sl.st. over first 2 ch. of 5 ch. loop, work 1 d.c., 5 ch. and 1 d.c. into next ch., * 5 ch., work 1 d.c., 5 ch. and 1 d.c. into centre ch. of next 5 ch. loop; rep. from * ending 5 ch., 1 d.c. into first d.c.
3rd round: sl.st. over first 2 ch. of 5 ch. loop, 1 d.c. into next ch., * 5 ch., 1 d.c. into centre ch. of next 5 ch. loop; rep. from * ending 5 ch., 1 d.c. into first d.c.
4th round: sl.st. over first 2 ch. of 5 ch. loop, work 1 d.c., 5 ch. and 1 d.c. into next ch., * 5 ch., 1 d.c. into centre ch. of next 5 ch. loop, 5 ch., work 1 d.c., 5 ch. and 1 d.c. into centre ch. of foll. 5 ch. loop; rep. from * ending 5 ch., 1 d.c. into centre ch. of last 5 ch. loop, 5 ch., 1 d.c. into first d.c.
5th and 6th rounds: as 3rd round.
Break 2nd C.
7th round: join 1st C. to centre ch. of next 5 ch. loop with a d.c., * 5 ch., 1 d.c. into centre ch. of next 5 ch. loop, 5 ch.,
1 d.c. into centre ch. of foll. 5 ch. loop, 5 ch., work 1 d.c., 5 ch. and 1 d.c. into centre ch. of next 5 ch. loop; rep. from * ending 5 ch., work 1 d.c., 5 ch. and 1 d.c. into first d.c.
8th round: as 3rd round.
9th round: sl.st. over first 2 ch. of 5 ch. loop, 1 d.c. into next ch., * 5 ch., work 1 d.c. and 5 ch. into centre ch. of each of next three 5 ch. loops, work 1 d.c., 5 ch. and 1 d.c. into centre ch. of next 5 ch. loop; rep. from * ending work 1 d.c., 5 ch. and 1 d.c. into first d.c.
10th, 11th and 12th rounds: as 3rd round.
Break 1st C.
13th round: join M. to centre ch. of next 5 ch. loop with a d.c., * 5 ch., 1 d.c. into centre ch. of next 5 ch. loop; rep. from * ending 5 ch., 1 d.c. into first d.c.
14th–19th rounds: as 3rd round.
20th round: sl.st. over first 2 ch. of 5 ch. loop, 1 d.c. into next ch., * 3 ch., 1 d.c. into centre ch. of next 5 ch. loop; rep. from * ending 3 ch., 1 d.c. into first d.c.
Fasten off. Sew in ends.

Three-colour scarf

MATERIALS

4 balls (25 gr. each) Twilleys Cortina Super Crochet Wool in main shade, 3 balls in first contrasting shade, and 1 oz. in second contrasting shade. One crochet hook International Standard Size 4.50.

MEASUREMENTS

Scarf measures approx. 50 in. long, 7 in. wide.

Striped scarf and hat (see opposite).

TENSION
9 tr. and 5 rows to 2 in.

ABBREVIATIONS
See page 19; M., main shade; C., contrast shade.

TO MAKE
With M., make 42 (50, 53) ch.

1st row: 1 tr. in 4th ch. from hook, 1 tr. in each ch. to end: 40 (48, 56) tr.

2nd row: 3 ch. (to form first tr.), 1 tr. in 2nd tr., 1 tr. in each tr. to end.

This row forms the tr. patt. and is repeated throughout.

Work 20 more rows in M.

Now work in stripe patt. as follows:

Work 14 rows 1st C., 6 rows 2nd C., 22 rows M.

Rep. last 42 rows 3 times more.

Fasten off. Sew in ends. Press lightly.

Ring collar

MATERIALS
1 ball (20 gr.) Wendy Courtellon Double Knit. One crochet hook International Standard Size 4.00. Sixteen curtain rings, 1½ in. in diameter.

MEASUREMENTS
Length of inside edge approximately 19 in.

TENSION
A 5-tr. gr. measures 1 in.

ABBREVIATIONS
See page 19.

TO MAKE
Commence with 96 ch. made loosely and join with sl.st. to form a ring, taking care not to twist sts.

1st round: * miss 2 ch., 3 ch., 1 d.c. into next ch.; rep. from * to end.

2nd round: 3 ch. (to stand as first tr.), 2 tr. into next loop, 3 tr. into each loop to end, sl.st. to top of 3 ch.

3rd round: * 4 ch., miss 3 tr., 1 d.c. between last and next tr.; rep. from * to end.

4th round: 3 ch., 3 tr. into next loop, 4 tr. into each loop to end, sl.st. to top of 3 ch.

5th round: as 3rd round, but miss 4 tr. instead of 3 tr.

6th round: as 4th round, but work 3 ch. and 4 tr. into first loop then 5 tr. into each rem. loop.

Fasten off.

With yarn, work buttonhole st. round each curtain ring.

Sew rings round lower edge of collar 2 patts. apart (see photograph below, left).

Buckled choker

MATERIALS
1 oz. Twilleys Goldfingering. One crochet hook International Standard Size 2.50. One 1-in. buckle.

MEASUREMENTS
To fit average size neck.

ABBREVIATIONS
See page 19.

TO MAKE
Work Band as given for Sequin-trimmed Choker (below). Sew buckle to one end.

Sequin-trimmed choker

MATERIALS
1 oz. Twilleys Goldfingering. One crochet hook International Standard Size 2.50. Four 1-in. square sequins. One hook and eye.

MEASUREMENTS
To fit average size neck.

ABBREVIATIONS
See page 19.

TO MAKE
Band

Make 6 ch.

1st row: 1 d.c. into 2nd ch. from hook, 1 d.c. into each ch. to end, 1 ch.; turn.

Pendant-style choker

MATERIALS
1 oz. Twilleys Goldfingering. One crochet hook International Standard Size 2.50. Thirteen $\frac{1}{2}$-in. curtain rings and three 1-in. curtain rings. One hook and eye.

MEASUREMENTS
To fit average size neck.

ABBREVIATIONS
See page 19.

TO MAKE
Work Band as given for Sequin-trimmed Choker.

To Cover Rings
Crochet round each ring by working d.c. through the ring, then when ring is completely covered, slip stitch into first d.c. Fasten off.

2nd row: 1 d.c. into each d.c. to end, 1 ch.; turn. Repeat last row until work measures $11\frac{1}{2}$ in. (or length required). Fasten off.

TO COMPLETE
Sew sequins to lower edge of front of choker, as shown in photograph above. Sew hook and eye at back to fasten.

Beaded choker

MATERIALS
1 oz. Twilleys Goldfingering. One crochet hook International Standard Size 2.50. One packet of small beads. One hook and eye.

MEASUREMENTS
To fit average size neck.

ABBREVIATIONS
See page 19.

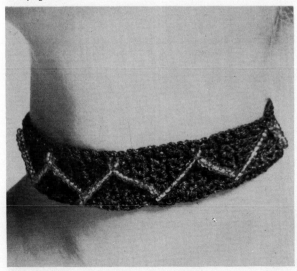

TO MAKE
Work Band as given for Sequin-trimmed Choker.
Sew a zig-zag of beads right round choker, as shown in photograph above, having 12 beads in each arm of the zig-zag. Sew hook and eye at back of choker to fasten.

TO COMPLETE
Sew rings together to form pendant motif, as shown in photo-graph above: i.e. three large rings will form centre of motif; the thirteen smaller motifs will form outer 'frame'. Sew top two rings of motif to centre of lower edge of band.
Sew hook and eye to back of choker to fasten.

Blue top with matching long skirt (see page 105).

Bolero and skirt (see page 108) and long button-up dress in pink (see page 106).

Ring belt

MATERIALS
Oddments of double knitting yarn in assorted colours. Twenty-one 1-in. curtain rings. One crochet hook International Standard Size 4.00. A waist length of petersham ribbon 1½ in. wide. Two hooks and eyes.

MEASUREMENTS
Finished belt is 24½ in. long (or any length required).

ABBREVIATIONS
See page 19.

TO MAKE
Crochet round each ring by working d.c. through the ring. When ring is completely covered, sl.st. to first d.c.
Fasten off.
Sew rings together to make a long strip. (Alternatively, do not break yarn after crocheting round each ring, but start immediately to crochet round next ring, thus joining them together as you work.)
Sew covered rings to petersham ribbon.
Hem ribbon at each end, then sew on hooks and eyes to fasten belt at the back.
If a longer belt is required, then add more rings.

Tie belt

MATERIALS
1 ball (20 gr.) Coats Chain Mercer-Crochet No. 20 in each of three contrasting shades. One steel crochet hook International Standard Size 1.75.

MEASUREMENTS
To fit any waist size.

TENSION
3 sps. to 1 in.

ABBREVIATIONS
See page 19; A., first shade; B., 2nd shade; C., 3rd shade.

TO MAKE
1st row: with B. and C. tog., commence with 8 ch., 1 tr. into 8th ch. from hook, 5 ch., 1 tr. into same place as last tr., * 5 ch.; turn; miss 2 ch. of previous 5 ch., 1 tr. into next ch.; rep. from * until the row measures 1½ in. less than waist measurement required, and having an uneven number of sps., 7 ch.; turn; miss 2 ch., sl.st. into next ch.
2nd row: 3 d.c. into each sp. to within end sp., 12 d.c. into end sp., working along opposite side of sps. 3 d.c. into each sp. to within end sp., 12 d.c. into end sp., sl.st. into first d.c.
3rd row: 1 d.c. into next d.c., * 3 ch., miss 2 d.c., 1 d.c. into

next d.c. *; rep. from * to * along side working last d.c. into 2nd of 12 d.c., (4 ch., miss 2 d.c., 1 d.c. into next d.c.) 3 times; rep. from first * ending with 3 ch., sl.st. into first d.c.

4th row: work 3 d.c. into each 3-ch.sp. and 6 d.c. into 4-ch.sp. at ends, sl.st. into first d.c. Fasten off.

5th row: with A. and B. tog. attach to first free d.c. after last sl.st., 1 d.c. into same place, * 3 ch., miss 2 d.c., 1 d.c. into next d.c.; rep. from * all round omitting 1 d.c. at end of last rep., sl.st. into first d.c.

6th row: work 3 d.c. into each sp. along side and 5 d.c. into 5 sps. at each end, sl.st. into first d.c. Fasten off.

Tie
With 2 strands A., commence with * 5 ch., leaving the last loop of each on hook work 2 tr. into 5th ch. from hook, y.o.h. and draw through all loops on hook; rep. from * until work measures length of Belt plus ends for tying. Fasten off.

TO COMPLETE
Thread tie through sps. on first row. Damp and press.

Reversible hipster belt
illustrated in colour overleaf

MATERIALS
3 oz. Hayfield Gaylon Double Knitting in cream (or any other main shade, as wished), 1 oz. in each of four contrasting colours. One crochet hook International Standard Size 4.50.

MEASUREMENTS
Finished belt, excluding centre front fastening, measures 33 in. long, 5 in. wide.

TENSION
One motif measures 4½ in. square.

ABBREVIATIONS
See page 19.

TO MAKE
With first contrast shade, make 8 ch., and join into a ring with sl.st.

1st round: 6 ch., (1 tr., 3 ch.) 7 times into ring, sl.st. to join.
2nd round: join in 2nd contrast shade and work 2 ch., 3 tr., 2 ch. into first sp., * 4 tr., 2 ch. into next sp.; rep. from * to end of round, sl.st. to join.
3rd round: with first contrast shade, 3 ch., 5 tr., 1 ch. into first sp., * 6 tr., 3 ch. into next sp., 6 tr., 1 ch. into next sp.; rep. from * to end of round, sl.st. to join.
4th round: with 2nd contrast shade, 2 ch., 1 tr., 3 ch., 2 tr. into 3 ch.sp. at corner, * 3 ch. 1 d.c. between 3rd and 4th tr. in next group, 3 ch., 1 d.c. into 1 ch.sp., 3 ch., 1 d.c. between 3rd and 4th tr. of next group, 3 ch., (2 tr., 3 ch., 2 tr.) into 3 ch.sp. at corner; rep. from * 3 times and from * excluding instructions in brackets once more, sl.st. to join. Fasten off.
Make 2 more motifs with first and 2nd contrast shades, then make 4 motifs with 3rd and 4th contrast shades.

Reverse Side of Belt
With cream (or main shade chosen) make 18 ch.
1st row: 1 d.c. in 2nd ch. from hook, 1 d.c. in each ch. to end of row.
2nd row: 2 ch., 1 d.c. in each d.c. to end of row. Continue working each row in d.c. until belt measures 32 in. Fasten off.

TO COMPLETE
Press the motifs, and press the long strip in main shade. Join the motifs into a long strip, alternating colours, and using cream (or main shade) yarn to join the motifs. Place motif strip to plain strip, wrong sides together, and with cream (or main shade) yarn work d.c. all round edges to join the strips together.
Next row: 4 ch., 1 sl.st. into same st., sl.st. over 3 sts., 4 ch., 1 sl.st. into same st. as last sl.st. Continue in this way all round the edges of belt. Fasten off.
Make 3 crochet chains with cream (or main shade) yarn, each 15 in. long. Thread these through 3 of the loops down each end of belt, and tie ends of each chain in a bow, to form centre front fastening.

Embroidered belt
illustrated in colour overleaf

MATERIALS
3 oz. Hayfield Gaylon Double Knitting in main shade, oddments in each of five different shades for the embroidery. One crochet hook International Standard Size 3.00. Piece of canvas, 4½ in. by 25½ in., for stiffening. Piece of lining fabric, 4½ in. by 25½ in.

MEASUREMENTS
Finished belt measures just over 4½ in. by 25½ in.

TENSION
5 sts. and 5 rows to 1 in.

ABBREVIATIONS
See page 19; M., main shade.

TO MAKE
With M., make 26 ch.
1st row: 1 h.tr. in 3rd ch. from hook, 1 h.tr. in each ch. to end of row.
2nd row: 2 ch., 1 h.tr. in each h.tr. to end of row.
Repeat 2nd row until work measures 26 in. Fasten off.

continued on page 122

1 square = 1 half treble

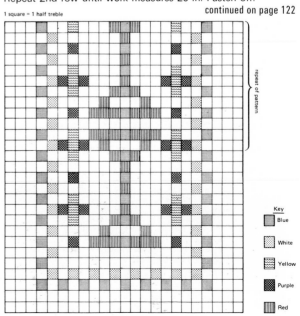

repeat of pattern

Key
Blue
White
Yellow
Purple
Red

centre front of belt

A pair of pretty belts – the brown-based belt has embroidery worked on it in cross stitch; the reversible hipster belt is made up of motifs on one side, a plain-coloured continuous strip on the other (see previous page).
Opposite: *golden party sweater (see page 104).*

To Work Embroidery

Using contrast shades as wished, embroider pattern on belt in cross stitch, following chart on page 119 for position of the blocks of cross stitch. One square on the chart represents 1 h.tr. on the crocheted fabric.

TO COMPLETE

Place canvas stiffening centrally against wrong side of belt, and then place lining on top of canvas, wrong side of lining facing the canvas. Baste in place, then turn over edges of crochet to wrong side of belt and stitch neatly all the way round.

With one of the contrast shades, work 2 rows of crochet at each end of belt to make lace-up holes, as follows:

1st row: 4 ch., * miss next st., 1 tr., 1 ch. in next st.; rep. from * to end of row.

2nd row: 2 ch., 1 d.c. in each sp. and each tr. to end of row. Fasten off.

Working with 2 other contrast shades together, make a crocheted chain 44 in. long, and lace this through alternate holes, to fasten belt at centre front.

Cloche hat

MATERIALS

3 balls (20 gr. each) Coats Chain Mercer-Crochet No. 10 in main shade and 3 balls in a contrasting shade. One steel crochet hook International Standard Size 2.00. Small quantity lining material for wheels (optional).

MEASUREMENTS

To fit an average size head.

TENSION

First 5 rows 2 in. in diameter.

ABBREVIATIONS

See page 19; M., main shade; C., contrasting shade.

Note. Use thread double throughout.

MAIN SECTION

1st row: with C., commence with 4 ch., 13 tr. into 4th ch. from hook, sl.st. into 4th of 4 ch.

2nd row: 1 d.c. into same place as sl.st., 1 d.c. into back loop of each tr., sl.st. into first d.c. Fasten off.

3rd row: attach M. to same place as sl.st., 1 d.c. into same place as join, * 3 ch., 1 d.c. into next d.c.; rep. from * ending with 1 tr. into first d.c.: 14 loops.

4th to 6th rows: 1 d.c. into loop just made, * 3 ch., 1 d.c. into next loop; rep. from * ending with 1 tr. into first d.c.

7th row: sl.st. into loop just made, 6 ch., 1 tr. into same loop (a V st. made), * 1 ch., into next loop work 1 tr., 3 ch. and 1 tr. (another V st. made); rep. from * ending with 1 ch., sl.st. into 3rd of 6 ch.

8th row: sl.st. into next ch., 1 d.c. into same loop, * 3 ch., 1 d.c. into next 1-ch.sp., 3 ch., 1 d.c. into next loop; rep. from * omitting 3 ch. and 1 d.c. at end of last rep., 1 tr. into first d.c.

9th to 12th rows: as 4th to 7th rows.

13th row: sl.st. into next ch., 1 d.c. into same loop, * 3 ch., 1 d.c. into next 1-ch.sp., (3 ch., 1 d.c. into next loop) twice; rep. from * omitting 3 ch. and 1 d.c. at end of last rep., 1 tr. into first d.c.

14th to 17th rows: as 4th to 7th rows.

18th row: sl.st. into next ch., 1 d.c. into same loop, * 3 ch., 1 d.c. into next 1-ch.sp., (3 ch., 1 d.c. into next loop) 7 times; rep. from * omitting 3 ch. and 1 d.c. at end of last rep., 1 tr. into first d.c.

19th to 22nd rows: as 4th to 7th rows.

23rd row: as 18th row working rep. in brackets 8 times instead of 7.

24th to 26th rows: as 4th to 6th rows.

27th row: sl.st. into loop just made, 6 ch., 1 tr. into same loop, a V st. into each loop, sl.st. into 3rd of 6 ch.

28th row: sl.st. into next ch., 1 d.c. into same loop, * 3 ch., 1 d.c. into next loop; rep. from * ending with 1 tr. into first d.c. Rep. from 24th row twice more.

39th row: as 27th row.
Fasten off.

ROPE BRAID

With C., commence with * 5 ch., leaving the last loop of each on hook work 3 d.tr. into 5th ch. from hook, y.o.h. and draw through all loops on hook (a cl. made); rep. from * 13 times more.

Cut thread leaving an end. Thread braid through first row of V sts. made. Using cut end, join last cl. to base of first cl. and fasten off.

Make 7 more lengths of Braid, one for each V-st. row, having a cl. for every V st. Thread through as before.

WHEEL MOTIFS (make 2 alike)

With C., commence with 7 ch., join with sl.st. to form a ring.

1st row: 3 ch., 15 tr. into ring, sl.st. into 3rd of 3 ch.

2nd row: 3 ch., a 2-d.tr.cl. into same place as sl.st., * 5 ch., miss 1 tr., a 3-d.tr.cl. into next tr.; rep. from * ending with 5 ch., sl.st. into first cl.

3rd row: 1 d.c. into same place as sl.st., * 5 d.c. into next loop, 1 d.c. into next cl.; rep. from * ending with 5 d.c. into next loop, sl.st. into first d.c.

4th row: 3 ch., 1 tr. into each of next 2 d.c., * 2 tr. into next d.c., 1 tr. into each of next 5 d.c.; rep. from * omitting 3 tr. at end of last rep., sl.st. into 3rd of 3 ch.

5th row: 3 ch., into same place as sl.st. work 1 d.tr., 3 ch. and 1 sl.st., * 1 d.c. into each of next 6 tr., into next tr. work 1 sl.st., 3 ch., 1 d.tr., 3 ch. and 1 sl.st.; rep. from * ending with 1 d.c. into each of next 6 tr., sl.st. into last sl.st. on previous row.
Fasten off.

TO COMPLETE

Line wheels if desired.
Place one wheel at each side of hat having centre of wheel to lower edge. Sew in position.

Reversible beret
illustrated in colour overleaf

MATERIALS

2 oz. Hayfield Gaylon Double Knitting in each of two contrasting shades. One crochet hook International Standard Size 5.00. Short length shirring elastic.

MEASUREMENTS

To fit an average size head.

TENSION

6½ tr. to 2 in.

ABBREVIATIONS

See page 19; A, first shade; B, 2nd shade.

TO MAKE
First Side

With A commence with 6 ch. and join with sl.st. to form a ring.

1st round: 3 ch., 11 tr. into ring, sl.st. to 3rd of 3 ch.: 12 sts.

2nd round: 3 ch., 1 tr. into same st., 2 tr. into each st. to end, sl.st. to 3rd of 3 ch.: 24 sts.

3rd round: 4 ch., * 1 tr. into next tr., 1 ch.; rep. from * to end, sl.st. to 3rd of 4 ch.

4th round: as 3rd round.

5th round: sl.st. into first ch.sp., * 4 ch., 1 d.c. into next ch.sp.; rep. from * to end, 4 ch., sl.st. to beg. of round.

6th round: sl.st. to centre of ch.loop, * 4 ch., 1 d.c. into centre of next ch. loop; rep. from * to end, 4 ch., 1 d.c. into centre of first ch.loop.

7th round: as 6th round.

8th round: as 6th round.

9th round: as 6th round but work 5 ch. instead of 4 ch.

10th round: as 9th round.

11th round: as 9th round.

12th round: as 9th round, but work 6 ch. instead of 5 ch.

13th round: as 12th round.

14th round: as 12th round but work 7 ch. instead of 6 ch.

15th round: as 14th round.

16th round: as 12th round.

17th round: as 9th round.

18th round: as 6th round.

19th round: as 18th round.

20th round: as 6th round but work 3 ch. instead of 4 ch.

21st round: as 20th round.
Fasten off.

Second Side

With B, work as first side.

TO COMPLETE

Insert one side of the beret inside the other and secure at crown. With crochet hook and either A or B, insert hook through ch. loops on outer edges of both sides of beret and work 1 d.c. and 1 ch. into each loop all round. Fasten off. Thread 2 strands shirring elastic round edge of beret.

Peaked beret
illustrated in colour overleaf

MATERIALS

4 oz. Hayfield Gaylon Double Knitting. One crochet hook International Standard Size 5.00.

MEASUREMENTS

To fit an average size head.

continued on page 126

Opposite: *reversible beret and peaked beret (see page 123).*

Right: *motif cushion (see page 140).*

Below: *coffee table mat (see page 135).*

ABBREVIATIONS
See page 19.

TO MAKE
Commence with 6 ch. and join with sl.st. to form a ring.
1st round: 3 ch., 11 tr. into ring, sl.st. to 3rd of 3 ch.: 12 sts.
2nd round: 3 ch., 1 tr. into same st., 2 tr. into each st. to end, sl.st. to 3rd of 3 ch.: 24 sts.
3rd round: 1 tr. into each tr.sp. to end, sl.st. to first tr.: 24 sts.
4th round: * 1 tr. into first tr.sp., 2 tr. into next tr.sp.; rep. from * to end, sl.st. to first tr.: 36 sts.
5th round: 1 tr. into each tr. sp. to end, sl.st. to first tr.
6th round: * 1 tr. into each of first 2 tr.sps., 2 tr. into next tr.sp.; rep. from * to end, sl.st. to first tr.
7th round: as 6th round but work 3 tr. between each inc.
8th round: as 5th round.
9th round: as 6th round but work 4 tr. between each inc.
10th round: as 5th round.
11th round: as 6th round but work 5 tr. between each inc.
12th round: as 5th round.
13th round: as 6th round but work 6 tr. between each inc.: 96 sts.
14th round: as 5th round.
15th round: as 5th round.
16th round: * 1 tr. into each of next 7 tr.sps., miss 1 tr.sp.; rep. from * to end, sl.st. to first tr.: 84 sts.
17th round: as 5th round.
18th round: as 5th round.
19th round: as 16th round but work 6 tr. between each dec.
20th round: as 5th round.
21st round: as 16th round, but work 5 tr. between each dec.: 60 sts.
22nd round: as 5th round.
23rd round: as 5th round.
24th round: 1 h.tr. into each st. to end, sl.st. to first h.tr.
25th round: as 24th round.
26th round: as 24th round.
Fasten off.
Fold last 3 rounds to wrong side to form an inside band.
Rejoin yarn and work 1 round of d.c. along folded edge to hold band in place.

Peak
Next row: sl.st. over 10 sts., 1 d.c. into next st., * 2 d.c. into next d.c., 1 d.c. into next d.c.; rep. from * 17 times; turn.
Next row: sl.st. over 2 sts., 1 d.c. into each st. to last 2 sts.; turn.
Rep. last row 9 times. Fasten off.

TO COMPLETE
Beg. at centre back, work 1 round of d.c. round back edge and peak. Fasten off.

Drawstring bag

MATERIALS
Two 4-oz. hanks Twilleys Lyscot cotton yarn. One crochet hook International Standard Size 4.00. Twelve 1-in. curtain rings.

MEASUREMENTS
Bag measures approx. 22 in. all round and 14 in. deep.

TENSION
2 patts. to approx. 1 in. in width.

ABBREVIATIONS
See page 19.

TO MAKE
Make 4 ch. and join with sl.st. into a ring.
1st round: (1 d.c. into next ch., 2 d.c. into next ch.) twice. Now work in rounds of d.c., working 2 d.c. into every alternate d.c. until there are 43 d.c. in the round.
Next round: work 1 d.c. into each d.c. of previous round.
Next round: 4 ch., * 1 d.tr. into next d.c., 1 ch.; rep. from * ending with a sl.st. into top of 3rd ch.
Patt. round: 4 ch., * 1 d.tr. into next d.tr., 1 ch.; rep. from * ending with sl.st. into top of 3rd of 4 ch.
Rep. last round 11 times more.
With wrong side of work facing, now work as follows: * (1 d.c. in next sp., 1 d.c. in next d.tr.) 3 times, now place a curtain ring at back of work and work a d.c. into next sp., working through ring as well, 1 d.c. in next d.tr.; rep. from * 9 times, then rep. between brackets twice, place a ring at back of work and work a d.c. into next sp. and ring as before, 1 d.c. into next d.tr. Fasten off.

TO COMPLETE
Press work with a damp cloth and hot iron.
Sew a ring to centre of base. Make a twisted cord by cutting 3 strands of yarn, each 150 in. long, and twisting them tightly together. Fold in half and allow to form into a cord. Thread cord through rings at top and join ends.

Après ski socks

MATERIALS
3 oz. Emu Scotch Double Knitting. Crochet hook International Standard Size 3.50. One pair of insoles. Small quantity of felt to match yarn colour. Piece of foam rubber, ⅜ in. thick. Fabric glue.

MEASUREMENTS

To fit an average size foot. (Work more or less ch. for bigger or smaller sizes.)

TENSION

5 spaces to 2 in.

ABBREVIATIONS

See page 19.

FOOT

Make 108 ch. and join into ring with a sl.st.

1st round: 2 ch., then work 1 d.c. on each ch. all round, join with sl.st.

2nd round: 4 ch., miss 1 d.c., 1 tr. into next d.c., * 1 ch., miss 1 d.c., 1 tr. into next d.c.; rep. from * all round, join with sl.st.

3rd round: (mark centre space with coloured thread) now work tr. on tr. with 1 ch. between each tr., omitting tr. on centre tr.

4th round: work as 3rd round, but omitting 3 alt. tr. at centre.

5th and 6th rounds: as 4th round but omitting 2 extra tr. as before on each round. Break off yarn and fasten off.

LEG

Beginning at centre back, work in patt. over 12 spaces, make 5 ch., then work over 12 spaces on other side to meet at centre back, join with sl.st.

Next round: patt. over 12 spaces, 1 ch., miss 2 ch., 1 tr. into next ch., 1 ch., patt. to end. Work in rounds until 8 rounds of leg have been worked. Break off yarn and fasten off.

ROSETTE

Make 60 ch. and work 1 row of d.c., then 1 row of tr. spaces. Work 1 row of d.c. on each tr. and ch. of previous row. Break off yarn and fasten off.

TO COMPLETE

Cut foam to fit insoles and two pieces of felt for each insole. Stick felt to one side of each sole, then stick foam to each sole. Finally stick second piece of felt on top of foam. Cut strips of felt ¾ in. wide and long enough to fit all round outside edge of soles. With matching thread oversew felt strip to edge of sole and close seam at back of heel. Pin sock in position round top edge of felt strip and oversew. Allow rosette to curl naturally and sew to centre front.

Red, white and blue bag

illustrated opposite

MATERIALS

3 oz. Hayfield Gaylon Double Knitting in red, 2 oz. in white, and 2 oz. in blue. Crochet hooks International Standard Sizes 3.00 and 4.00. Three large press fasteners. ½ yd. lining material, 36 in. wide. Piece of card, approx. 11 in. by 28 in., for stiffening. A 2-in. pronged buckle.

MEASUREMENTS

Finished bag measures approx. 12 in. long, 11 in. wide, excluding handles.

TENSION

2 rows of tr. and 4 sts. measure 1 in. on No. 4.00 hook.

ABBREVIATIONS

See page 19; R., red; W., white; B., blue.

TO MAKE

With No. 4.00 hook and R., make 45 ch.
Foundation row: 1 d.c. in 2nd ch. from hook, 1 d.c. in each ch. to end of row, 3 ch., turn.
1st row: 1 tr. in each d.c. to end of row, 3 ch., turn.
2nd row: 1 tr. into each tr. of previous row.
Continue in tr., working 2 rows W., then 2 rows in B. These 6 rows form patt.
Work 9 more patts.

Front Flap

Work 1 more patt. but dec. 1 st. at each end of every row, then 2 more rows in R., still dec. at each end of row. Fasten off.

Strap and Gusset (make 2 alike)

With No. 3.00 hook and R., make 130 ch.
1st row: 1 d.c. in 2nd ch. from hook, 1 d.c. in each ch. to end of row, 2 ch., turn.
Work 3 more rows of d.c. Fasten off.

Tag for Buckle

Fold and mark centre of flap.
Join in R. 5 sts. from centre of flap, and with No. 3.00 hook work 10 d.c. (i.e. 5 each side of centre).
Cont. on these sts. for 10 more rows, working in d.c., then dec. at each end of alt. rows 3 times. Fasten off.

TO COMPLETE

Press all pieces. Using 2 strands of yarn together, threaded on to a large-eyed darning needle, work darning sts. lengthwise between each tr. over all main piece of bag, alternating the darn or weave on each row (i.e. stitches are taken evenly over and under the trebles on each line, so if you start one line of darning

sts. with a stitch on the right side of work, in order to alternate the weave, the first stitch on the next line will be on the wrong side. The first stitch on the third line will then be on the right side, as the first line – and so on).
Start lines of darning sts. on 4th line of trebles in from one side edge. Work 3 lines of darning in red, then 3 lines in blue, then 3 lines in white. Continue in this sequence until the 5th band of red darning stitches has been worked (39 rows of darning stitches altogether). Leave final 4 rows of tr. free.
Using the worked main piece of bag as a pattern, cut the card stiffening to exactly the same size and shape. Cut lining to the same shape but add ½ in. to all edges for turnings. Turn in ½ in. on all raw edges on lining, then place lining and crocheted fabric together, wrong sides facing. Sl.st. together round all sides but leave the short straight edge open. Slip the card inside between lining and bag and then sl.st. remaining edge closed. Count down 10½ stripes from short straight edge and make a fold in work – this represents front of bag. Make another fold the width of the crocheted strap to form bag base.

Side Gusset

Pin one of the straps in position placing end of strap at the 10½ stripe fold. Stitch firmly in place stitching one side of strap to front and the other side to back of bag, thus making side gusset. The remaining part of strap forms the handles. Stitch other strap to opposite side of bag, in a similar way. If wished, a row of d.c. may be worked all round gusset and handle edges, to give a firmer neater edge. Stitch the stud part of 2 press fasteners on one strap, one at the end, and one 3 in. further along. Stitch the matching parts of the fasteners on the other strap in a similar position so that when clipped together a shoulder strap is formed. Stitch the 3rd press fastener, one part each side of gusset near top of bag so that when ends of strap are clipped to these a handbag effect is achieved.
Count to 3rd red stripe down front of bag and stitch buckle in centre. Slip tag through buckle to fasten.

Bag with cane handles

illustrated overleaf

MATERIALS

8 oz. Twilleys D42 dishcloth cotton. One crochet hook International Standard Size 4.00. One pair of 10-in. cane handles. A piece of cardboard, 11 in. by 2½ in., for base.

MEASUREMENTS

Finished bag measures approx. 9½ in. long, 13 in. wide at widest point (excluding handles).

TENSION

5 d.c. to 1 in. and 4 rows to 1 in.

ABBREVIATIONS

See page 19.

TO MAKE

Make 42 ch. and work 12 rows d.c.: this forms base of bag.
Work now continues in rounds, working round all edges of the base, and always ending round with a sl.st. into the first st. of the round. Mark the beg. of each round with a coloured thread. Work round all edges of the base in d.c. for 2 rounds, then work d.c. into the back loop of each st. for 18 rounds. Cont. in d.c. into both loops of each st. for 3½ in. Divide work into 2 pieces from the centre of one short side of base to the centre of the other short side, and finish each side separately, working back and forth in rows. Work 1½ in. in d.c., and then work 3 rows in d.c. on the first 12 sts. at each end of work. Break yarn and rejoin on the centre sts. and work 4 rows in d.c.
Break yarn.
Work the other side of bag in a similar way.

Shell Trimming

With the right side of bag facing, attach yarn to first free loop on the 3rd round of d.c. (counting from the base up). Work as follows: * 4 ch., (y.o.h., insert hook into next ch. and draw loop through) 3 times working into the same ch. each time, y.o.h. and draw through all loops on hook, sl.st. into base of shell, then sl.st. over next 2 ch.; rep. from * to end of round.

Repeat this round on every 2nd round of d.c. loops until 8 rounds in all are completed.

TO COMPLETE

Fold the 12 sts. at each end of both sides of bag in half towards the inside and sew last row together. Fold the 4 rows on centre of front and back over the bar of the handle and sl.st. Push the shaped metal and cane ends into the gusset formed by the fold of 12 sts. at each end.

Cut a piece of cardboard, 11 in. by 2½ in., and stick to the bottom of the bag with a spot of fabric glue.

Chapter nine
HOME SWEET HOME
furnishings and decorations to grace your home

Elegant curtain worked in fine crochet cotton (instructions start overleaf).

Curtain
illustrated on previous page

MATERIALS
13 balls (20 gr. each) Coats Chain Mercer-Crochet No. 20. One steel crochet hook International Standard Size 1.25. (8 motifs can be worked from 1 ball.)

MEASUREMENTS
31½ in. by 38½ in. excluding casing.

TENSION
1 motif 3½ in. square.

ABBREVIATIONS
See page 19; p., picot.

FIRST MOTIF
Commence with 4 ch., join with sl.st. to form a ring.
1st row: 5 ch., * into ring work 1 tr. and 2 ch.; rep. from * 6 times, sl.st. into 3rd of 5 ch.
2nd row: sl.st. into first sp., 4 ch., 2 d.tr. into same sp., * 2 ch., 3 d.tr. into next sp., 5 ch., 3 d.tr. into next sp.; rep. from * omitting 3 d.tr. at end of last rep., sl.st. into 4th of 4 ch.
3rd row: 3 ch., 1 d.tr. into same place as sl.st., * 1 d.tr. into each of next 2 d.tr., 1 ch., 1 d.tr. into each of next 2 d.tr., leaving the last loop of each on hook work 2 d.tr. into next d.tr., y.o.h. and draw through all loops on hook (a 2-d.tr.cl. made), 3 ch., into next sp. work 1 d.tr., 4 ch. and 1 d.tr., 8 ch., remove loop from hook insert hook into 2nd last d.tr. made and draw loop through, 3 d.c. into loop just made, 3 ch., sl.st. into last d.c. (a p. made), into same loop work (3 d.c. and a p.) twice and 2 d.c., sl.st. into next d.tr., 3 ch., a 2-d.tr.cl. into next d.tr.; rep. from * omitting a 2-d.tr.cl. at end of last rep., sl.st. into first d.tr.
4th row: 4 ch., leaving the last loop of each on hook work 1 d.tr. into each of next 4 d.tr. and into next cl., y.o.h. and draw through all loops on hook (a 5-d.tr.cl. made), * 9 ch., sl.st. into next p., 14 ch., miss next p., sl.st. into next p., 9 ch., miss next sp., a 6-d.tr.cl. working 1 d.tr. into each of next cl., 4 d.tr. and cl.; rep. from * omitting a cl. at end of last rep., sl.st. into first cl.
5th row: * into next loop work 6 d.c. and 5 d.c., into next loop work 6 d.c., (a p., 5 d.c.) twice, into next loop work 6 d.c., a p. and 5 d.c.; rep. from * ending with sl.st. into first d.c.
6th row: sl.st. into each of next 4 d.c. and into p., * 9 ch., sl.st. into next p., 12 ch., sl.st. into next p., (9 ch., sl.st., into next p.) twice; rep. from * working last sl.st. into same place as first sl.st.
7th row: * into next loop work 6 d.c., a p. and 5 d.c., into next loop work 8 d.c., a p. and 7 d.c. (into next loop work 6 d.c., a p. and 5 d.c.) twice; rep. from * ending with sl.st. into first d.c. Fasten off.

SECOND MOTIF
Work as First Motif for 6 rows.

7th row: into next loop work 6 d.c., a p. and 5 d.c. into next loop work 8 d.c., 1 ch., sl.st. into corresponding p. on first motif, 1 ch., sl.st. into last d.c. on second motif (a joining p. made), 7 d.c. into same loop, (into next loop work 6 d.c., a joining p. and 5 d.c.) 3 times, into next loop work 8 d.c. a joining p. and 7 d.c.; complete as first motif.

OTHER MOTIFS
Make 11 rows of 9 motifs, joining each as second motif was joined to first. Where 4 corners meet, join 3rd and 4th motifs to previous joining.

CASING
1st row: with wrong side facing attach thread to p. at corner of last row, 1 d.c. into same p., * 10 ch., 1 d.c. into next p., (8 ch., 1 d.c. into next p.) twice, 10 ch., 1 d.c. into next joining p.; rep. from * working last d.c. into corner p., 3 ch.; turn.
2nd row: miss first st., 1 tr. into each st., 3 ch.; turn.
Rep. last row 7 times more omitting turning ch. at end of last row. Fasten off.

TO COMPLETE
Turn back last 4 rows of casing and slip st. neatly to base of first row.
Damp and pin out to measurements.

Motif tablecloth

MATERIALS
12 balls (25 gr. each) Twilleys Lysbet cotton yarn. One crochet hook International Standard Size 3.00.

MEASUREMENTS
Finished tablecloth measures 36 in. square.

TENSION
2 motifs measure 7 in. across.

ABBREVIATIONS
See page 19.

TO MAKE
First Motif
Make 6 ch., join with sl.st. into a ring.
1st round: 3 ch. (for first tr.), 15 tr. into ring, join with sl.st.
2nd round: 3 ch., 1 tr. into same tr. as sl.st., 2 ch., * miss 1 tr., 2 tr. into next tr., 2 ch.; rep. from * to end, sl.st. to top of ch.

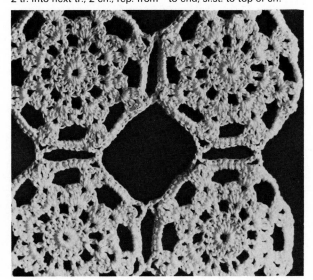

3rd round: sl.st. between tr., 3 ch., 1 tr., 2 ch., 2 tr. into same sp., * 2 ch., 1 d.c. into sp., 2 ch., 2 tr., 2 ch., 2 tr. between next 2 tr.; rep. from * to end, finishing 2 ch., sl.st. into top of 3 ch.

4th round: sl.st. into next tr. and sp., 3 ch., 1 tr., 2 ch., 2 tr. into same sp. as sl.st., * 4 ch., 2 tr., 2 ch., 2 tr. into sp. between tr.; rep. from * to end, finishing 4 ch., sl.st. into top of 3 ch.

5th round: * 5 ch., miss 1 tr., 1 ch., 1 tr., 1 d.c. into next tr., 5 d.c. into sp., 1 d.c. into tr.; rep. from * to end, join with sl.st. Fasten off.

Second Motif

Work as for first motif as far as end of 4th round.

5th round: 2 ch., 1 d.c. into 5 ch.sp. on first motif, 2 ch., 1 d.c. into tr. on second motif, 5 d.c. into sp., 1 d.c. into tr., 2 ch., 1 d.c. into next 5 ch. on first motif, 2 ch., 1 d.c. into tr. on second motif; continue to end as 5th round of first motif. Join 10 motifs in this way to make one complete strip.

Next Strip

Work first motif, joining it to first motif of first strip, as second motif was joined to the first.

To join second motif on second strip, work as usual to end of 4th round.

5th round: 2 ch., 1 d.c. into 5 ch.sp. on first motif, 2 ch., 1 d.c. into tr. on second motif, 5 d.c. into sp., 1 d.c. into tr., 2 ch., 1 d.c. into 5 ch.sp. on first motif, 2 ch., 1 d.c. into tr. on second motif, 5 ch., 1 d.c. into sp., 1 d.c. into tr., 2 ch., 1 d.c. into 5 ch. on next motif, 2 ch., 1 d.c. into tr. on second motif, 5 d.c. into sp., 1 d.c. into tr., 2 ch., 1 d.c. into 5 ch.sp. on next motif, 2 ch., 1 d.c. into tr. on second motif, 5 d.c. into sp., 1 d.c. into tr., continue to end as 5th round of first motif.

Work 10 strips of 10 motifs each altogether.

TO COMPLETE

Press with a warm iron over a damp cloth on the wrong side.

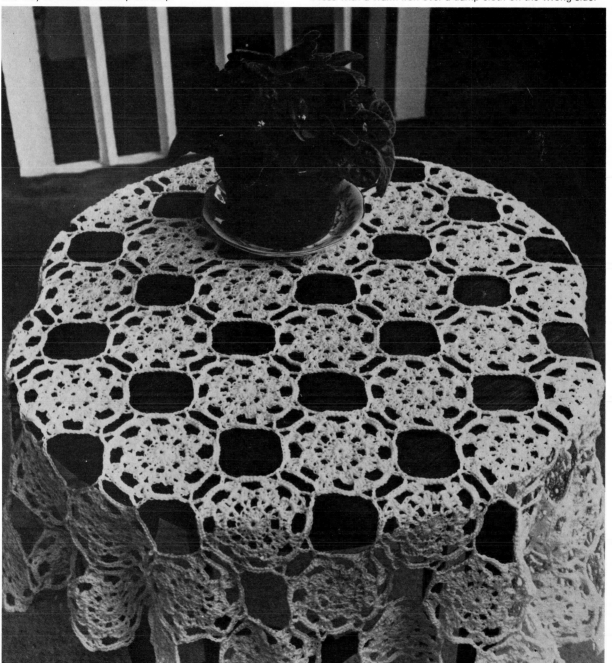

Cheval set

MATERIALS
3 oz. Twilleys Crysette cotton yarn. One crochet hook International Standard Size 3.00.

MEASUREMENTS
Round mat is 7½ in. in diameter. Oval mat is 11 in. by 15 in.

TENSION
First 3 rounds measure 2½ in.

ABBREVIATIONS
See page 19.

ROUND MAT (make 2 alike)
Commence with 10 ch., sl.st. into first ch. to form ring.
1st round: 16 d.c. into ring, sl.st. into first d.c.
2nd round: 4 ch., leaving last loop of each d.tr. on hook make 2 d.tr. into same place as sl.st., yarn over hook and draw through all loops on hook, * 5 ch., miss next d.c., leaving last loop of each d.tr. on hook make 3 d.tr. into next d.c., y.o.h., and draw through all loops on hook: a cluster formed; rep. from * ending with 5 ch., sl.st. into top of first cluster: 8 sps.
3rd round: 7 d.c. into each 5 ch.sp., sl.st. into first d.c.
4th round: 1 d.c. into same place as sl.st., 1 d.c. into each of next 6 d.c., * 4 ch., 1 d.c. into each of next 7 d.c.; rep. from * ending with 4 ch., sl.st. into first d.c.
5th round: 1 sl.st. into next d.c., * 1 d.c. into each of next 3 d.c., 2 ch., (3 tr., 2 ch., 3 tr.) all into next 4 ch.sp., 2 ch., miss next 2 d.c.; rep. from * ending with sl.st. into first d.c.

6th round: * 1 d.c. into next d.c., 4 ch., miss next 2 tr., 1 tr. into next tr., (2 tr., 2 ch., 2 tr.) all into next 2 ch.sp., 1 tr. into next tr., 4 ch., miss next 2 tr., miss next d.c.; rep. from * ending with sl.st. into first d.c.
7th round: 7 ch., * miss 2 tr., 1 tr. into next tr., (2 tr., 2 ch., 2 tr.) all into next 2 ch.sp., 1 tr. into next tr., 4 ch., miss 2 tr., 1 tr. into next d.c., 4 ch.; rep. from * omitting 1 tr. and 4 ch. at end of last rep., sl.st. into 3rd of 7 ch.
8th round: 8 ch., * miss 2 tr., 1 tr. into next tr., (2 tr., 1 ch., 2 tr.) all into next 2 ch.sp., 1 tr. into next tr., 5 ch., miss 2 tr., 1 tr. into next tr., 5 ch.; rep. from * omitting 1 tr. and 5 ch. at end of last rep., sl.st. into 3rd of 8 ch. Fasten off, or if it is wished to make a bigger mat, then cont. in patt. working 8th round and inc. chain lengths by 1 ch. on every rep. until mat is the required measurement. Fasten off.

OVAL MAT
First motif
Work as for Round Mat until the 2nd round is completed. Fasten off.

Second motif
Work as for Round Mat until the first round is completed.
Next round: 4 ch., leaving last loop of each d.tr. on hook make 2 d.tr. into same place as sl.st., y.o.h. and draw through all loops on hook, * 2 ch., 1 tr. into any loop on first motif, 2 ch., miss next d.c. on second motif, a cluster into next d.c., 2 ch., 1 d.c. into next loop on first motif, 2 ch., miss next d.c. on second motif, a cluster into next d.c., 2 ch., 1 tr. into next loop on first motif, 2 ch., miss next d.c. on second motif, a cluster into next d.c., complete as for first motif. Fasten off.

Third motif

Work as for second motif but work joining on 2nd round into appropriate loops on other side of first motif. Fasten off.

Edging

1st round: with right side of work facing, attach yarn to free loop on first motif, 1 d.c. into same place as join, 7 ch., 7 d.c. into each 5 ch. loop on next motif, 7 ch., 1 d.c. into next free 5 ch. loop on first motif, 7 ch., 7 d.c. into each 5 ch. loop on next motif, 7 ch., 1 sl.st. into first d.c.

2nd round: 7 d.c. into next loop, (4 ch., 1 d.c. into each of next 7 d.c.) 5 times, (4 ch., 7 d.c. into next loop) twice, (4 ch., 1 d.c. into each of next 7 d.c.) 5 times, 4 ch., 7 d.c. into next loop, 4 ch., 1 sl.st. into first d.c.

3rd round: 1 sl.st. into next d.c., * 1 d.c. into each of next 3 d.c., 2 ch., (3 tr., 2 ch., 3 tr.) all into next 4 ch. loop, 2 ch., miss next 2 d.c.; rep. from * omitting 'miss 2 d.c.' at end of last rep., sl.st. into first d.c.

Work 6th and 7th rounds of Round Mat, then work 2 rounds of 7th rounds of Round Mat, followed by 2 rounds of 8th round. Fasten off, or if it is wished to make a bigger mat, then cont. in patt. inc. chain lengths by 1 ch. on next and every alternate rep. of 8th round until mat is the required measurement. Fasten off.

TO COMPLETE ALL MATS

Starch lightly and press.

Coffee table mat

illustrated in colour on page 125

MATERIALS

11 balls (25 gr. each) Twilleys Lysbet cotton yarn in brown, and 7 balls in cream. One crochet hook International Standard Size 2.00.

MEASUREMENTS

Finished mat measures 36 in. square.

TENSION

1 motif in brown measures 3 in. across.

ABBREVIATIONS

See page 19; B., brown; C., cream.

TO MAKE
Lattice motif

With C., make 23 ch.

1st row: miss 7 ch., 1 tr. in next ch., (2 ch., miss 2 ch., 1 tr. into next ch.) 5 times.

2nd row: 5 ch., miss 2 ch., 1 tr. in tr., (2 ch., miss 2 ch., 1 tr. in tr.) 4 times, 2 ch., miss 2 ch., 1 tr. in next ch.

3rd row: 5 ch., miss 2 ch., 1 tr. in tr., (2 ch., miss 2 ch., 1 tr. in tr.) 5 times.

Repeat last row 3 times more.

7th row: 3 d.c. into each of next 3 sp., * 6 ch., 3 d.c. into each of next 3 sp., 6 ch., 3 d.c. into same sp. as last 3 d.c., 3 d.c. into each of next 2 sp.; rep. from * to end, 6 ch., sl.st. to d.c.

Break yarn and fasten off.

Rose motif

With B., make 8 ch., and join into a ring with sl.st.

1st round: 12 d.c. into ring, join with sl.st., 9 ch., turn, 1 sl.st. into sl.st. to form a loop; * turn, 1 d.c., 5 tr. and 3 d.tr. all into 9 ch. loop, 6 ch., 1 sl.st. on top of last d.tr. worked, 3 d.tr., 5 tr. and 1 d.c. all into same loop, 1 d.c. into next d.c. of ring, 5 ch., 1 d.c. into each of next 2 d.c. of ring, 9 ch., turn, 1 sl.st. into last d.c. worked; rep. from * twice; turn, 1 d.c., 5 tr. and 3 d.tr. into loop, 6 ch., 1 sl.st. on top of last d.tr., 3 d.tr., 5 tr. and 1 d.c. all into same loop, 1 d.c. in next d.c. of ring, 5 ch., 1 d.c. in next d.c., join with sl.st. to sl.st.

Break yarn and fasten off.

With B., join yarn with sl.st. to one of the corner loops, * 5 ch., 1 d.c. into same loop, 3 ch., miss 3 d.tr., 1 tr. in next tr., 1 d.tr. into loop between petals, 3 ch., miss 5 tr. on next petal, 1 d.c. into next tr., 3 ch., 1 d.c. into corner loop; rep. from * 3 times more, join with sl.st., ** 3 d.c., 6 ch., 3 d.c. into loop of 5 ch., 3 d.c. into each of next 2 loops, 6 ch., 3 d.c. into each of next 2 loops; rep. from ** once more, 3 d.c. into corner loop.

Join motifs

Join rose motif to lattice motif as follows: continuing with B., 3 ch., 1 d.c. into corner of lattice motif, 3 ch., 3 d.c. into same loop as before, 3 d.c. into each of next 2 loops, 3 ch., 1 d.c. into centre loop of side of lattice motif, 3 ch., 3 d.c. into each of the next 2 loops, 3 d.c. into corner loop, 3 ch., 1 d.c. into next corner loop of lattice motif, 3 ch., 3 d.c. into same loop as before, 3 d.c. into each of next 2 loops, 6 ch., 3 d.c. into each of next 2 loops, sl.st. to d.c. Break off yarn and fasten off.

Make 81 B. motifs, and 64 C. motifs. Continue joining the motifs alternately until until you have 9 rows of B. motifs, 9 motifs to a row, and 8 rows of C. motifs, 8 motifs to a row (or whatever size you wish the finished mat to be).

TO COMPLETE
Edging

With C., work the edging as follows: * into loop at point make (1 d.c., 5 ch., 1 d.c.), 5 ch., miss 4 d.c. of previous row, 1 d.c. into next d.c., 5 ch., (1 d.c., 5 ch., 1 d.c.) into loop, 5 ch., miss 4 d.c., 1 d.c. into next d.c., 5 ch., 1 d.c. into loop of next square, 5 ch., miss 4 d.c., 1 d.c. into next d.c., 5 ch., (1 d.c., 5 ch., 1 d.c.) into loop, 5 ch., miss 4 d.c., 1 d.c. into next d.c., 5 ch.; rep. from * to end. Join with sl.st.

Next row: * (5 ch., 1 d.c., 7 ch., 1 d.c., 5 ch., 1 d.c.) into loop on point, 5 d.c. into each of next 2 loops, (5 ch., 1 d.c., 7 ch., 1 d.c., 5 ch., 1 d.c.) into next loop, 5 d.c. into each of next 4 loops, (5 ch., 1 d.c., 7 ch., 1 d.c., 5 ch., 1 d.c.) into next loop, 5 d.c. into each of next 2 loops; rep. from * all round.

Press with a hot iron and a damp cloth.

Kneeler

MATERIALS

5 balls (20 gr. each) Coats Chain Mercer-Crochet No. 20. One steel crochet hook International Standard Size 1.25. One kneeler. (If desired, kneeler may be covered with contrasting fabric taking ¾ yard 36-in. wide fabric.)

MEASUREMENTS

14 in. by 10 in. by 5 in.

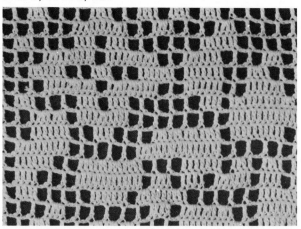

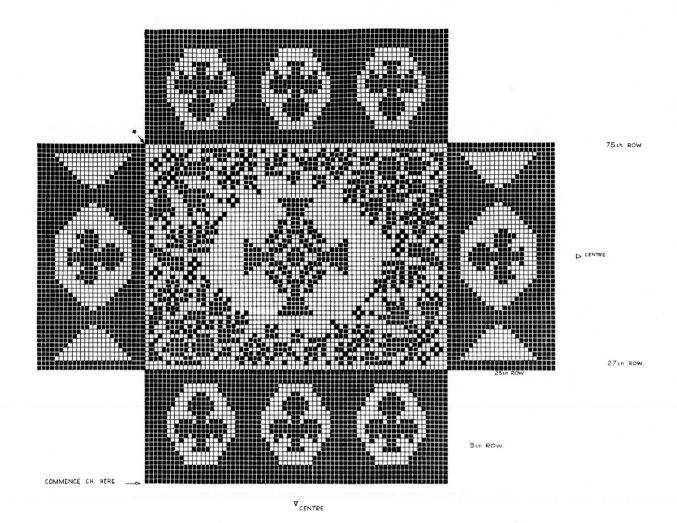

75th ROW.

▷ CENTRE.

27th ROW.

25th ROW.

9th ROW.

COMMENCE CH. HERE →

▽ CENTRE

TENSION
5 sps. and 5 rows to 1 in.

ABBREVIATIONS
See page 19; sp(s)., space(s): 2 ch., miss next 2 ch. or tr., 1 tr. into next ch. or tr.; blk(s)., block(s): 4 tr., then 3 tr. for each additional blk.

TO MAKE
Make 75 ch.; fasten off and leave aside.
Commence with 213 ch.
1st row: 1 tr. into 4th ch. from hook, 1 tr. into each ch. (70 blks. made), 3 ch.; turn.
2nd to 4th rows: miss first tr., 1 tr. into each tr., 1 tr. into next ch. (70 blks. made over 70 blks.), 3 ch.; turn.
5th row: 9 blks., (2 ch., miss 2 tr., 1 tr. into next tr.) 8 times (8 sps. made over 8 blks.), (14 blks., 8 sps.) twice, 9 blks., 3 ch.; turn.
6th row: 9 blks., (2 ch., 1 tr. into next tr.) 8 times (8 sps. made over 8 sps.), (14 blks., 8 sps.) twice, 9 blks., 3 ch.; turn.
7th row: 8 blks., (10 sps., 12 blks.) twice, 10 sps., 8 blks., 3 ch.; turn.
8th row: 7 blks., 4 sps., (2 tr. into next sp., 1 tr. into next tr.) 4 times (4 blks. made over 4 sps.), (4 sps., 10 blks., 4 sps., 4 blks.) twice, 4 sps., 7 blks., 3 ch.; turn.
Cont. to follow chart from 9th to 25th row, turning with 77 ch. at end of last row.
26th row: 1 tr. into 4th ch. from hook, 1 tr. into each ch., 1 tr.

into next tr. (25 blks. made), 70 sps., attach 75 ch. already worked to base of last tr., 1 tr. into each ch. (25 blks. made), 3 ch.; turn.
Cont. to follow chart from 27th to 75th row. Fasten off.
Attach thread to position marked by * on chart and cont. to follow chart to top. Fasten off. Damp and pin out to measurements. Place crochet over kneeler and sew in position.

Table mats
illustrated overleaf

MATERIALS
For 1 large and 2 small mats: 2 balls ($\frac{3}{4}$ oz. each) Templeton's Antler Double Crêpe in main shade and 1 ball in contrasting shade. One crochet hook International Standard Size 4.00.

MEASUREMENTS
Large mat $8\frac{1}{2}$ in. square; small mats $6\frac{1}{2}$ in. square.

TENSION
A 4-d.tr. gr. measures $\frac{3}{4}$ in.; 1 d.tr. is 1 in. deep.

ABBREVIATIONS
See page 19; cl., cluster: leaving the last loop of each on hook, work 3 d.tr. into next sp., y.o.h. and draw through all 4 loops on hook; M., main shade; C., contrasting shade.

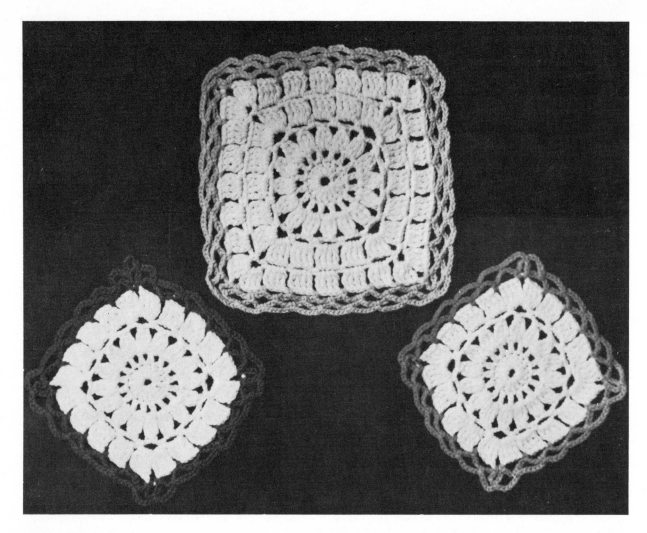

LARGE MAT

With M. commence with 7 ch. and join with sl.st. to form a ring.

1st round: 3 ch. (to stand as first tr.), work 15 tr. into ring, sl.st. to top of 3 ch.

2nd round: 4 ch., * 1 tr. into next tr., 1 ch.; rep. from * 14 times, sl.st. to 3rd of 4 ch.

3rd round: sl.st. into next sp., 4 ch., leaving last loop of each on hook, work 2 d.tr. into same sp., y.o.h. and draw through all 3 loops on hook, 3 ch., * 1 cl. into next sp., 3 ch.; rep. from * 14 times, sl.st. to top of first cl.

4th round: sl.st. into centre of next loop, * 4 ch., 1 d.c. into next loop.; rep. from * to end, working last d.c. into sl.st.

5th round: sl.st. into next loop, 4 ch., 3 d.tr. into same loop, 3 ch., 4 d.tr. into same loop (corner), 1 ch., (4 d.tr. into next loop, 1 ch.) 3 times, * into next loop work 4 d.tr., 3 ch. and 4 d.tr., 1 ch., (4 d.tr. into next loop, 1 ch.) 3 times; rep. from * twice, sl.st. to top of 4 ch.

6th round: sl.st. over next 3 d.tr. and into corner sp., 6 ch., 1 d.c. into same sp., (4 ch., 1 d.c. into next sp.) 5 times, * 6 ch., 1 d.c. into same sp., (4 ch., 1 d.c. into next sp.) 5 times; rep. from * to end.

7th round: as 5th round, but work rep. in brackets 5 times. Fasten off.

8th round: join C. to a corner sp., 6 ch., 1 d.c. into same sp., * 6 ch., 1 d.c. into next sp.; rep. from * to next corner, 6 ch., 1 d.c. into same corner sp.; rep. from * to end.

9th and 10th rounds: sl.st. into centre of next loop, * 6 ch., 1 d.c. into next loop; rep. from * to end. Fasten off.

SMALL MATS (make 2 alike)

Work as Large Mat until 5th round has been completed. Fasten off. Now work 8th and 9th rounds as for Large Mat. Fasten off.

TO COMPLETE

Pin out and press very lightly on wrong side.

Two-colour rug

MATERIALS

9 balls (2 oz. each) Twilleys Knitcot cotton yarn in main shade, and 9 balls in a contrasting shade. One crochet hook International Standard Size 5.00.

MEASUREMENTS

Finished rug measures approx. 30 in. by 54 in.

TENSION

$3\frac{1}{2}$ sts. to 1 in.

ABBREVIATIONS

See page 19; M., main shade; C., contrast shade.

TO MAKE

With M., commence with 86 ch. (to measure 24 in.).

Foundation row: 4 d.c. into 2nd ch. from hook, 1 d.c. into each ch., 4 d.c. into last d.c., turn work round and make 1 d.c. into each rem. loop on commencing ch., 1 d.c. into first d.c.

2nd round: 1 d.c. into each d.c. until 3rd d.c. of 4 d.c. group is reached, 4 d.c. into next d.c., 1 d.c. into each d.c.; rep. from * ending with sl.st. into first d.c. Fasten off.

3rd round: join in C. and attach yarn to any st., 1 d.c. into next d.c., * 1 d.c. into next d.c. on row immediately 2 rows below, miss the d.c. above and make 1 d.c. into each of next 2 d.c.; rep. from * omitting last d.c. of last rep., 1 d.c. into first d.c.

** **4th round:** 1 d.c. into each d.c. all round but making 8 incs. of 1 d.c. evenly round rug, 1 d.c. into first d.c.

Rep. last row twice more being careful not to work an inc. immediately over an inc. of the previous round. **

Rep. from ** to ** until work measures 15 in. from commencing ch. Fasten off.

Motif cushion

illustrated in colour on page 125

MATERIALS

2 balls (50 gr. each) Patons Double Knitting in each of two contrasting shades. One crochet hook International Standard Size 3.50. One 16-in. square cushion pad or ½ yd. cotton material and kapok for stuffing.

MEASUREMENTS

16 in. square.

TENSION

1 square 3⅛ in.

ABBREVIATIONS

See page 19; A, first shade; B, 2nd shade.

FIRST SQUARE (make 25 alike)

With A. commence with 6 ch. and join with sl.st. to form a ring.
1st round: 4 ch., 3 d.tr. into ring, 5 ch., * 4 d.tr. into ring, 5 ch.; rep. from * twice, sl.st. to top of 4 ch.; turn and work next round on wrong side.
2nd round: working into back loops only of all sts., * 1 d.c. into each of next 2 ch., 3 d.c. into next ch., 1 d.c. into each of next 2 ch., 1 d.c. into each of next 4 d.tr.; rep. from * 3 times, sl.st. to first d.c.: 44 sts. Break A and turn to right side.
3rd round: join B to 1 corner st., working into back loops only of all sts., 3 ch., 2 tr. into same st., * 1 tr. into each of next 10 sts., 3 tr. into corner st.; rep. from * twice, 1 tr. into each of next 10 sts., sl.st. to top of 3 ch. Fasten off.

SECOND SQUARE (make 25 alike)

Work as First Square, but work first 2 rounds with B and 3rd round with A.

TO COMPLETE

Pin out and press each square on wrong side, using a warm iron and a damp cloth.
Take 13 squares with A centres and 12 squares with B centres. St. tog. in 5 rows of 5 squares each, alternating the A and B centres as shown in photograph on page 125. Take rem. 25 squares and st. tog. in similar way. Press the 2 pieces on wrong side. With wrong sides facing, st. tog. round 3 sides, then turn right side out.

If necessary cut lining material into two 17-in. squares; join tog. round 3 sides with ½-in. turnings. Turn right side out and insert cushion pad inside crochet, or stuff with kapok. Stitch 4th side of crochet.

Motif bedspread

MATERIALS

61 oz. Twilleys Lyscordet fine cotton yarn. One crochet hook International Standard Size 2.50.

MEASUREMENTS

Finished bedspread measures approx. 70 in. by 90 in.

TENSION

One motif measures 2½ in. square.

ABBREVIATIONS

See page 19.

TO MAKE
Motif
Commence with 6 ch., sl.st. into first ch. to form a ring.
1st round: 4 ch., 4 d.tr. into ring, (5 ch., 5 d.tr. into ring) 3 times, 5 ch., sl.st. into 4th of 4 ch.
2nd round: 1 d.c. into same place as sl.st., 1 d.c. into each of next 4 d.tr., (7 d.c. into 5 ch. loop, 1 d.c. into each of next 5 d.tr.) 3 times, 7 d.c. into next 5 ch. loop, sl.st. into first d.c.
3rd round: 4 ch., miss first d.c., 1 tr. into next d.c., (1 ch., miss 1 d.c., 1 tr. into next d.c.) 3 times, * (1 ch., 1 tr.) twice into same place as last tr., (1 ch., miss 1 d.c., 1 tr. into next d.c.) 6 times; rep. from * twice, (1 ch., 1 tr.) twice into same place as last tr., 1 ch., miss 1 d.c., 1 tr. into next d.c., 1 ch., sl.st. into 3rd of 4 ch. Fasten off.
Make 1008 motifs in all.

TO COMPLETE

Join a line of 28 motifs, then add to this 36 more rows of 28 motifs each.

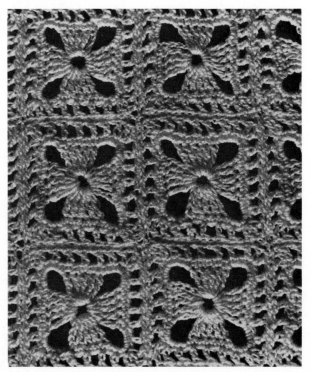

Edging

With right side facing, attach yarn to one corner of bedspread.
1st round: 4 ch., 1 tr. into same place, 1 ch., * 1 tr. into next tr.,
1 ch.; rep. from * until next corner tr. is reached, (1 tr., 1 ch.) 3
times into next tr.; rep. from * twice more; ** 1 tr. into next tr.,
1 ch.; rep. from ** ending with 1 tr. into same place as first tr.,
sl.st. into 3rd of 4 ch., turn.
Rep. last round once more.
2nd round: 1 d.c. into same place as sl.st., * 1 d.c. into next
sp., 3 ch., sl.st. into last d.c.; rep. from * all round, sl.st. into first
d.c. Fasten off.
Press work lightly on the wrong side with a warm iron over a
damp cloth.

*Note. A baby shawl could be made instead of a bedspread from
the above pattern. 17 oz. Lyscordet cotton would be required.
Work 256 motifs and join into 16 rows of 16 motifs each. Work
edging as given for bedspread.*

Easter table decoration

MATERIALS

3 balls (20 gr. each) Coats Chain Mercer-Crochet No. 20. One steel crochet hook International Standard Size 1.25. Four candles ½ in. in diameter at base. Four saucers. Four squares of felt 1 in. larger than diameter of saucer.

MEASUREMENTS

Base approx. 7 in. in diameter; height of candle holder 4 in.

TENSION

1 motif 1½ in. in diameter.

ABBREVIATIONS

See page 19; p., picot.

BASES (make 4 alike)

FIRST MOTIF (make 12 for each base)

Commence with 7 ch., join with sl.st. to form a ring.
1st row: * 1 d.c. into ring, 5 ch.; rep. from * 4 times, sl.st. into first d.c.
2nd row: * into next loop work 1 d.c., 1 h.tr. and 2 tr., (5 ch., sl.st. into last tr.) 3 times (a triple p. made), into same loop work 1 tr., 1 h.tr. and 1 d.c.; rep. from * ending with sl.st. into first d.c.: 5 petals.
3rd row: 2 ch., * working from the back of petals work 1 d.c. into ring at centre of next petal, 5 ch.; rep. from * 4 times, sl.st. into first d.c.
4th row: as 2nd row.
Fasten off.

EDGINGS (make 4 alike)

Commence with a length of ch. to fit round outer edge of saucer, join with sl.st. to form a ring.
1st row: 1 d.c. into same place as sl.st., 1 d.c. into each ch., sl.st. into first d.c., 3 ch.; turn.
2nd row: 1 tr. into each d.c., sl.st. into 3rd of 3 ch. Fasten off.

CANDLE HOLDERS (make 4 alike)

MAIN SECTIONS (make 2 alike)

Commence with 10 ch., join with sl.st. to form a ring.
1st row: 3 ch., 4 tr. into ring, remove loop from hook, insert hook into 3rd of 3 ch. and draw dropped loop through (a starting popcorn st. made), * 3 ch., 5 tr. into ring, remove loop from hook, insert hook into first of 5 tr. and draw dropped loop through (a popcorn st. made); rep. from * 6 times, 3 ch., sl.st. into first popcorn st.: 8 popcorn sts.
2nd row: * into next loop work 1 d.c., 3 ch. and 1 d.c.; rep. from * ending with sl.st. into first d.c.
3rd row: sl.st. into first loop, into same loop work a starting popcorn st., 3 ch. and a popcorn st., * into next loop work a popcorn st., 3 ch. and a popcorn st.; rep. from * ending with sl.st. into first popcorn st.
4th row: sl.st. into first sp., * 3 ch., 6 tr. into same loop, 3 ch.; turn; 1 tr. into first tr., 1 tr. into each tr., 2 tr. into 3rd of 3 ch., ** 3 ch.; turn; miss first tr., 1 tr. into each tr., 1 tr. into 3rd of 3 ch., **; fasten off; miss next loop on previous row, attach thread to next loop; rep. from * 3 times ending last rep. at second **; rep. from ** to ** 8 times, 3 ch.; turn; 1 tr. into first tr., 1 tr. into each tr., 2 tr. into 3rd of 3 ch.; rep. from ** to ** once; do not turn.
5th row: 2 d.c. over each of next 13 row-ends, * 1 d.c. between next 2 popcorn sts., 2 d.c. into next loop, 3 ch., sl.st. into last d.c. (a p. made), 1 d.c. into same loop, 1 d.c. between next 2 popcorn sts. **, 2 d.c. over each of next 3 row-ends, 2 d.c. into st. at corner, 1 d.c. into each of next 7 tr., 2 d.c. into next st. at corner, 2 d.c. over each of next 3 row-ends; rep. from * 3 times ending last rep. at **, 2 d.c. over each of next 13 row-ends, 2 d.c. into next st. at corner, 1 d.c. into each of next 9 tr., 2 d.c. into next st. at corner, sl.st. into first d.c.
Fasten off.
Damp and pin out to measurements.

TO COMPLETE

Cut circle of felt 1 in. larger than diameter of upturned saucer. Cut hole in centre of felt ½ in. in diameter for candle. Sew a row of small running sts. ¼ in. in from edge of felt circle and draw up ro fit curve of saucer. Steam gathers out flat and remove gathering sts. Trim to fit neatly over saucer.
Place first row of edging to edge of felt having 2nd row overlapping edge and sew in position. Place motifs on felt (see photograph opposite) and sew at centre of each motif. Place wrong sides of candle holder sections tog. and working into inside loops of d.c. only, sew sides up to top picots, leaving base and top open to insert candle. Place felt over upturned saucer, insert candle into holder, and stand candle on saucer at centre of felt.

WOOLS AND YARNS
an important note

It is recommended that wherever possible the brand name and weight of yarn quoted in each pattern is used. Where it is not possible to obtain these particular yarns, the following general equivalents may be satisfactorily substituted. It is essential however whether using the original brand-name yarn, or one of the general equivalents listed below, that you make a careful tension check before you embark on any pattern. Only by achieving the correct tension can you hope to make a successful, well-fitting garment. Remember that the hook size quoted in the pattern is only given as a guide – depending on the yarn you are using and whether you work tightly or slackly, you may well have to use a hook two or even three sizes bigger or smaller than the size quoted in order to achieve the correct tension measurement.

Coats yarns
Mercer-Crochet Nos. 10, 20 and 40 should be readily available almost everywhere. In USA substitute J. & P. Coats 6/c Crochet Cotton or 3/Mercerised Nos. 10, 20 and 40.

Emu yarns
For Baby Nylon 3-ply use a good-quality standard 3-ply yarn. For 4-ply crochet wool use a good-quality standard 4-ply yarn. For Machine Washable Baby Quickerknit or Double Knit Crochet Wool use a good-quality standard double knitting. For Tricel with Nylon use a standard Tricel yarn. For Filigree use any mohair yarn.

Hayfield yarns
For Gaylon Double Knitting, Courtier Bri-Nova Double Knitting or Diane, use any good-quality standard double knitting yarn.

Lee Target yarns
For Loch Isle Double Knitting, use any good-quality random-dyed double knitting yarn.

Lister yarns
For Lavenda 4-ply Wool use any good-quality standard 4-ply yarn.
For Bel Air Starspun 4-ply use any good-quality glitter yarn which works to a 4-ply tension.
For Lavenda Double Knitting use any good-quality standard double knitting yarn.

Patons yarns
For Promise use any Tricel yarn preferably with a 'crinkle' finish.
For Double Knitting, Brilliante Double Knitting or Fiona, use any good-quality standard double knitting yarn.

Pingouin yarns
For Classique Crylor use any good-quality standard double knitting yarn.
For Jaspee or Multipinguin use any good-quality chunky double knitting or triple knitting yarn.

Robin yarns
For Tricel-Nylon Perle 4-ply use any good-quality standard 4-ply yarn.
For Super Crimp Bri-Nylon Double Knitting, Vogue Double Knitting, Tricel-Nylon Double Knitting or Camille Crêpe Double Knitting use any good-quality standard double knitting yarn.
For Aran Pure New Wool use any good-quality Aran knitting yarn.

Templeton's yarns
For Antler Double Crêpe use any good-quality standard double knitting yarn.

Twilley yarns
Lysbet, Lyscordet, Crysette, Stalite, Knitcot and Lyscot are all cotton yarns, ranging in weight from Lysbet which is very fine through to Lyscot which is fairly thick in the order given above. Any good-quality cotton yarns may therefore be substituted provided the weight is carefully chosen and the tension measurement checked.
D42 is a medium-weight dishcloth cotton.
For Afghan Wool use any Afghan pure wool.
For Mohair use any random-dyed mohair yarn.
For Goldfingering use any good-quality medium-weight glitter yarn.
For Cortina Super Crochet Wool use any good-quality medium-weight wool with a firm twist.

Wendy yarns
For Invitation Cotton use any good-quality medium-weight cotton yarn.
For Courtelle Crêpe 4-ply use any good-quality standard 4-ply yarn.
For Courtelle Double Knitting, Double Knit Nylonised or Tricel Nylon Double Knitting use any good-quality standard double knitting.

Ball quantities
Many knitting and crochet yarns are now being sold in 20 or 25 gram balls instead of in ounce quantities. If you are buying balls of yarn to make up a particular pattern take care that you buy sufficient – i.e. if the quantity given in the pattern is for ounce balls, and the yarn manufacturer has meanwhile gone over to gram measurements, you will need to buy more balls of the new measure than of the old. The exact conversion for one ounce is 28.35 grams which means that a 25-gram ball will be nearest in weight to the old ounce ball, but still slightly under. If you therefore want to buy 4 oz. of a yarn being sold in 25-gram balls, then you should buy five balls to make sure you will have enough. If the yarn is being sold in 20-gram balls, then buy six.